Corpus Linguistics in Chinese Contexts

New Language Learning and Teaching Environments
Series edited by Hayo Reinders

Titles include:

Hayo Reinders (*editor*)
DIGITAL GAMES IN LANGUAGE LEARNING AND TEACHING

Marie-Noëlle Lamy and Katerina Zourou (*editors*)
SOCIAL NETWORKING FOR LANGUAGE EDUCATION

Mark Pegrum
MOBILE LEARNING

Geoffrey Sockett
THE ONLINE INFORMAL LEARNING OF ENGLISH

Tasha Bleistein and Marilyn Lewis
ONE-ON-ONE LANGUAGE TEACHING AND LEARNING
Theory and Practice

Regine Hampel and Ursula Stickler (*editors*)
DEVELOPING ONLINE LANGUAGE TEACHING
Research-Based Pedagogies and Reflective Practices

Shona Whyte
IMPLEMENTING AND RESEARCHING TECHNOLOGICAL INNOVATION IN
LANGUAGE TEACHING
The Case of Interactive Whiteboards for EFL in French Schools

Bin Zou, Simon Smith, and Michael Hoey (*editors*)
CORPUS LINGUISTICS IN CHINESE CONTEXTS

New Language Learning and Teaching Environments
Series Standing Order ISBN 978–0–230–28249–0 hardback
978–0–230–28250–6 paperback
(*outside North America only*)

You can receive future titles in this series as they are published by placing a standing order. Please contact your bookseller or, in case of difficulty, write to us at the address below with your name and address, the title of the series and the ISBN quoted above.

Customer Services Department, Macmillan Distribution Ltd, Houndmills, Basingstoke, Hampshire RG21 6XS, England

Corpus Linguistics in Chinese Contexts

Edited by

Bin Zou
Xi'an Jiaotong-Liverpool University, China

Simon Smith
Coventry University, UK

and

Michael Hoey
University of Liverpool, UK

First published 2015 by
PALGRAVE MACMILLAN

Palgrave Macmillan in the UK is an imprint of Macmillan Publishers Limited,
registered in England, company number 785998, of Houndmills, Basingstoke,
Hampshire RG21 6XS.

Palgrave Macmillan in the US is a division of St Martin's Press LLC,
175 Fifth Avenue, New York, NY 10010.

Palgrave Macmillan is the global academic imprint of the above companies and has companies
and representatives throughout the world.

Palgrave® and Macmillan® are registered trademarks in the United States,
the United Kingdom, Europe and other countries.

ISBN 978–1–137–44002–0

This book is printed on paper suitable for recycling and made from fully managed and
sustained forest sources. Logging, pulping and manufacturing processes are expected to
conform to the environmental regulations of the country of origin.

A catalogue record for this book is available from the British Library.

Library of Congress Cataloging-in-Publication Data

Corpus linguistics in Chinese contexts / edited by Bin Zou, Simon Smith, Michael Hoey.
pages cm

"On 28-30 June 2012, Xi'an Jiaotong-Liverpool University (XJTLU) had the honour of hosting
an international conference on Corpus Technologies and Applied Linguistics, CTAL-2012, in
Suzhou. The event, co-sponsored by the University of Liverpool and the Corpus Linguistics
Society of China, was a great success on at least two counts: it was the first major international
corpus linguistics conference in China, and the first international conference hosted by XJTLU.
There were more than 100 paper submissions, of which 68 were accepted for presentation
by the Programme Committee. A total of 6 plenary speeches were given by international and
Chinese corpus linguists of renown. For the first time ever at a single event, workshops on
two popular corpus tools, Sketch Engine and Wordsmith Tools, were given by their designers.
The contributions to this edited volume represent the best of CTAL-2012. A post conference
call for full papers was issued, and after a rigorous proces! s of double blind peer review, by an
international panel of experts, 9 articles were selected for inclusion in the volume."

Summary: "Rapid advances in computing have enabled the integration of corpora into
language teaching and learning, yet in China corpus methods have not yet been widely
adopted. Corpus Linguistics in Chinese Contexts aims to advance the state of the art in the
use of corpora in applied linguistics and contribute to the expertise in corpus use in China.
Uniquely, this book includes corpus studies on both Chinese and English, addressing the use of
corpora in language teaching, analysis of learner language, as well as examinations of patterns
of Chinese and English. Topics addressed include the novel extension of Lexical Priming theory
to Chinese, textual analyses of both Chinese and English, and learner corpus studies. The book
will appeal to all those interested in teaching or researching language using corpora, where
either the target language, learners or teaching context is Chinese. "— Provided by publisher.

ISBN 978–1–137–44002–0 (hardback)

1. Chinese language—Data processing. 2. Chinese language—Topic and
comment. 3. Corpora (Linguistics)—Data processing. I. Zou, Bin, editor. II. Smith, Simon,
III. Hoey, Michael, editor.

PL1074.5.C68 2015
495.101'88—dc23   2015002659

Typeset by MPS Limited, Chennai, India.

Corpus Linguistics in Chinese Contexts is dedicated to the memory of Dr Adam Kilgarriff, who died on May 16, 2015 after a battle with cancer. Adam was a plenary speaker at the CTAL-2012 Conference, and lead author of Chapter 3 of this volume. Adam was a corpus linguist, computational linguist, and lexicographer, best known for the design of the Sketch Engine, the powerful and multilingual corpus query tool whose application to Chinese teaching and learning is the subject of the chapter.

As an academic, he was widely published, and much in demand as a reviewer and keynote speaker. His passion for his work inspired many people in corpus linguistics and lexicography. As a friend and colleague, Adam was always quick to offer a supportive or encouraging word, always tempered with exactly the right degree of constructive criticism. Everyone who knew him would agree that he was a very clear thinker, who would see his way easily to the core of an issue or problem. Adam was always happy to give advice, whether professional or personal, and his special insight meant that he invariably turned out to be right.

Adam was a man of great courage, who accepted the reality of his illness and impending death with fortitude, wit, and aplomb. He will be sorely missed by many readers of this volume, as well as all those involved in producing it.

The editors,
May 2015

Contents

List of Figures and Tables

Figures

Tables

Foreword

Corpus linguistics in China: theory, technology and pedagogy

I feel greatly honoured to have been invited by Dr Bin Zou to write a foreword for the present volume. As Chairman of the Corpus Linguistics Society of China, I helped Dr Zou and his colleagues to orchestrate the landmark international conference on Corpus Technologies and Applied Linguistics, the CTAL-2012 at Suzhou, China, where I witnessed the impressive success of this commendable event. Although I did not contribute a chapter to this book, as expected by Dr Zou, I do feel nonetheless delighted at the news of its publication. The book comprises a selection of the top-quality papers presented at the conference, which can be expected to give corpus linguistics practitioners an insight into what is going on in China, and the central concerns, theoretical positions and methodologies of the Chinese corpus research community in particular. In my view, the book has dealt with, to varying degrees, some pressing issues facing corpus researchers in China, if not facing colleagues in other parts of the globe. These issues have always been of central importance, and, as I see it, will continue to be of importance for the foreseeable future. These include, among other things, the issues of theory, technology and pedagogy in corpus linguistics studies. In the next few paragraphs, I will briefly express my concerns and views about these issues.

In the first place, theory. Do corpus linguists need to be theoretically minded? Or more specifically, can we design and address research questions, whether applied linguistic questions or other types, with more theoretical concerns, and will our findings be treated as having more theoretical significance? A consensus is lacking for these seemingly simple questions. In the past two decades, within the circle of Chinese language studies, a great number of Chinese corpora have been constructed. Obviously, however, no substantial corpus-based language description has started, and most research seems to keep going on along traditional well-trodden roads without using corpora. Within the circle of foreign language teaching and research, numerous corpus-based studies have found their way into various journals, which are, however, often accused by scholars in other linguistic disciplines of being strong in data but weak in theorizing. It seems to me that these phenomena call forth the necessity of rethinking the theoretical weight of our research and of the discipline of corpus linguistics itself. As far as I can see, corpus linguistics essentially represents a new approach, compared with that of traditional linguistic studies, to linguistic issues. In the strict sense of the term, a linguistic approach encompasses its theories, both macro and micro, along with its characteristic methods. It cannot be just a theory-free neutral method which is amenable to whatever kind of enquiry one wishes to make. As a new approach to language issues, corpus linguistics offers us new ways of looking at language and doing linguistics, making it possible to discover new facts and patterns of language in use. For this point, let us listen to the respected Geoffrey Leech again, who insightfully cautioned 22 years ago that corpus linguistics is 'not just a newly emerging methodology for studying language, but a new research enterprise, and in fact a new philosophical approach to the subject' (Leech, 1992: 106).

Indeed, the first generation corpus linguists, say, Randolph Quirk, Jan Svartvik, Geoffrey Leech, John Sinclair and Michael Halliday, are all theoretically minded. During the heyday of Chomskyan linguistics, they undertook to build their corpora because they were not satisfied with the prevailing ideology at the time. They more or less regarded their corpora as a theoretical construct as against constructs of the mainstream linguistics (see Halliday, 1992). For corpus researchers in China, theory-mindedness cannot be over-emphasized. Even if we agreed with Tony McEnery and Andrew Hardie's (2012) corpus-linguistics-as-method position, we would have to be aware that not all methods are entirely theory-free. We cannot forget that our routine practice of counting word frequency is explicitly rejected as pointless by Chomsky (see Halliday, 1991). In actual fact, methods and theories can hardly be divorced. Rather, they are mutually informed, though to differing degrees. An increased awareness of theory and an appropriate use of theory can be expected to add to the theoretical weight of research, turn our abundant corpus data into higher-quality research products, and, hopefully, blaze new paths for research as well.

Having said that, I must say I am very happy to recognize that studies reported on in *Corpus Linguistics in Chinese Contexts* have strong theoretical significance, appropriately addressing relevant theoretical concerns and offering readers useful insights for similar studies. Particularly, Michael Hoey and Juan Shao's examination on the applicability of Hoey's Lexical Priming theory to Chinese data adds much theoretical weight to the whole book. Drawing on insights from psycholinguistics and firmly based on findings of corpus-based studies, Hoey's theory attempts to account for collocation in terms of psycholinguistic behaviour. His research manifests all the important characteristic features of a corpus linguistic study but goes on further to arrive at a new potentially powerful theory of language. Hoey and Shao's chapter convincingly shows that the corpus linguist is quite theoretically minded and corpus studies can pose serious challenges to current linguistic theories. To paraphrase Kilgarriff (2013: 96), corpus linguistics can make an impact across linguistics.

Secondly, technology. Beyond doubt, technology has played an important role in the booming development of corpus linguistics. Today we rely on concordancers for the co-textual profiles of words, POS taggers for the grammatical class of words, and parsers for the internal structural relationships of texts. These apparatus have constructed a work-face for the corpus linguist, at which he or she digs into the depth of patterns and meanings of the text, and so forth. However, current corpus tools need to be improved in various ways. For example, automatically extracting attitudinal meanings, particularly implicit attitudinal meanings, from texts remains a thorny task, and current tools for extracting multi-word units from texts suffer weaknesses of different sorts. As corpus linguistics strides into newer research territories, we are in need of a wider variety of tools for extracting and processing more types of information. For these reasons, it is commendable that this book has attached great importance to corpus technology in research and teaching. It contains contributions from Adam Kilgarriff, Maocheng Liang and Bin Zou, who have done remarkable work in developing a wealth of software packages, for example, the Sketch Engine and Textsmith Tools, for extracting data from corpora. As the name of the CTAL-2012 conference indicates, developing better technologies is an important concern of the corpus research community, and is particularly true for the Chinese corpus linguistics community. In a word, better tools can mean better data for higher-quality-studies. And it is not unlikely that better tools will entirely change our work-face and give us a new way of doing research.

Finally, pedagogy. From its birth corpus linguistics in China has been inseparably linked with foreign language teaching and research. The initial objective of the JDEST corpus project in the 1980s under the directorship of Professor Huizhong Yang at Shanghai Jiao Tong University was to develop a word list for specifying the then new College English syllabus. The construction of the Chinese Learners English Corpus (CLEC) in late 1990s was also focused on the status of language knowledge and skills of the learners, with a clear aim to provide feedback information for English teaching in the country. As a matter of fact, a good number of corpus construction projects are pedagogy-oriented. However, there are causes for concern. On the face of it, it is very encouraging sign that an avalanche of papers and books on the features of the learner interlanguage have been published as a result of the learner corpora projects, bringing to our attention the unique usage patterns and characteristic errors of the learners. The other side of the coin, however, is that due to various factors these research results are still lying dormant today. Almost no one has made serious endeavour to convert the research findings into real pedagogical behaviour, with, perhaps, the honourable exception of Professor Anping He and her team, who have been steadfastly carrying out pedagogic processing of corpus data for use in classroom teaching. On the whole, corpus research projects in recent years have left a great deal undone in the direction of improving foreign language pedagogy. There is no denying that corpus linguistics has not brought about a significant change, as expected by many, in the way language teaching is planned, organized, and implemented. And in this regard, it is praiseworthy that the present volume has made worthwhile effort in exploring the possibilities of utilizing corpus technology and other resources to improve pedagogy.

To conclude, the publication of *Corpus Linguistics in Chinese Contexts* is a welcome delight; the book has a lot of merits deserving a positive comment. As readers may realize, most chapter authors are key corpus linguists in China, doing interesting research projects, exerting influence on other scholars, and helping shape corpus linguistics in China. Moreover, most are good friends and trustworthy colleagues of mine, for example Wenzhong Li, Maocheng Liang, and Anping He, to name just a few. Many a time, we have put our heads together to tackle problems in joint research. Many brainstorms saw us debating and arguing heatedly. But we have worked together to make the Corpus Linguistics Society of China a harmonious society, to use a popular term in Chinese politics, but in its true sense. Some other authors are well-known scholars on the international academic arena, for example, Michael Hoey and Richard Xiao. Michael Hoey has done ground-breaking work in formulating the influential lexical priming model of language while Richard Xiao has done remarkable work in contrastive studies of Chinese and English. But I must also mention that Michael was always a respected teacher of mine when I was doing my MA at Birmingham University 20 years ago and Richard is a long-time friend of mine in both research

and life. Needless to say, I am filled with delight at the publication of this interesting book.
I wish the present book, like its preceding CTAL-2012 conference, will be a great success.

Naixing Wei
Beihang University, China; Corpus Linguistic Society of China

References

Halliday, M. A. K. 1991. Corpus studies and probabilistic grammar. In K. Aijmer & B. Altenberg (Eds). *English Corpus Linguistics: Studies in honor of Jan Svartvik.* London: Longman. 30–43.

Halliday, M. A. K. 1992. Language as system and language as instance: The Corpus as a theoretical construct. In J. Svartvik (Ed.). *Directions in Corpus Linguistics: Proceedings of the Nobel Symposium 82 Stockholm, 4–8 August 1991.* New York & Berlin: Mouton de Gruyter. 61–77.

Kilgarriff, A. 2013. Review of *Corpus Linguistics: Method, Theory and Practice* by Tony McEnery and Andrew Hardie. *International Journal of Lexicography.* 26 (1). 95–97.

Leech, G. 1992. Corpora and theories of linguistic performance, In J. Svartvik (Ed.). *Directions in Corpus Linguistics: Proceedings of the Nobel Symposium 82 Stockholm, 4–8 August 1991.* New York & Berlin: Mouton de Gruyter. 104–122.

McEnery, T. & Hardie, A. 2012. *Corpus Linguistics: Method, Theory and Practice.* Cambridge: Cambridge University Press.

Series Editor's Preface

The 'New Language Learning and Teaching Environments' book series is dedicated to recent developments in learner-centred approaches and the impact of technology on learning and teaching inside and outside the language classroom. It offers a multidisciplinary forum for presenting and investigating the latest developments in language education, taking a pedagogic approach with a clear focus on the learner, and with clear implications for both researchers and language practitioners.

The focus of the series is thus squarely on innovations, of all kinds, in our field. Although undoubtedly many innovations in language education practice and research take place everywhere in the world, few of these from outside inner circle countries (Kachru, 1992) are reported. Surprisingly this applies even to China, where the scale of the instructional system is enormous and where an increasingly active research culture is making significant contributions to our understanding of language and its acquisition. For this reason I am very pleased to welcome *Corpus Linguistics in Chinese Contexts*, edited by Bin Zou, Simon Smith, and Michael Hoey into this series as it provides valuable insights that will – undoubtedly – benefit researchers and practitioners around the world.

Professor Hayo Reinders

Reference

Kachru, B. 1992. *The Other Tongue: English across cultures*. University of Illinois Press, Champaign, IL.

Preface and Acknowledgements

On 28–30 June 2012, Xi'an Jiaotong-Liverpool University (XJTLU) had the honour of hosting an international conference on Corpus Technologies and Applied Linguistics, CTAL-2012, in Suzhou. The event, co-sponsored by the University of Liverpool and the Corpus Linguistics Society of China, was a great success on at least two counts: it was the first major international corpus linguistics conference in China, and the first international conference hosted by XJTLU. There were more than 100 paper submissions, of which 68 were accepted for presentation by the programme committee. A total of six plenary speeches were given by international and Chinese corpus linguists of renown. For the first time ever at a single event, workshops on two popular corpus tools, the Sketch Engine and Wordsmith Tools, were given by their designers.

The contributions to this edited volume represent a selection of the best of CTAL-2012. A post conference call for full papers was issued, and after a rigorous process of double blind peer review, by an international panel of experts, nine articles were selected for inclusion in the volume.

As is not uncommon with post-conference edited volumes, this book has been a long time in the making. It will stand as a permanent record of a conference which was rewarding for all participants, at times demanding for those organizing it, and led to some lifelong friendships being forged. The editors would like to acknowledge once again the invaluable contributions of Samantha Ng, Gloria Molinero, Li Xiaoli, and Peng Wangheng, and of course Nicole Keng and her team of student helpers. Also, we thank all the plenary speakers and conference presenters, whether or not their individual contribution has been included in this volume.

Special thanks go to our peer review team: Alex Boulton (University of Lorraine), Jozef Colpaert (University of Antwerp), Mike Cribb (Coventry University), Sheena Gardner (Coventry University), One-Soon Her (National Chengchi University), Mike Scott (Lexical Analysis Software Ltd.), Serge Sharoff (University of Leeds), Claire Simmons (Coventry University), Richard Xiao (Lancaster University), Wenzhong Li and Jiajin Xu (both of Beijing Foreign Studies University), and Ying Liu (City University of Hong Kong).

Whether you're a corpus aficionado or as yet unconvinced, from China, a 中国通 (old China hand) or you've never even been there: we commend *Corpus Linguistics in Chinese Contexts* to you!

Notes on Contributors

Yiyan Cai is a lecturer at Xianda College of Economics and Humanities, Shanghai International Studies University, and has been teaching English as a foreign language for ten years. Her publications include journal articles on English Language Teaching.

Anping He is Professor of English at South China Normal University, Guangzhou, and Vice Chair of the Corpus Linguistics Society of China. Her current research interests include corpus linguistics, curriculum and teaching material development, and discourse analysis. She has published 11 books and more than 80 articles, covering topics ranging from the application of corpus linguistics to English teaching and learning.

Michael Hoey is Emeritus Professor of English Language and Pro Vice-Chancellor for Internationalization at the University of Liverpool, UK. He has lectured in applied linguistics in over 40 countries. Hoey has authored a number of textbooks on linguistics including *Signalling in Discourse* (1979), *On the Surface of Discourse* (1983), *Patterns of Lexis in Text* (1991) (which was awarded the Duke of Edinburgh English-Speaking Union Prize for the best book on Applied Linguistics in 1991), *Textual Interaction* (2001), and *Lexical Priming: A New Theory of Words and Language* (2005), which proposes a new way of looking at language based on evidence from corpus linguistics. It was shortlisted for best book in applied linguistics by the British Association for Applied Linguistics.

Nicole Keng has a wealth of experience teaching both General and Academic English to students of all levels, in China, the UK, and Finland. She completed her PhD at the University of York. She currently teaches Academic English and Study Skills at Coventry's partner institution in Guangzhou. In her teaching, she focuses on what Chinese students really need to succeed in their academic programmes. Research interests include corpora in language teaching and learning, corpus linguistics, individual differences between learners in the classroom, group dynamics in the language classroom, cross-cultural communication, and education policy.

Adam Kilgarriff was Director of Lexical Computing Ltd, Brighton, UK. He led the development of the Sketch Engine (http://www.sketchengine. co.uk), a leading tool for corpus research used for dictionary-making at

Oxford University Press, Cambridge University Press, HarperCollins, Le Robert, and elsewhere. His scientific interests lay at the intersection of computational linguistics, corpus linguistics, and dictionary-making. Following a PhD on 'Polysemy' from Sussex University, he worked at Longman Dictionaries, Oxford University Press, and the University of Brighton. He was a Visiting Research Fellow at the University of Leeds. He was active in moves to make the web available as a linguists' corpus and was the founding chair of ACL-SIGWAC (Association for Computational Linguistics Special Interest Group on Web as Corpus). He was also chair of the ACL-SIG on the lexicon and a board member of EURALEX (the European Association for Lexicography). (See also http://www.kilgarriff.co.uk.)

Wenzhong Li is a full-time professor and researcher at the National Research Centre for Foreign Language Education of Beijing Foreign Studies University. His major research fields are in corpus linguistics, applied linguistics, and computer assisted language instruction. Since 2002, he has co-authored and published several books in China, including *Introduction to Corpus Linguistics* (2002), *Research on the Chinese College Learner Spoken English Corpus* (2005), *Applied Corpus Research* (2005), and *A Coursebook for Corpus Applications* (2010).

Maocheng Liang is Professor of Applied Linguistics at the National Research Centre for Foreign Language Education, Beijing Foreign Studies University, China. He is Vice-President of the Corpus Linguistics Society of China, the Secretary-general of the China Language Testing Research Society, and the Associate Editor-in-chief of *Foreign Language Education in China*. His research interests include corpus linguistics, language testing, and natural language processing, language assessment, and second language writing.

Zhaoyang Mei is a language teacher in the Department of Foreign Languages at The Third Military Medical University, Chongqing. Her current research interests include corpus linguistics, foreign language teaching, and critical discourse analysis. Through the use of corpus linguistics, she is trying to analyse ideological aspects of journalistic discourse.

Wangheng Peng is an English Tutor at the Language Centre, Xi'an Jiaotong-Liverpool University, China. He obtained his PhD degree in 1999 and MA degree in 1994 from the University of Liverpool, UK. His research interests include bilingual language teaching and learning, systemic functional grammar, computational linguistics, and corpus studies.

Juan Shao is a lecturer in the School of Foreign Studies, Xi'an Jiaotong University, and has been teaching English as a foreign language for over ten years. She has also taught Chinese to students at all levels in the UK. Now she is a PhD candidate at the School of English, University of Liverpool. Her current research interests include corpus linguistics, foreign language teaching, and comparative language studies.

Simon Smith is a corpus linguist and a language teacher. He currently teaches Chinese and Academic English at Coventry University, and previously taught at XJTLU in Suzhou, where the CTAL-2012 conference was held. He encourages his students to learn autonomously, discovering linguistic patterns for themselves, rather than memorizing grammar patterns and vocabulary. Recent published work has focused on both Chinese and English learning, including data-driven learning, corpus construction by learners, and the acquisition of classical-origin vocabulary.

Haiping Wang holds a PhD from Shanghai International Studies University's Institute of English Language and Literature. She is a lecturer at East China University of Political Science and Law, Shanghai. She was a visiting research student at University of Bristol's Graduate School of Education. Her publications include journal articles on Applied Corpus Linguistics.

Richard Xiao is Lecturer in the Department of Linguistic and English Language at Lancaster University in the UK. His main research interests cover corpus linguistics, contrastive and translation studies of English and Chinese, and tense and aspect theory. In addition to dozens of journal articles, he has published numerous books including *Aspect in Mandarin Chinese* (2004), *Corpus-Based Language Studies* (2006), *A Frequency Dictionary of Mandarin Chinese* (2009), *Using Corpora in Contrastive and Translation Studies* (2010), *Corpus-Based Contrastive Studies of English and Chinese* (2010), and *Corpus-Based Studies of Translational Chinese in English-Chinese Translation* (2012).

Baixiang Yu is Professor at the Department of Foreign Languages and Literatures, National University of Defense Technology, Changsha, China. His current research interests include semantics, corpus linguistics, and relevance theory.

Ren Zhang is a language teacher at the National University of Defense Technology. She obtained her PhD at Shanghai Foreign Languages University. Her interests are predominantly in the fields of cognitive linguistics and culture studies.

Yuanyuan Zheng is a lecturer at Shanghai International Studies University's Xianda College, and a visiting scholar at the English Department of Western Oregon University. Her publications include journal articles on foreign language teaching and research.

Bin Zou is a senior tutor at the Language Centre, Xi'an Jiaotong-Liverpool University in China, a joint venture between the University of Liverpool and Xi'an Jiaotong University. He is the Editor-in-Chief of the *International Journal of Computer-Assisted Language Learning and Teaching*. Zou's research interests include Applied Linguistics, ELT, EAP, CALL, corpus, and ICT. He has authored one book, edited two books, and published widely in journals including *Computer-Assisted Language Learning, System*, and the *Chinese Journal of Applied Linguistics*. He is a committee member of the China Computer-Assisted Language Learning Association. He was the Conference Chair of 2012 Corpus Technologies and Applied Linguistics in Suzhou, China, jointly organized by the University of Liverpool and the Corpus Linguistics Society of China.

Introduction

Wenzhong Li and Simon Smith

Corpora have become increasingly important in the last few decades. Initially, they were widely used in language technology and lexicography. Rapid advances in computing have enabled the integration of corpora into language teaching and learning. New tools for corpus construction and consultation help researchers, translators, lexicographers, teachers and language learners collect and analyse data and use corpora more effectively. However, in China corpus methods have not yet been widely adopted. Outside the corpus linguistics community there is, to date, a lack of awareness of what corpora can offer, whether in the compilation of dictionaries, the creation of corpus-informed materials, or data-driven learning tasks and approaches for use in the classroom or self-study. *Corpus Linguistics in Chinese Contexts* aims to advance the state of the art in the use of corpora in applied linguistics and to spread awareness of and expertise in corpus use in China.

The book serves as a vehicle for nationally and internationally renowned experts to share their work on corpora and technology in language teaching and research. It seeks to make an important contribution to integrating corpora and technology in language teaching and research in China, and to appeal to a wide variety of readers, including anyone who is interested in teaching languages with the use of corpora and technology. It targets, in particular, language teachers who are in China, or whose students are Chinese, or who are learning Chinese, helping them to use corpus technologies, encouraging the students to learn more autonomously or through exposure to more authentic texts. It is hoped, too, that the book will appeal to the corpus research community internationally, as well as to educational organizations and Higher Education (HE) institutions who are integrating corpus technologies into their existing syllabuses. The four chapters which do not directly address pedagogical issues will also be of interest to general corpus linguists in China and beyond.

These four chapters (by Hoey, Xiao, Liang, and Mei et al.) could be characterized as research oriented, while all the remaining chapters are practitioner (teacher) oriented, and we did consider adopting this distinction as the organizing principle for the book. Since our chapter contributions all focused on corpus-informed analysis of either Chinese or English, it was however finally decided that the chapters should be grouped according to language treated, with work on Chinese presented first.

The remainder of this introductory chapter gives an account of corpus-informed research on the Chinese language, followed by a brief treatment of English language corpus work in China, with special attention paid to learner corpora of English built by Chinese scholars. Finally, a short summary of each chapter is provided.

I.1 Chinese language corpora

While Biber et al. (1998: 21) attribute the first English use of a corpus to Dr Johnson in 1755, the earliest corpora or concordance books in China date back rather further. They often take the form of book compilations, or 类书 *Lei Shu* (Encyclopedias of Books). One of the first such publications, 皇览 *Huang Lan*, which appeared in about the 2nd century A. D., was effectively a concordance of various books, based on a list of carefully selected key words or terms indexed either by thematic or prosodic categories, for convenient use by the royals. This tradition of concordancing books was adopted in both official and private circles in the later imperial dynasties. Different from concordances of the Bible or classic works in the western tradition, which were basically complete concordances of a specific single book, the Chinese *Lei Shu* usually concordanced miscellaneous books. For example, 北堂书钞 *Bei Tang Shu Chao* (North Hall Book Notes), compiled by Yu Shinan by the end of the Sui Dynasty (about 600 A. D.), concordanced over 800 books; and 艺文类聚 *Yi Wen Lei Ju* (A Collection of Literary Texts), compiled by Ouyang Xun and his colleagues in the beginning of the Tang Dynasty (624 A. D.), concordanced 1,431 books. These compilations ensured that the contents of many of the ancient books that were subsequently lost or damaged were preserved for posterity.

The earliest systematic collection of data for grammatical study, according to Teubert and Čermáková (2004), was Quirk's *Survey of English Usage*, which began in the 1950s. The first use of corpora in

China for language education or public literacy pre-dates this by several decades, and can be traced back to the 1920s, when there was nation-wide campaigning for universal education. Chen Heqin, a prominent educator of the time, was the first person to have used a manually created corpus, and compiled statistics on the Chinese characters in it. The questions on Chen Heqin's mind were: how many commonly used Chinese characters are there? Among them, how many are from ancient classic written Chinese, and how many are from modern vernacular Chinese, how many are shared in both, how many are the most common or uncommon characters, and finally, how many common characters are needed for primary school pupils and ordinary people striving for literacy? Chen applied his work in corpus creation and application not only for the advancement of adult and child literacy, but also in test design. Between 1920 and 1925, Chen Heqin and his assistants manu-ally collected Chinese texts from different genres and set about inves-tigating the use of characters in modern vernacular Chinese, with an initial classification of Chinese characters into two groups: single char-acters and character combinations. Within a year and a half, they had collected a corpus of 554,478 running characters from six categories of texts (children's books, newspapers and magazines, women's magazines, extracurricular readings for primary school children, novels, and mis-cellaneous), and obtained a list of 4,261 character types (Chen, 1928). From the list Chen was able to get the 1,165 most common Chinese characters whose frequency of occurrence is above the threshold 101 times per million characters (Tao, 1998: 154). The result of Chen's research was a report by the name of 语体文应用字汇 *Common Characters in Use in Vernacular Chinese*, published in 1928 by the Commercial Press. Based on this work, a course book 平民千字课本 *Texts of 1000 Characters for the Common People* was edited by Tao Xingzhi and Zhu Jingnong and put to use even before the report was formally published.

The first widely known computerized corpus of English, the Brown corpus (Francis and Kucera, 1964), became available in the mid-60s, fol-lowed by LOB (Lancaster-Oslo-Bergen) in the 1970s (Johansson et al., 1978). In the meantime, in the late 1970s and the beginning of the 1980s various machine-readable corpora of the Chinese language began to gain development momentum. In the period of time between 1979 and 1983, altogether four electronic corpora were constructed: 汉语现代文学作品语料库 *The Modern Chinese Literary Works Corpus* (5.27 million running characters) completed in 1979 at Wuhan University, 现代汉语语料库 *The Modern Chinese Corpus* (20 million) completed in 1983 at Beijing University of Aeronautics & Astronautics, 中学语文教材语料库

The Corpus of High School Chinese Coursebooks (1.068 million) completed in 1983 at Beijing Normal University, and 现代汉语词频统计语料库 *The Corpus of Statistics of Word Frequencies of Modern Chinese* (1.82 million) completed in 1983 at Beijing Institute of Languages (since 1996, Beijing Language and Culture University) (Feng, 2002: 46).

Chinese text features consecutive character strings with no spaces separating each individual character; a great number of Chinese words are combinations of two or more characters, so word segmentation is a non-trivial problem for Chinese language processing. The early corpora were created and intended primarily for language engineering: initially computing the frequency and distribution of Chinese characters across different genres of texts, and segmenting and tokenizing Chinese character strings for the disambiguation of Chinese words, in an attempt to set up an initial standard for automatic word segmentation (Feng, 2002: 48). According to Feng, as one of the major accomplishments of the early corpus research on Chinese, two fundamental segmentation ambiguity types were identified: overlapping ambiguous strings and combinatorial ambiguous strings. While the former indicates the possibility of a bi-directional segmentation of a continuous string (e.g., for the string ABC, either AB or BC is a possible segmentation), the latter indicates an alternative segmentation of a two-character string (e.g., for the string AB, either AB, or A and B are possible segmentations).

From the 1990s, there has been rapid growth in corpus construction both in terms of size and variety of corpus types. Due to the growing awareness that large corpora are a must, both methodologically and technologically, for Chinese language processing, a number of large (multi-million character) corpora, along with huge archives of newspapers and book series, as well as texts of specific genres, have been made available for annotation and parsing. Dozens of institutions and universities, supported and funded by governmental organizations, have become involved in corpus construction and applications. Corpora have been segmented (tokenized), POS tagged and Proper-name tagged (in the case of the Modern Chinese Corpus at Beijing University), or parsed (as with the Treebank of the Chinese Language constructed in collaboration between Beijing University and the National University of Singapore). At the same time, a great number of parallel corpora with multi-level alignment (paragraphs, sentences, and phrases) together with databases of sentence pairs have been created for bilingual dictionary making and machine translation. Besides the development of various corpora for Chinese, a handful of specialist corpora of minority languages of China, such as Uyghur, Tibetan, and Mongolian, have contributed to the nation's corpus resources. Yet it is a fact that while many Chinese corpora are reported to have been constructed, few of them have been made available for public use. One of the earliest tagged corpora of Chinese was the Academia Sinica Balanced Corpus, described by Chen et al. (1996). A subsequent endeavour of Academia Sinica was the segmentation and tagging of the Linguistic Data Consortium's (LDC) Gigaword corpus. Ma and Huang (2006) give an account of this work. The corpus consists of newswires from both Taiwan (Central News Agency) and mainland China (Xinhua), as well as Singapore (Lianhe Zaobao). The interface implemented by Academia Sinica for Gigaword was the Sketch Engine corpus query tool (see Kilgarriff et al., this volume), which offers access to Gigaword and a number of other Chinese corpora.

The LDC provides a number of other corpora of Chinese, including the Call Home speech corpus used by Xiao (this volume). In his chapter, Xiao also makes use of the Lancaster Corpus of Mandarin Chinese which was created by himself and colleagues at Lancaster (McEnery et al., 2003). This is a balanced corpus, composed of the same proportions of text genres as the English LOB and FLOB corpora.

Corpus construction and use in Chinese language studies can be summarized as follows: (1) most of the corpora constructed are primarily focused on language engineering: information processing, machine translation, and data-mining. Therefore the most active participants in the various projects are computational linguists or scientists in computer science. Few linguists in China are involved in corpus-based research on the language per se, and little achievement has been seen so far in the application of corpora to Chinese language analysis, and still less in Chinese language learning; (2) There has been a great focus on the technological aspects: word segmentation, POS tagging, and parsing, many of which are based on probability models formulated from a limited number of manually tagged texts; (3) Chinese grammar poses a serious challenge to the POS tagging of Chinese. It is often the case that an individual word can be assigned three or four different POS tags, i.e., a word can be a noun, a verb, an adjective, and an adverb. This syntactic ambiguity is often exacerbated by the segmentation ambiguity referred to above; it is in the nature of the Chinese language that POS tagging can be an error-prone affair.

I.2 Corpus research in China on the English language

Much corpus research on the English language and on EFL has been conducted in China. In the first part of the 1980s, Yang Huizhong led a small team at Shanghai Jiaotong University to collect English texts in science and technology. Their initial objective was to obtain a list of common vocabulary for the English learning of science students. The result was the JDEST (Jiao Da English Corpus for Science and Technology), a balanced corpus of one million running words, with 2,000 randomly sampled texts of 500 words each, from 10 subject fields (electronics, metallurgy, machinery, shipbuilding, aeronautics, architecture, electricity, chemical industry, atomic energy, and physics), and across different genres (textbooks, monographs, articles, reports, booklets, abstracts, advertisements, and news articles) (Yang and Huang, 1982; Huang and Yang, 1984, 1985). In 1984, Yang Huizhong, as a visiting scholar in the University of Birmingham supported by the Hornby scholarship through the British Council, participated in a project headed by John Sinclair and Tim Johns for the automatic identification of scientific/technical terms. He postulated the hypothesis that:

> since scientific/technical terms are sensitive to subject matter, they should have fairly high frequencies of occurrence in texts where they occur, but vary dramatically from one subject area to another. It is therefore possible to identify scientific/technical terms solely on the basis of their statistical behaviour. (Yang, 1986: 94–97)

Based on the statistics and comparison of the frequency of distribution of words across different subject areas against a reference corpus, a list of technical words was extracted. To get a list of multi-word terms, a rule-system was designed and applied to the tagged texts, so that only nominal combinations were retained after a post hoc manual editing. Yang found that 'a multi-word key word system is better and more efficient than a single word key word system, because [it is] more revealing of the contents or the "aboutness" of the text' (Yang, 1986: 103). This research work, together with the construction of JDEST, as a pioneering accomplishment in the field of corpus development for specific purposes, was instrumental in the syllabus design and testing development for college English teaching in China. This early corpus research also inspired other empirical studies of English, targeting English education in the Chinese context, and foreshadowed a booming development of corpus research in China over 10 years later. Moreover, it marked the beginning of a long term collaboration and cooperation, as well as personal friendship, between western corpus linguists, such as John Sinclair, Antoinette Renouf, and Wolfgang Teubert (who was the Chair of Corpus Linguistics from 2000, and has been frequently invited to give lectures and seminal talks in many Chinese universities since 2003) at the University of

Birmingham, and Yang Huizhong and a cohort of home-grown corpus researchers tutored by Yang himself and Gui Shichun at Guangdong University of Foreign Studies. There was a gap of over 10 years before JDEST came into the public eye again. It was in the mid-1990s that Yang Huizhong had successfully recruited his first group of PhD students for his 'corpus linguistics specialty'. And at the same time, Gui Shichun, another pioneer corpus linguist in China, together with Yang Huizhong, obtained funding from the national government for their Chinese Learner English Corpus (CLEC), of which the primary objective was to diagnose the typical problems encountered by Chinese learners of English in their writing. The corpus was designed to include English texts written by learners of different proficiencies, including high school students, college English learners (non-majors), English majors, and graduate students. The project involved over 100 participants from a dozen universities in China, and the task of keyboarding the students' handwritten texts was formidable. Each text was marked up with meta information related to it. The CLEC has one million running words and was made available as both raw and error-tagged texts on a CD, as part of Gui and Yang (2005). The first corpus of its kind in China, the CLEC was manually tagged for errors with the aid of a self-written MS word macro. The tag set consists of over 60 preset error types in nine groups, namely word forms, nouns, verbs, adjectives, adverbs, prepositions, connectives, collocations, and sentence fragments. The error tags are placed in square brackets immediately following the errors identified. The corpus, ever since the time of its completion in 1998, has been a great resource and testbed for empirical investigation of learner language, and has motivated a battery of research on learner collocations and grammatical problems within the framework of Contrastive Interlanguage Analysis (Li, 2009).

The CLEC was followed by the College Learner English Spoken Corpus (shortened as COLSEC) in 2003, a project funded by the National Social Science Fund of China and headed by Yang Huizhong at Shanghai Jiaotong University, described by Yang & Wei (2005). The COLSEC, with 700,000 tokens in total, consists of transcribed oral texts from on-the-spot video recordings of the National Oral English Test, which has three types of interactions, namely teacher-student conversation, student-student discussion, and teacher-student discussion, around designated topics. The video clips were clustered according to the testees' universities, test scores and topics assigned, before random sampling. The transcription was carried out by participants from three universities under a policy of 'authenticity, completeness, and accuracy' with ad hoc tagging of prosodic features, such as pronunciation, intonation and pauses, as well as discursive features, such as turn-takings, hesitations and interruptions, as part of the transcribing process. The transcribed texts were then re-formatted in XML format (Li, 2005; Wei et al., 2007). In parallel with the COLSEC construction, another learner corpus of both written and spoken English by English majors was completed, a project directed by Wen Qiufang at Nanjing University. The corpus, published in 2005 with the general title of SWECCL, consists of two sub-corpora, a written corpus (WECLL, one million tokens) and a spoken corpus (SECCL, one million tokens). The corpus was POS tagged using CLAWS and made available alongside the raw texts (Wen et al., 2005).

As a consequence of the boom in learner corpora in China, there was an abrupt growth in corpus-based studies. An increasing number of books and journal articles were published from 1999 onwards, and more national and provincial projects related to corpus research were funded. A simple count of the corpus research articles and theses on the mainland (Figure I.1, retrieved from China National Knowledge Infrastructure http://www.cnki.net/) since 1980 shows that the number grew from two in 1981 to over 8,000 in 2012.

According to statistics from CiteSpace, the most frequent topics emerging in corpus research in recent years are foreign language teaching, learner corpora, collocation, verb-noun collocations, chunks, corpus construction, English writing, English corpora, teaching innovation, CLEC, interlanguage corpora, corpus typology, English teaching, and translation studies (Xu et al., 2012: 2–3). Such topics reflect the main areas of interest of the researchers, as most of them are English teaching practitioners.

The three learner corpora have also had a great influence on learner language analysis. The major research areas are the following:

(1) Interlanguage collocation analysis. Compared with grammatical accuracy, the learner's idiomaticity and fluency in language use is of greater importance. Many of the difficulties and problems the learners have lie in the fact that they are not aware of the collocational constraints on node words that native speakers take for granted.
(2) Interlanguage grammatical analysis. Frequent research objectives are to identify the errors in learners' written and spoken English, such as learners' misuse of verb tense, anaphora, and function words, and attribute them to learners' deviation from the native speaker's norm.

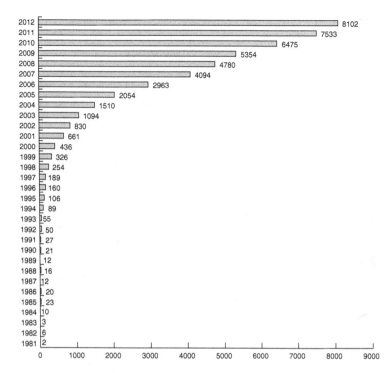

Figure I.1 A simple count of the corpus research articles in mainland journals
Note: Retrieved November 5, 2013 from http://www.cnki.net. The count does not include papers published in international journals, or those of Taiwan and Hong Kong.

(3) Co-relational analysis. This type of study attempts to relate learners' features to their language development. It is suggested that remedial teaching specific to diagnosed inadequacies be implemented to help learners achieve greater progress.

Most interlanguage research is diagnostic: the problems are always assumed to be with the students, they are wrong when they are found to deviate from the native speaker norm. This is a common practice in which researchers tend to highlight contrasts in learner language with native speech, and label the learner features as 'overuse', 'underuse', or 'misuse'. Such a research orientation is not without criticism. In a critical review, the Contrastive Interlanguage Analysis approach is called into question for its theoretical inadequacy and practical deficiency (Li, 2009).

The fact that in the early 2000s some of the current corpus software tools, such as Concordance, Wordsmith Tools, and ParaConc, were commercial programs and somewhat inaccessible to many of the corpus researchers in China gave rise to a series of self-developed software packages, such as BFSU PowerConc (a concordancing software suite by Xu Jiajin, Jia Yunlong, and Liang Maocheng), BFSU ParaConc (a parallel corpus concordancer by Xu Jiajin and Jia Yunlong), ColloExplorer (an automatic collocation concordancing tool by Liang Maocheng), developed at the National Centre for Foreign Language Education of Beijing Foreign Studies University, and the Open Corpus Platform, Multimedia Corpus Parallel Positioning Concordancer, developed by Li Wenzhong and Hang Zhaoyang at Henan Normal University. These software tools are freely available for downloading.

Besides learner corpus construction, it is worth mentioning that some large scale parallel corpora and specialized corpora are also gaining momentum in China, such as the parallel corpus developed by Wang Kefei at Beijing Foreign Studies University (2003), the parallel corpus for Dreams of Red Mansions by Liu Zequan at Yanshan University, the parallel corpus by Wei Naixing at Shanghai Jiaotong University (2009), and China English Corpus (2009) by Li Wenzhong at Henan Normal University. What characterizes these corpora is that they are all funded by the National Social Science Fund of China and have become corpus research resources for PhD students and graduate students in the universities where the corpora are hosted.

Another distinctive feature of corpus research in China is the national collaborative effort at popularizing corpus applications. Since 2006, two summer seminars, respectively, on 'Corpora and English Teaching' and 'Corpora and Language Research', targeted at young researchers in Chinese universities, have been hosted in Beijing by the National Centre for Foreign Language Education and the Foreign Language Teaching and Research Press, and again supported by the Ministry of Education, having involved so far (2006-2014) about 3600 participants from over 1000 universities in China.

While western corpus researchers are seemingly divided into corpus-based and corpus-driven camps, Chinese corpus researchers do not seem so partisan, and tolerate different approaches. The common attitude is: within the discipline of Corpus Linguistics, a corpus is a tool, and corpus-based and corpus-driven research are complementary in terms of methodology (Wei et al., 2014). This flexibility of approach is very much reflected in the selection of papers presented in this volume.

I.3 Chinese language corpus chapters in this volume

The first chapter, written by Hoey and Shao, highlights the impact that corpus linguistic research has had on traditional linguistic theories and descriptions. The chapter focuses on one theory that has been developed in response to the insights derived from corpus linguistics, that of Lexical Priming. Lexical Priming is unusual as a (corpus-driven) theory in that it builds upon long-standing and widely accepted psycholinguistic research, and uses it to account for collocation, colligation, and semantic preference. The theory generates hypotheses that have not been previously explored in a systematic fashion by corpus linguists. The psycholinguistic claims of Lexical Priming theory are not culture- or language-specific, and this chapter presents preliminary observations on the applicability of Lexical Priming theory to Chinese.

The chapter by Xiao presents a contrastive corpus analysis of English and Mandarin Chinese. Xiao looks at the distribution and use of passive voice and classifiers in these two very different languages. It is argued that, contrary to one's expectations, English can be considered a classifier language, like Chinese. Corpus-based evidence is provided for this claim, including a genre analysis of classifiers and passives. Xiao concludes his chapter by setting out future directions for contrastive corpus linguistics.

Chapter 3 is by Kilgarriff, Keng and Smith. The Sketch Engine is a widely used tool in lexicography and, increasingly, the teaching and learning of English. Its Chinese resources are more recent and less widely known. The chapter shows how Sketch Engine can be used to teach the use of homonyms, using authentic text, and how the character search function can find all words containing a given character. The reader can also learn how to find the measure word/classifier associated with a particular noun. In brief, the chapter has a lot to offer teachers of Chinese who are planning to use corpus resources in class.

I.4 English language corpus chapters in this volume

The fourth chapter is by Liang. He argues that research in corpus linguistics and genre analysis does not fully reveal the rhetorical structure of corpus texts, especially the lexico-grammatical patterns belonging to different sections of a text. The chapter then goes on to introduce a newly developed corpus analysis tool which is used to conduct a study on a corpus of research articles in the field of Applied Linguistics.

The chapter by He describes a pedagogical approach whereby students of corpus linguistics are involved in identifying target phrasal verbs and analysing their patterns of use. They are then asked to use this material to develop multimedia courseware, for use in English language teaching in Chinese middle schools. The study innovatively shows how the work of one group of learners can be exploited to help a second group, and how corpus research can feed naturally into pedagogical practice.

Peng's chapter draws on data from a number of corpora, including two native and two learner corpora. His study was conducted at XJTLU (the Sino-British university in Suzhou where CTAL-2012 was hosted), and investigates students' use and misuse of count and non-count nouns. The chapter contains some interesting findings on the countability of nouns, noting that forms that might seem wrong (such as plural *researches*) are in fact found in native speaker corpora. It is concluded that learners are more likely to use non-count nouns as if they were count nouns, and it is suggested that the corpus could be used as a pedagogical resource to help students acquire the correct usage. The chapter also describes the ongoing construction of the XJTLU learner corpus.

Zou and Peng's chapter looks at the writing of students at XJTLU. The students' writing is compared with two published corpora of English academic writing, one by mostly native speakers, the other a (Chinese native speaker) learner corpus. The study focuses on the use of conjunctions in academic writing, and concludes that the writing of the XJTLU students, over their four years of study, moves towards a distribution that more closely resembles English native speaker writing than Chinese university writing, in terms of conjunction use.

Wang, Zheng and Cai report on the construction of an 'open-ended' corpus and its use in teaching reading. They carried out an experimental classroom study to determine whether a corpus construction task helped learners to improve their reading skills. Participants in the experimental group were required to select and tag texts to create the corpus, and a pretest and posttest were given. The authors conclude that their approach stimulates students' interest in reading, as well as helping them to read more autonomously and critically.

The chapter by Mei, Zhang and Yu exploits Appraisal Theory to investigate the treatment of Chinese military affairs in an American newspaper. The authors show that while news reports may appear to relate events objectively, there are in fact latent evaluations which are conveyed to the reader. Twenty news stories, each on China's military development, the US–China military relationship or the naval mission in the Gulf, are analysed in terms of the three subcategories of appraisal (attitude, engagement, and graduation).

The chapters of this volume, then, showcase a variety of corpus-informed work: work on both Chinese and English, both pedagogical and text-analytic, both practical and theoretical. The diversity of the book reflects that of the CTAL-2012 conference that inspired it. Since the conference, in fact, there has been a succession of China-hosted conferences on related themes, all of which attained a high standard of scholarship and participation. Beijing was the venue for the June 2013 Corpus Discourse conference, and will host the 3rd Asia Pacific Corpus Linguistics Conference in 2016—the second in the series took place in Hong Kong in 2014. The acclaimed CLIC (Corpus Linguistics in China) conference was organized by the Corpus Linguistics Society of China (the sponsors of CTAL-2012) in Shanghai in 2013, and Xi'an in 2014. Corpora and corpus tools are now emerging as a standard methodology in textual analysis in Chinese, both theoretical and practical. The scholarship exemplified by these conferences, and the papers in the present volume, suggest strongly that corpus linguistics will play an ever more significant role in the teaching of Chinese, English and other languages in Chinese contexts.

References

Biber, D., Conrad, S., & Reppen, R. 1998. *Corpus Linguistics: Investigating Language Structure and Use*. Cambridge: Cambridge University Press.

Chen, H. Q. 1928. *Yutiwen yingyong zi hui (The Common Characters in Use in Vernacular Modern Chinese)*. Beijing: The Commercial Press.

———. 1992. *Chen Heqin quanji (The Complete Works of Chen Heqin)*. Vol.6. Nanjing: Jiangsu Education Press.

Chen, K., Huang, C., Chang, L. & Hsu, H. 1996. Sinica corpus: design methodology for balanced corpora. *Proceedings of PACLIC 11th Conference* (1996), pp. 167–176.

Feng, Z. W. 2002. Evolution and present situation of corpus research in China. *Journal of Chinese Language and Computing*, 12(1): 43–62.

Francis, W. N. & Kucera, H. 1964. A standard corpus of present-day edited American English, for use with digital computers (Brown). Providence, RI: Brown University.

Gui, S. C. & Yang, H. Z. 2005. *Chinese Learner English Corpus*. Shanghai: Shanghai Foreign Language Education Press.

Huang, R. J. & Yang, H. Z. 1984. A primary computer analysis of english technical words. *Foreign Languages*, 29(1): 46–51.

———. 1985. A statistical analysis of English technical words. *Journal of Foreign Language Teaching and Research*, 61(1): 34–39.

Johansson, S., Leech, G., & Goodluck, H. 1978. *Manual of Information to Accompany the Lancaster-Oslo/Bergen Corpus of British English*. Oslo: University of Oslo.

Li, W. Z. 2005. The design and framework of the COLSEC. In: Yang, H. Z. & Wei, N. X. (eds).

————. 2009. A critical review of the CIA approach. *Computer-assisted Foreign Language Education*, (3): 13–17.

Ma, W.-Y., & Huang, C.-R. 2006. Uniform and effective tagging of a heterogeneous Gigaword corpus. In *Proceedings of the 5th International Conference on Language Resources and Evaluation* (LREC2006). Genoa, Italy, May 2006, pp. 24–28.

McEnery, T., Xiao, R., & Mo, L. 2003. Aspect marking in English and Chinese: Using the Lancaster corpus of Mandarin Chinese for contrastive language study. *Literary and Linguistic Computing*, 18(4), 361–378.

Tao, X. Z. 1998. *Tao Xingzhi quanji (The Complete Works of Tao Xingzhi)* Vol. 11. Chengdu: Sichuan Education Press.

Teubert, W. & Čermáková, A. 2004. *Corpus Linguistics: A Short Introduction.* London: Continuum.

Wei, N. X., Li, W. Z., Pu, J. Z., Liang, M. C. & He, A. P. 2014. The changing corpus linguistics. *Journal of PLA University of Foreign Languages*, 37(1): 1–9.

Wei, N. X., Li, W. Z. & Pu, J. Z. 2007. The design and tagging of the COLSEC. *Contemporary Linguistics*, (3): 235–246.

Wen, Q. F., Wang, L. F. & Liang, M. C. 2005. *Spoken and Written English Corpus of Chinese Learners.* Beijing: Foreign Language and Teaching Research Press.

Xu, J. J., Liu, X., & Liu, L. 2012. A review of the corpus linguistic research in China based on CiteSpace II. *Corpus Linguistics Research Highlights*, 1(1): 2–6.

Yang, H. Z. 1986. A new technique for identifying scientific/technical terms and describing science texts (an interim report). *Literary and Linguistic Computing*, 1(2): 93–103.

Yang, H. Z. & Huang, R. J. 1982. JDEST as a computer corpus of science and technology. *Journal of Foreign Language Teaching and Research*, (4): 60–62.

Yang, H. Z. & Wei, N. X. 2005. *The Construction of and Research on the COLSEC.* Shanghai: Shanghai Foreign Language Education Press.

1

Lexical Priming: The Odd Case of a Psycholinguistic Theory that Generates Corpus-Linguistic Hypotheses for Both English and Chinese

Michael Hoey and Juan Shao

1.1 Corpus linguistics at the crossroads

Corpus linguistic research has had an iconoclastic effect on traditional linguistic theories and descriptions. Intuitions about the language have been found to be untrustworthy for over 20 years (e.g. Sinclair, 1991; Stubbs, 1995), and, in the wake of the methodological innovations associated with discourse analysis and sociolinguistics, attention has decisively shifted from guesswork about what an idealized speaker can theoretically say to hard evidence about what many thousands of speakers and writers actually do say. Whereas linguistics was once, for many, virtually synonymous with the study of grammar, the study of lexis is now widely accepted to be as important as grammar, with the role of collocation repeatedly recognized not only as ubiquitous but as central to our understanding of the way language works (Sinclair, 1991, 2004; Stubbs, 1995, 1996; Partington, 1998; Hoey, 1997, 2003, 2005). The generative linguist's identification of competence as key to understanding linguistic creativity has been replaced by the corpus linguist's identification of performance as key to understanding linguistic fluency (e.g. the idiom principle proposed by Sinclair, 1991; pattern grammar proposed by Hunston & Francis, 2000).

The energy with which traditional ideas have been knocked down has not however been matched by equivalent energy in rebuilding theories, and where theories have been proposed, they have often been incomplete or unconvincing. Although, for example, Sinclair's idiom principle articulates an important truth about the way we construct our utterances, it leaves unarticulated the mechanism whereby one might fall back onto grammar when idioms fail to serve the speaker's communicative process; nor is it convincing about why we should, as children, develop a grammatical system as a security mechanism for when our idioms fail. (Sinclair & Mauranen, 2006, admittedly offer a subtler picture.) On the whole, corpus linguistics has either ignored theoretical questions or (less commonly) related itself to pre-existing theoretical perspectives that appeared capable of accommodating corpus linguistic findings, e.g. cognitive linguistics and connectionism (Ellis, 2005; Gries & Stefanowitsch, 2006). There is of course nothing wrong with the latter course of action, but it may be premature until we have explored further what a corpus-based theory might look like.

1.2   A theory for corpus linguistics

One theory that has been developed in response to the insights derived from corpus linguistics, and in particular the work of John Sinclair, is that of Lexical Priming (Hoey, 2003, 2004a, 2004b, 2005; Hoey et al., 2007). If in due course this theory proves to be inadequate, it is to be hoped that it will nevertheless encourage more corpus-driven theoretical formulation. Lexical Priming is unusual as a (corpus-driven) theory in that it builds both upon corpus linguistic analysis and upon long-standing psycholinguistic research into the ways word recognition may be accelerated or retarded by previous exposure to other words, research which is widely accepted by psychologists but apparently little-known amongst corpus linguists.

Much of the psycholinguistic literature used by linguists is arguably more linguistic than psychological. But there are two research threads in psycholinguistics that may be of relevance, that are perhaps more psychological than linguistic: work on semantic priming and work on repetition priming.[1]

In semantic priming experiments, informants are shown a word or image (referred to as the prime) and then shown a second word or image (referred to as the target word). The speed with which the target word is recognized is measured. Some primes appear to retard informants' recognition of the target and others appear to accelerate informants' recognition of the target. For example, the prime word *wing* may be shown to inhibit the recognition of the word *pig* but to accelerate the recognition of the word *swan*.

As Pace-Sigge (2013) shows, the semantic priming literature is extensive and has an important pre-history; his book should be consulted by those interested in the psycholinguistic background. What is offered in this chapter is simply an outline account designed to explain the psycholinguistic underpinning of lexical priming theory before we consider its applicability to Chinese. The pioneering work on semantic priming was conducted by Meyer and Schvaneveldt (1971); they were the first to show that priming was scientifically demonstrable. Their work was followed through by Shelton and Martin (1992) (among others), who appear to show that semantic priming only works when the priming word and the target are associated in the informant's mind. McRae and Boisvert (1998) argue, however, that if the words in question have closely related meanings there will be a priming effect even without such association. It will be noted that the earliest of the papers we have just cited is now over 40 years old and the phenomenon has not been refuted, even if the constraints upon its operation are still under discussion. While semantic priming does not explain the phenomenon of collocation, and is not necessarily the product of collocation, it is reasonable to look for a common explanation of both phenomena. This we find in repetition priming.

Repetition priming is rather different from semantic priming, in that the prime and the target are identical. Experiments with repetition priming centre on exposing informants to word combinations and then, sometimes after a considerable amount of time and after they have seen or heard a great deal of intervening material, measuring how quickly or accurately the informants recognize the combination when they finally see or hear it again. For example, a listener may be shown the word ALARMING followed by the word SUNSHINE. A day later, if s/he is shown the word ALARMING again, the informant may be found to recognize SUNSHINE more quickly than other words equivalently positioned after ALARMING. The assumption in such a case must be that s/he would be remembering the combination from the first time, since a combination of words such as ALARMING SUNSHINE will only rarely have occurred before, and quite probably not in the earshot or reading of the informant, and is therefore unlikely to comprise a learnt expression.

Again, we refer the reader to Pace-Sigge (2013) for a fuller account of the relevant literature. Key papers on these facets of repetition priming, though, are those of Jacoby and Dallas (1981), who observed greater accuracy in the identification of the target, and Scarborough et al. (1977), who noted a faster response time. Forster and Davis (1984) observed that these effects of repetition priming were more noticeable when the words in question were of low frequency in the language. As with the semantic priming research, it will be observed that several of the key papers are more than 30 years old and that again the phenomenon they report has not been challenged.

Repetition priming potentially provides an explanation of both semantic priming and collocation. If a listener or reader encounters two words in close proximity in a text (spoken or written), and stores them together, then the ability of one of the words to accelerate recognition of the other is explained. If close proximity includes adjacency, as it must, then the storage is presumably of the combination, which would account for the development of collocations in the mind. If the listener or reader then draws upon this combination in his or her own utterances, then the reproduction and spread of collocations are also explained.

Hoey (2005) looks at the relationships explored in semantic priming research from a slightly different angle. Where the attention in the psycholinguistic work cited above is on the recognition effects of a particular prime on a particular target, lexical priming theory is more interested in the way the target may accumulate such primes. Likewise, the theory draws on corpus linguistic evidence to suggest that the combinations stored and recovered in repetition priming experiments go beyond collocational combinations and include colligations (Firth, 1957; Halliday, 1959; Sinclair, 1996, 2004; Hoey, 1997, 2005), semantic preferences (which Hoey rechristens semantic associations) (Sinclair, 1999; Hoey, 2005), and pragmatic associations (Hoey, 2005), amongst a number of other kinds of association. In so doing the theory seeks to account for the existence of these phenomena. The argument is not circular, though it is not complete either. It is not circular in that we have triangulation between the psycholinguistic experimentation and the corpus-linguistic evidence; it is not complete because it has still be to be demonstrated psycholinguistically that colligation and semantic association have the same kind of psychological validity as collocation has. However the theory makes a number of claims that lead to testable hypotheses, one of which is the subject of this chapter.

1.3   Six lexical priming claims

There are a number of claims that lexical priming theory makes. The first lexical priming claim is that whenever we encounter a word or syllable or a combination of words, we note subconsciously the linguistic context in which it occurs and, when it is repeatedly encountered, we begin to identify the features of the context and (particularly) the co-text that are also being repeated with it. It is this claimed identification that research into repetition priming provides evidence for. More precisely, the claim is that as we have an increasing number of encounters with the word, syllable, or word combination in question, we come to identify the word or words that characteristically accompany it (its collocations), the grammatical patterns with which it is associated (its colligations), the meanings with which it is associated (its semantic associations), and the pragmatics with which it is associated (its pragmatic associations). These do not exhaust the features of the co-text and context that we recognize as a result of our repeated encounters (see, for example, Hoey, 2005; Hoey & Brook O'Donnell, 2008, for accounts of larger textual associations that are claimed to be recognized), but this chapter will concern itself with only the four types of priming mentioned.

The second lexical priming claim is that because all our encounters with a piece of language prime us in the way just described, we are likely, when we come to use the piece of language ourselves, to use it in the same kinds of way as it was used in those encounters. These two claims are central to the argument of Hoey (2005).

The third claim, touched upon in Hoey (2005) but not fully developed there, is that grammar and semantics are outputs from our primings, not inputs, and differ from person to person. Simplifying slightly, every word has its own local grammar and semantics and what we think of as the grammatical/semantic systems are the products of all these local grammars and local semantics. Hoey (2007, 2009) explores this claim in slightly more detail as regards local grammars and their acquisition. Lewis (2000: 137) articulates a similar position when he notes that 'language consists of grammaticalised lexis, not lexicalised grammar'.

The fourth lexical priming claim is that every time we encounter a piece of language we note the genre, domain, style, co-text, and context in which it occurs and associate the word, phrase or syllable with those genres, domains, and so on in which it is normally encountered, a point also made by Conzett (2000) (though without, of course, reference to priming). To use a couple of examples from Conzett, we learn to associate re-entry into society with prisons and incentive schemes with the workplace (p. 80). A sentence such as *He's tied up at the moment* will normally only occur in Business English and a sentence beginning with the words *Recent findings support* ... will be more likely to occur in academic articles than anywhere else (examples again from Conzett p. 81–2). The implication is that there are a large number of hugely overlapping but non-coterminous language varieties, only some of which any particular speaker will have familiarity with. For some speakers these genres, domains and styles may not be distinct while for other speakers they may be divisible, depending on the richness and variety of their priming.

The fifth claim echoes the fourth, though it is not tied to it. This claim is that everybody's linguistic experience is unique; we have different parents and friends, who say different things to us, we read different books, signs, advertisements and websites and we watch different films and TV programs; in addition, we do all these things with different levels of attention. The effect is that everybody's primings are slightly different from everybody else's. In lexical priming theory, the idiolect is accordingly central.

The final claim is quite an important one and is different in kind from the others, in that it concerns the relationship of a scientist's methodology to the language under study. This claim is that a corpus does not represent anybody's linguistic experience and that therefore, although a corpus description may be used to identify potential primings, only psychological experimentation can demonstrate whether the potential is realized. What follows therefore cannot be taken as evidence of the correctness of the psychological claims but as evidence of the kinds of psychological claims that can reasonably be made.

It is perhaps an irony that a theory designed to account for the discoveries of corpus-linguistics should end up placing a limit on what corpus linguistic description can tell us. However, because the theory builds upon general psycholinguistic claims about the way language is stored and accessed, its implications extend beyond the phenomena characteristically described by corpus linguists and it may generate hypotheses that have not been previous explored in a systematic fashion, thereby fruitfully extending the scope of corpus linguistics. The investigation of one of these hypotheses will be reported on in this chapter.

1.4   English versus Chinese

Because the psycholinguistic claims briefly outlined above are not culture- or language-specific, the theory ought to generate hypotheses about all languages, not only Indo-European ones. But Chinese and English are usually regarded as very different along a number of parameters. English, for example, makes a fairly clear distinction between words and morphemes whereas the distinction is blurred in Chinese. In English, intonation is a discourse feature, but in Chinese tone is a feature of the lexicon. English marks tense and number grammatically, in contrast to Chinese which marks them lexically.

Nevertheless the hypothesis generated by lexical priming theory is that the Chinese and English languages are in many important matters alike and can be described in the same lexico-grammatical terms as each other, not because a Western description is being imposed on a non-Western language but because the corpus-derived categories of description that lexical priming utilizes are language-neutral. More specifically, it is hypothesized that Chinese and English will be alike in displaying evidence of collocations, colligations, and semantic associations. If such relations were as apparent in Chinese as they are in English, there would presumably be the same need to account for their existence in the language, and lexical priming would be offered as a possible explanation. The absence of collocation, colligation, and semantic association in Chinese, on the other hand, would constitute a challenge to the theory, since the theory assumes that these would be necessary outcomes of being lexically primed and it is improbable that Chinese is acquired in wholly different ways from English. (The presence of collocation, colligation and semantic association in Chinese would not, though, by itself, demonstrate the theory's correctness.)

1.5   Collocation in English and Chinese

As we have seen, the starting point of Lexical Priming theory is that, as we have more and more encounters with a word or combination of words (or as we shall see later, components of words), we come to identify its collocations. The starting point of any consideration of whether lexical priming applies to Chinese, and whether Chinese and English share lexical properties, must therefore also be collocation.

One example should suffice to illustrate how collocation operates in English, since it is unlikely that any reader of this chapter will be unfamiliar with the concept or the evidence of its ubiquity in the language (Sinclair, 1991, 2004; Stubbs, 1995, 1996; Partington, 1998, etc.). A search in Google for combinations of words occurring with the word *wine* threw up the following data in the form of Google hits (see Table 1.1).

These data show that *wine* collocates with *red, white, dry,* and (less strongly) *sweet*; it seems probable that these associations have psychological validity for most native speakers of English as well as statistical validity.

The question of whether collocation is a natural phenomenon in the Chinese language does not need answering here, as the existence of collocation has already been demonstrated for Chinese by Xiao

Table 1.1 Most frequent word combinations including *wine*, according to Google search

red wine	16,900,000
dry red wine	338,000
white wine	10,600,000
dry white wine	1,140,000
sweet wine	587,000
red dry wine	952
dry wine	266,000
white dry wine	935
sweet red wine	66,200
red sweet wine	8,500
sweet white wine	99,100
white sweet wine	225

and McEnery (2006). Here, therefore, we seek only to explore further instances of the way collocation operates in the language.

Here and in subsequent sessions we make use of Sketch Engine, an online corpus query system (Kilgarriff et al., 2004) that can handle a character-based writing system like that of Chinese. Like most corpus query systems, it provides concordances for search terms; it also incorporates a 'Word Sketch' facility, a one-page automatic summary of the grammatical and collocational behaviour of the lexical item under investigation. In addition to meeting the essential criterion of handling character-based writing systems, the software also provides access to ready-made Chinese corpora for research purposes.

zhTenTen11 is a Chinese corpus in simplified characters collected in 2011. It is the largest simplified Chinese corpus available on Sketch Engine, containing 2,106,661,021 tokens. The data in this corpus were retrieved by Web crawling and processed with the latest boilerplate cleaning and de-duplication tools. One problem with web-crawling data is that 'none of the dates on a web page reliably state when it was written – unless it is one of a few types of text such as newspaper, blog, or press release' (Jakubíček et al., 2013). It is also not possible to calculate accurately the numbers of instances of text types or genres in the corpus nor to work out their relative weighting. However, while these defects would be damaging if a general description of the Chinese lexicon were being attempted, they are less of a problem in a paper that focuses on the applicability and relevance to Chinese of categories of description utilized by lexical priming theory.

The word we chose to explore was 好 (*hao*), which occurs in Chinese with several tones. (In what follows we present the character first, followed by its Pinyin representation in brackets, Pinyin being an institutionalized Roman alphabet transcription of what is said in Mandarin.) So in the combination 好斗 (*hàodòu*), 好 (*hào*) occurs with a falling tone

(tone four in the Chinese categorization of tones), but in most of its uses, it occurs with a fall-rise tone (tone three), and it is that variant, which is of course different to the Chinese ear from the falling tone variant, that we primarily examine here. There are 5,750,122 hits of 好 (2,729.5 per million) in the corpus, which is a reflection of the fact that 好 (*hao*) is a very frequent lexical item in Chinese. Table 1.2 shows the most frequent collocates modified by 好 (hǎo). The figures in column 2 of the table show the frequency of the collocates, for example, the number 21727 means there are 21727 instances of 效果 (xiàoguǒ) co-occurring with 好 (hǎo), where 好 (hǎo) functions as the modifier of 效果 (xiàoguǒ). The figures in column 3 are association scores for collocational strength, measured by logDice, which has been argued to be more reliable since it will not be biased by either too high or too low frequency of the items in the query (Rychlý, 2008).

We shall look at a few of these in more detail, but before we do, we note, simply, that if collocation is self-evidently present in Chinese, as indeed Xiao and McEnery (2006) noted, our hypothesis is supported.

Table 1.2 Most frequent collocates modified by 好 in zhTenTen11 corpus

Collocates	Frequency	Score
效果 xiàoguǒ (effect)	21727	9.86
成绩 chéngjī (achievement)	10171	8.77
作用 zuòyòng (use, effect)	10411	8.25
做法 zuòfǎ (way, method)	4739	8.22
建议 jiànyì (suggestion)	5067	8.16
机会 jīhuì (chance)	5690	8.15
办法 bànfǎ (way, method)	5699	7.91
选择 xuǎnzé (choice)	4430	7.91
方法 fāngfǎ (way, method)	6910	7.67
经验 jīngyàn (experience)	5406	7.61
效益 xiàoyì (effect and profit)	3999	7.56
意见 yìjiàn (advice)	3822	7.44
朋友 péngyǒu (friend)	2835	7.34
条件 tiáojiàn (condition)	4756	7.29
平台 píngtái (platform)	4283	7.24
成效 chéngxiào (achievement and effect)	2386	7.18
时候 shíhou (moment, time)	3217	7.14
东西 dōngxi (thing)	2503	7.14
基础 jīchǔ (basic)	6179	6.95
例子 lìzi (example)	1803	6.89
环境 huánjìng (environment)	6740	6.72
老师 lǎoshī (teacher)	3103	6.68
习惯 xíguàn (habit)	1855	6.67
机遇 jīyù (opportunity)	1707	6.67
前景 qiánjǐng (prospect)	1753	6.66

However, the majority of the items in the list above are made up of two characters and the question arises of whether collocations occur between characters as well as between words. We therefore looked at a particular sub-set of the collocations of 好 (*hǎo*) that had a similar meaning to see whether there was evidence of character collocations; the collocations chosen were those of 好 (*hǎo*) with 做法 (*zuòfǎ*), 办法 (*bànfǎ*) and 方法 (*fāngfǎ*), all of which mean 'way, method'; the reason for selecting these collocates was that they all share the character 法 (*fǎ*). This character can function as a self-standing word with the meaning of 'French' or 'law'. It can, more rarely, also mean 'way, method', particularly in a Buddhist context, but occurs more naturally in the combinations below.

做法 zuòfǎ (way, method)	4,739	8.22
办法 bànfǎ (way, method)	5,699	7.91
方法 fāngfǎ (way, method)	6,910	7.67

To investigate whether 好 (*hǎo*) collocates with 法 (*fǎ*) independently as well as with the words in which 法 (*fǎ*) occurs, we retrieved concordances of 好 (*hǎo*) with 法 (*fǎ*) in the context of 15 tokens on the right side. This decision took account of the fact that modifiers in Chinese have a strong tendency to appear before the words they modify (at least in the written form) and little tendency to occur on the right. But it was also based on a conviction by both authors that the traditional five-word span is not always appropriate in the search of collocations. Hoey (2014) argues more generally for a wider trawl for collocations than is permitted by a five-word span to left and right, and Shao (2014) argues a similar case for Chinese.

2,410 instances were found in the corpus of 好 (*hǎo*) co-occurring with 法 (*fǎ*) within 15 tokens to the right.[2] A sample of 250 instances of these was analysed at the preliminary stage to identify irrelevant pairings. Firstly, we identified as needing to be eliminated all lines where 法 (*fǎ*) was used in connection with 法语 (*fǎyǔ*) (French) or 法国 (*fǎguó*) (France), since there was no semantic common ground between these uses and those discussed above. Secondly, when 好 (*hǎo*) was used to modify verbs such as 执行 (*zhíxíng*) (conduct), 用 (*yòng*) (use), and 实施 (*shíshī*) (carry out), it was found that 法 (*fǎ*) was being used to refer to law or to aspects of a law. Although this suggests another collocational relationship between the two words, we eliminated these cases also. Finally, and more mechanically, there were instances in which 好 (*hǎo*) occurred in a separate clause from 法 (*fǎ*), with a comma between the clauses. Given the broader window being used to identify collocations, these instances were also removed from the data set, though it does not follow that they were always irrelevant to the argument. This left us with 51 instances of 好 (*hǎo*) occurring with 法 (*fǎ*), separate from its occurrences with 做法 (*zuòfǎ*), 办法 (*bànfǎ*) and 方法 (*fāngfǎ*), but still retaining, as we will show in the next section, the same general meaning of 'way, method'.

1.6 Semantic association in English and Chinese

Semantic association can be said to occur when a word (or group of words) regularly co-occurs with words or phrases drawn from the same semantic set. Usually (perhaps always) one or more members of the set will also be collocates with the word or group of words in question. Thus in English *dry* and *sweet* are collocates of *wine*, but they are also members of the semantic set of FLAVOUR, which *wine* has a more general association with – wines are regularly described (by wine merchants and aficionados) as *tart, spicy, woody, rich, fruity, tangy, musky, peppery*, and so on, few of which would be primed for the ordinary drinker as collocates. The FLAVOUR association also manifests itself as noun phrases – *pear and spice notes, lemony acidity, a few hints of coffee, a rapid expression of violet*. The assumption would be that collocations are identified by the language user first and that, as semantically related but hitherto unexpected items are encountered in the place of the expected collocate, the collocation is subsumed into a semantic association, of which the collocations are the unmarked members.

The question then is whether Chinese shows evidence of semantic association. Examining the data for 好 (*hǎo*) occurring with 法 (*fǎ*), with a view to answering this question, our findings were as follows.

Firstly, 27 out of 51 instances (53%) of the collocation concerned methods 法 (*fǎ*) of LOSING WEIGHT, of which 26 occurred in combination with either 减肥 (*jiǎnféi*) (lose weight) or 瘦身 (*shòushēn*) (go on a diet) or both. All but one of the occurrences of these two words appeared before 法 (*fǎ*), the exception appearing before 好 (*hǎo*). Some examples follow:[3]

(1)
我	给	你	说	一个	大好的	减肥	瘦身	法
wǒ	gěi	nǐ	shuō	yíge	dàhǎode	jiǎnféi	shòushēn	fǎ
I	to	you	say	a	good	lose-weight	diet	method

是	我	本身	切身	履历[4]	的	最	有用。	
shì	wǒ	běnshēn	qièshēn	lǚlì	de	zuì	yǒuyòng	
be	my	own		experience	PAR	most	effective	

The way of losing weight and keeping fit that I am telling you about is the most effective one that I tried myself.

(2) 减肥　　　效果　最　好　最　快　黄瓜　　香蕉　三　日　法

jiǎnféi　　xiàoguǒ zuì　hǎo　zuì　kuài huángguā xiāngjiāo sān　rì　fǎ

Lose weight effect　most good most quick cucumber banana　three days method

What has the best and most quick effect of losing weight (is) the method (of eating) cucumber and banana for three days.

We also found that 12 of the 51 hits occurred in the domain of EDUCATION, with words such as 教学 (*jiàoxué*) (teaching), 写 (*xiě*) (writing), 算 (*suàn*) (calculating), and 破解 (*pòjiě*) (solving) appearing before 法 (*fǎ*).

(3) 好　的　课堂　　教学　导入法，既　　　能够　集中　学 生　的　注意

hǎo　de　kètáng　jiàoxué　dǎorùfǎ jì　　nénggòu jízhōng xuésheng de　zhùyì

Good PAR classroom　teaching lead-in　not only can　focus　student　PAR attention

A good lead-in method in the classroom can not only focus students' attention...

Re-examination of the collocations of 好 (*hǎo*) with 做法 (*zuòfǎ*), 办法 (*bànfǎ*), and 方法 (*fangfǎ*) (the original collocations identified by Sketch Engine) revealed that words such as 减肥 (*jiǎnféi*) (losing weight) and 教学 (*jiàoxué*) (teaching) also occur before 方法 (*fāngfǎ*). Examining the original 6,910 instances of 方法 (*fāngfǎ*) we identified only seven instances with 瘦身 (*shòushēn*) (go on a diet), but 234 instances (0.1 per million) with 教学 (*jiàoxué*) (teaching), and 228 hits (0.1 per million) with 解决 (*jiějué*) (solving).

The data for 好 (*hǎo*) and 法 (*fǎ*) go beyond demonstrating that collocation exists in Chinese as well as English and take us, as intended, into the second area of investigation – semantic association. They suggest that 好 (*hǎo*) and 法 (*fǎ*) have a semantic association with DIET and also (separately) occur in the domain of EDUCATION; the domain in which the collocation occurs also appears to manifest itself as a semantic association, though we have not sought to investigate this in any detail.

1.7   Nesting in English and Chinese

We have also demonstrated in passing that the phenomenon of nesting, present in English, is also present in Chinese. Nesting is the phenomenon whereby a pair of words or word combinations may contract collocations (and other associations) of their own, independently of the collocations and associations that the individual items might contract.

So, for example, in English, in a concordance containing 133 instances, the collocating pair of words *high tide* has as its second highest collocate in L1 position *at* and as its fourth highest collocate in R1 position *mark*. The Chinese data we have been considering show, in similar fashion, that the nested combination of 好 (*hǎo*) and 法 (*fǎ*) has in turn semantic associations with DIET and EDUCATION, and also occurs in those domains. Thus nesting is another shared property of the two languages.

1.8 Collocation with word components in English

The above analysis however raises an interesting question. We noted earlier that one of the traditional contrasts between English and Chinese is that English is a language with a clear distinction between word and morpheme, while in Chinese the boundary is blurred. In the analysis of 好 (*hǎo*)'s relationship with 法 (*fǎ*), we have just seen that a Chinese word component may collocate and form semantic associations. The question then naturally arises as to whether the same is true for English or whether this remains a point of difference between the languages.

Hoey (forthcoming) presents data in support of the claim that –*eries* is associated with CRIME and SIN on the one hand (*chicaneries, adulteries, forgeries*) and PRODUCT CREATION on the other (*breweries, bakeries, distilleries*). In the combined corpora of *The Guardian* and the British National Corpus, 118,932 tokens of words ending –*eries* were identified, of which there were 142 separate types. Eleven of these types were classified as associating with NASTY SUBSTANCE and occurring within (arguable) UNPLEASANTNESS, including *snotteries, splatteries, miseries, sludgeries, slickeries, dysenteries, grotesqueries, goucheries, camperies, flummeries,* and *flatteries,* and they accounted for 8% of the total set of types. A further 24 out of 142 (17%) of the types ending in –*eries* associated with the closely related set CRIME/SIN/SOCIAL FAULT. Examples are *adulteries, trickeries, treacheries, mockeries,* and *snobberies.* Finally, 28 out of 142 (20%) of the types, including *wineries, potteries, tanneries, saddleries, rotisseries, crêperies, refineries,* and *perfumeries* were identified as PRODUCT CREATION.[5] Altogether, 45% of –*eries* were associated with these three meanings, which leads us to put a question mark with the assumption that English has clear boundaries between words and morphemes.

This is not an isolated or carefully chosen example. Looking again at *high tide*, the first and second highest collocates of the word combination are *the* in L1 position and *of* in R1 position (*the high tide of* ...);

this combination occurs 26 times and accounts for one in five of the instances of *high tide*. Of these 26 instances, 12 (46%) are followed by a nominal group whose Head ends –*ism* (*federalism, Thatcherism, idealism, interventionism,* etc.).

Or starting at the other end, looking this time at **ology*, there are 12,402 occurrences of **ology* in the Guardian newspaper between 1990 and 1995, excluding 13,686 instances of *technology*. The latter were removed from our analysis because the many instances of this single type represented slightly over 50% of the data for **ology*; no other type came close to *technology's* frequency. Had *technology* been included, we would have been confusing collocations of the word with collocations of the morphology. The analysis that follows is unaffected by the removal of instances of *technology*, except as regards the figures given for the overall proportion of the data set accounted for by the collocations. We used the WordSmith Tools concordancing software package (Scott, 2013) to calculate the collocations found for **ology*. WordSmith identified a number of collocates with **ology* and at least one semantic association was reflected in the collocational list. One of the collocations is with another word component, albeit one that is more straightforwardly lexical – *stud**. There are in our data 406 instances of *stud** (*student, students, studied, study, studying*) co-occurring with **ology* (accounting for 3.3% of instances of **ology*).[6] A near synonym of *study* in the context of university education is *read (for)*, as in *read theology* and *read for the degree of* ... (mainly a UK usage); there are a further 110 instances of *read** (excluding *reader* which is a formal (UK) academic title) that co-occur with **ology*. Together they account for 4.2% of instances of **ology* in our data.

As it happens, *reader* in the formal academic title sense is part of another semantic association with **ology*, along with *professor* and *researcher*. There are 512 professor(s), 48 reader(s), and 14 researcher(s) all in the vicinity of **ology*, together accounting for 4.6% of the data set. Students might be added to this list as 'workers in a university', which would add a further 107 to the semantic set, and would account for over one in 20 of instances of **ology*.

There is a need for much more research on the collocational (and other) properties of word-components in English, but on the basis of these analyses of –*eries* and –*ology* and of the presence of –*ism* as a collocate of *high tide*, we venture to suggest that the gap between Chinese and English, in respect of the way word components operate, may not be as large as their writing systems may suggest.

1.9 Colligation in English and Chinese

According to lexical priming theory, as noted above, grammar is an output of the accumulation of primings, in particular the colligational primings. Colligation can be defined as the grammatical patterns and positions that a word recurrently occurs in or with; it importantly implies that other patterns and positions do not often occur despite their apparent availability in the linguistic system. The lexical priming claim is that as we have our repeated encounters with a particular word, word-combination or word-component, we come to identify the grammatical patterns with which it is associated (its colligations). The psychological aspects of this claim cannot of course be demonstrated by corpus-linguistic means, but what can be demonstrated is the existence (or otherwise) of such lexico-grammatical patterns in a particular language and their consequent availability for the purposes of priming in that language.

The Google hits for *wine*, referred to above, are equivalent to a concordance of *wine* of 30,006,912 lines. Out of these hits the following are the results for *dry* and *wine*. Occurrences of *dry* in premodifying position are presented in Table 1.3.

In sum, the Google search threw up approximately 1,746,000 combinations of *dry* premodifying *wine* (5.8% of the hits). Compare these figures with those for *wine* and *dry* when the latter is performing a Complement function (i.e. *wine + BE + dry*). This occurs just 243,400 times in the data set (0.8%) (a 7:1 ratio between the two possible patterns). A similar picture pertains for *sweet*, though less markedly so. There are 761,025 instances of *sweet* premodifying *wine* as opposed to 326,600 predicative uses (a ratio of 7:3). (The ratios are predictably much more striking for *red* and *white*, it being rare that we wish to say *This wine is red*.) We conclude that *wine* colligates with adjectives describing flavour in premodifying position/function.

We now turn to Chinese. In the first place, 好(*hǎo*) is associated with 法 (*fǎ*) in the particular structure of 好 (*hǎo*) + X + 法 (*fǎ*), where X can

Table 1.3 Occurrences of *dry* pre-modifying *wine*, according to Google search

dry red wine	338,000
dry white wine	1,140,000
red dry wine	952
dry wine	266,000
white dry wine	935

be realized by 减肥 (*jiǎnféi*), 教学 (*jiàoxué*), 方 (*fang*), 办 (*bàn*), or 做 (*zuò*). This structure dominates the data.

A more complex example can be found by looking at the polarity of clauses containing 后悔 (*hòuhuǐ*) (regret, repent) + 事 (*shì*) (a general word with a range of vague senses, including 'matter', 'thing', 'affair'). There are 77 occurrences of 后悔 (*hòuhuǐ*) with 事 (*shì*) in the corpus. Two of these we eliminated from our analysis because their structures differed from the others, one of them being in question form and the other containing double negation. Of the remaining 75, 37 occurred in positive clauses and 38 in negative, the negation being explicitly marked by occurrences of 不 (*bù*) (no) or 没有 (*méiyǒu*) (have not). The ratio of positive to negative (almost 1:1) is striking. Halliday and James (1993) demonstrate in a detailed computational study that, in English, clauses distribute between positive and negative in a ratio of 9:1. Although it has yet to be established that this ratio is applicable to Chinese, it is highly unlikely in the opinion of the authors of this chapter, one of whom is Chinese, that the ratio 1:1 for 后悔 (*hòuhuǐ*) + 事 (*shì*) is not significant. Thus Chinese lexis has been shown to colligate in a manner very similar to that found for English.

1.10 Pragmatic association and Chinese

Pragmatic association occurs whenever a word, word combination or word component is regularly associated with the performance of a pragmatic function, such as uncertainty, expression of implicit attitude to the utterance, vagueness, and performance of a speech act. Examples in English include the association of *white wine* with REQUEST/MAKING AN ORDER in the context of pubs and bars and the association of *turn the tide* with beginning to solve a problem (in our data, the movement is to a better situation 113 times as opposed to a worse or neutral situation 16 times). So does pragmatic association occur in Chinese?

In the 38 negative instances of the 后悔 (*hòuhuǐ*)/事 (*shì*) collocation, 12 (31.6% of the negative instances) are concerned with MAKING A SUGGESTION/GIVING ADVICE, usually in the structure 'don't do something you will regret' or 'avoid doing something you may regret'. 后悔 (*hòuhuǐ*) on its own has the same pragmatic association. When in a negative clause it again has a positive pragmatic association with MAKING A SUGGESTION/GIVING ADVICE; on the other hand, no instance of 后悔 (*hòuhuǐ*) occurring in a positive clause is so used. Although there are likely to be more sentences that are used to make suggestions or give advice in Chinese than in English because of cultural differences, it is highly unlikely that nearly a third of clauses in Chinese would be so used. Examples from our data of 后悔 (*hòuhuǐ*)/事 (*shì*) used to make suggestions or give advice are the following:

(4) 不要   做   将来   后悔   的   事
    búyào   zuò   jiānglái   hòuhuǐ   de   shì
    Don't   do   future   regret   PAR   thing

Don't do anything you'll regret in the future.

(5) 以防止   做出   将来   后悔   的   事
    yǐfángzhǐ zuòchū   jiānglái   hòuhuǐ   de   shì
    avoid   do   future   regret   PAR   thing

Avoid doing something you'll regret in the future.

We conclude that there is evidence that pragmatic association occurs in Chinese as well as English.

1.11   Conclusion and implications

By looking at a few examples both from English and Chinese, we have argued that the corpus-driven categories of descriptions which lexical priming utilizes are culture- and language-neutral, not because we have imposed English description on Chinese, but because the two typologically different languages share properties when looked at from both a lexical and a psycholinguistic perspective. The implications for linguistic description and for language teaching seem to us considerable. If the lexical properties of the two unrelated languages are such that they can be described using a shared set of concepts and procedures, then it brings us a step closer to the universal description of language that proved so elusive in the 70s and 80s. And, more specifically, if teaching materials can be developed that emphasize the shared characteristics of English and Chinese rather than constantly drawing attention to their differences, it not only might mean that the lexis of each language would be learnt more effectively but also might improve the motivation of language learners, who are currently only too aware of the differences between the language they speak and the language they seek to speak, as each of the two authors of this chapter can painfully affirm.

Notes

1. One of the authors of this chapter briefly touched upon the psycholinguistic literature on semantic and repetition priming in his book on lexical priming theory (Hoey, 2005), but he is rightly reproached by Pace-Sigge (2013) for the inadequacy of his account.
2. Given the higher figures cited earlier, the statistics may seem strange but they are in fact reasonable, given the way that Sketch Engine operates. When a search is made of 好 (*hǎo*) in the context of 法 (*fǎ*), the only items that count as hits are those where 法 (*fǎ*) is found as a one-character word. Instances of combinations such as 做法 (*zuòfǎ*), which is tokenised as a two-character word in Sketch Engine, are therefore excluded from the count (Adam Kilgarriff, personal communication).
3. The Chinese is given first in character form, then in Pinyin, followed by a word-for-word translation and then a free translation.
4. 履历 (*lǚlì*) here appears to be a mistake for 经历 (*jīnglì*) which means 'experience' and can be used both as a verb and a noun. 履历 (*lǚlì*) also means experience but is only used as a noun (as can be seen in Chinese dictionaries). However we do encounter a few examples of 履历 (*lǚlì*) used as a verb on the Internet, so the example may be a non-standard or informal usage on personal websites or blogs.
5. Interestingly, these *–ies* words have differing etymologies. Some are derived from (and indeed still bear every evidence of being derived from) French forms with a singular *–ie*, while others have a more indirect relationship with French (or none). They are treated here synchronically, without reference to their origins.
6. Here and in subsequent discussion, **ology* refers to all words ending in *ology* except *technology*.

References

Conzett, Jane (2000) 'Integrating collocation into a reading & writing course' in M Lewis (ed.) *Teaching Collocation: Further Developments in the Lexical Approach.* Hove: LTP, pp. 70–87.

Ellis, Nick C. (2005) 'Constructions, chunking and connectionism: The emergence of second language structure' in Doughty, C.J. & M.H. Long (eds) *Handbook of Second Language Acquisition.* Oxford: Blackwell, pp. 63–103.

Firth, J. R (1957) 'A synopsis of linguistic theory, 1930–1955' in F. Palmer (ed.) *Selected Papers of J. R. Firth 1952–59.* London: Longman, pp. 168–205.

Gries, S.T. & A. Stefanowitsch (eds) (2006) *Corpora in Cognitive Linguistics: Corpus-Based Approaches to Syntax and Lexis.* Berlin: Mouton de Gruyter.

Halliday, M. A. K. (1959) *The Language of the Chinese 'Secret Society of the Mongols'.* Oxford: Blackwell.

Halliday, M. A. K. & James, Z. L. (1993) 'A quantitative study of polarity and primary tense in the English finite clause' in John M. Sinclair, Michael Hoey & Gwyneth Fox (eds) *Techniques of Description: Spoken and Written Discourse. A Festschrift for Malcolm Coulthard.* London: Routledge, pp. 32–66.

Hoey, Michael (1997) 'From concordance to text structure: new uses for computer corpora' in *PALC '97: Proceedings of Practical Applications of Linguistic Corpora Conference*. Lodz: University of Lodz Press.

Hoey, Michael (2003) 'Why grammar is beyond belief' in J.-P. van Noppen, C. Den Tandt, I. Tudor (eds) *Beyond: New Perspectives in Language, Literature and ELT*. Special issue of *Belgian Journal of English Language and Literatures*, new series 1:183–96.

Hoey, Michael (2005) *Lexical Priming: A New Theory of Words and Language*. Abingdon: Routledge.

Hoey, Michael (2007) 'Grammatical creativity: a corpus perspective' in Michael Hoey, Michaela Mahlberg, Michael Stubbs & Wolfgang Teubert (eds) *Text, Discourse and Corpora*. London: Continuum, pp. 31–56.

Hoey, Michael (2009) 'Corpus-driven approaches to grammar: a search for common ground' in Ute Römer & Rainer Schulze (eds) *Exploring the Lexis-Grammar Interface*. Amsterdam: John Benjamins, pp. 33–47.

Hoey, Michael (2014) 'Words and their neighbours' in John R Taylor (ed.) *Oxford Handbook of the Word* Oxford: OUP (currently published online at http://www.oxfordhandbooks.com/view/).

Hoey, Michael & Matthew Brook O'Donnell (2008) 'The beginning of something important: Corpus evidence on the text beginnings of hard news stories' in Barbara Lewandowska-Tomaszczyk (ed.) *Corpus Linguistics, Computer Tools, and Applications – State of the Art*. Bern: Peter Lang, pp. 189–212.

Hunston, Susan & Francis, Gill (2000) *Pattern Grammar*. Amsterdam: John Benjamins.

Jakubíček, Miloš, Kilgarriff, Adam, Kovář, Vojtěch, Rychlý, Pavel & Suchomel, Vit (2013) 'The TenTen corpus family' *Proceedings on the International Conference of Corpus Linguistics, 2013*. Lancaster: Lancaster University (last accessed on scholar.google.com/citations, November 20, 2014).

Kilgarriff, Adam, Rychlý, Pavel, Smrz, Pavel & Tugwell, David (2004) *The Sketch Engine Proceedings of EURALEX*. http://www.euralex.org/elx_proceedings/Euralex2004/ pp 105–114 (last accessed November 20, 2014).

Lewis, Michael (1993) *The Lexical Approach*. Hove: LTP.

Lewis, Michael (2000) 'Language in the lexical approach' in M Lewis (ed.) *Teaching Collocation: Further Developments in the Lexical Approach*. Hove: LTP, pp. 126–154.

Partington, Alan (1998) *Patterns and Meanings: Using Corpora for English Language Research and Teaching*. Amsterdam: John Benjamins.

Rychlý, Pavel (2008) 'A lexicographer-friendly association score' Proceedings of Recent Advances in Slavonic Natural Language Processing, RASLAN, 6–9.

Scott, Michael (2013) *Wordsmith Tools 6.0.0.166* available at http://www.lexically.net/wordsmith/ downloaded 7-12-13.

Shao, Juan (2014) 'Near synonymy and lexical priming', paper given at 6th International Conference on Corpus Linguistics, Universidad de Las Palmas de Gran Canaria, May 22–24, 2014.

Sinclair, John McH (1991) *Corpus, Concordance, Collocation*. Oxford: OUP.

Sinclair, John McH (1996) 'The search for units of meaning' *Textus IX*. 75–106.

Sinclair, John McH (1999) 'The lexical item' in E. Weigand (ed.) *Contrastive Lexical Semantics*. Amsterdam: John Benjamins, pp. 1–24.

Sinclair, John McH (2004) *Trust the Text: Language, Corpus and Discourse* (edited by R. Carter) London: Routledge.

Sinclair, John McH & Mauranen, Anna (2006) *Linear Unit Grammar: Integrating Speech and Writing*. Amsterdam: John Benjamins.

Stubbs, Michael (1995) 'Corpus evidence for norms of lexical collocation' in Cook, G. & Seidlhofer, B (eds) *Principle & Practice in Applied Linguistics*. Oxford: OUP, pp. 245–56.

Stubbs, Michael (1996) *Text and Corpus Analysis*. Oxford: Blackwell.

Xiao, Richard & McEnery, Tony (2006) 'Collocation, semantic prosody and near-synonymy: a cross-linguistic perspective' *Applied Linguistics*. 27.1.103–129.

2
Contrastive Corpus Linguistics: Cross-linguistic Contrast of English and Chinese

Richard Xiao

2.1 Introduction

English and Chinese are the two most widely spoken world languages that differ genetically. Compared with typologically related languages like English and French, cross-linguistic contrast of such distinctly different languages is more challenging yet promising. The promise relates to the difference – by studying such language pairs in contrast, we can gain a better appreciation of the scale of variability in the human language system. The challenge arises from that promise – theories and observations based on closely related language pairs can give rise to conclusions which seem certain but which, when studied in the context of a language pair such as English and Chinese, become not merely problematized afresh, but significantly more challenging to resolve.

This chapter demonstrates this promise and this challenge by presenting the major research outcomes of our corpus-based contrastive studies of English and Chinese. The research reported here is based on two ESRC-funded projects undertaken by us, which are concerned with cross-linguistic contrast of aspect-related grammatical categories, i.e. grammatical categories that contribute to aspectual meaning, including both 'situation aspect' at the semantic level and 'viewpoint aspect' at the grammatical level, covering core grammatical categories in English and Chinese. The research outcomes are published in Xiao & McEnery (2010). In this chapter we will focus on the major findings about passive constructions and classifiers in the two languages.

As stated earlier, we have taken a corpus-based approach to contrastive studies. The advantages of using corpora in language studies in general, and using comparable and parallel corpora for contrastive and translation studies in particular, have been explored in detail elsewhere (e.g. McEnery et al., 2006; McEnery & Xiao, 2007; Xiao, 2009). Here we will only present our corpus data. Four corpora are used in the two case studies reported in this chapter.

The Freiburg-LOB corpus (FLOB) is an update of LOB (Lancaster-Oslo-Bergen corpus of British English, see Johansson et al., 1978) which sampled texts published in 1991–1992 (Hundt et al., 1998). A second corpus, the Lancaster Corpus of Mandarin Chinese (LCMC), was designed as a Chinese match for FLOB, representing written Chinese published in China in the early 1990s (McEnery et al., 2003). Both corpora consist of 500 2,000-word samples taken proportionally from the same 15 genres in English and Chinese, with each totalling one million words. The two balanced comparable corpora have not only made it possible to compare English and Chinese in general, they have also allowed us to reveal more fine-grained genre distinctions between the two languages. The genres covered in FLOB and LCMC and their proportions are given in Table 2.1.

In addition to written corpus data, two spoken corpora of sampling periods similar to that of FLOB and LCMC are used in this chapter to compare writing with speech. We decided to use only typical spoken data, i.e. dialogue, while excluding hybrid genres such as written-to-be-spoken scripts or prepared speech. For English, we used the demographically sampled component of the British National Corpus (the

Table 2.1 Genres covered in FLOB and LCMC

Code	Genre	No. of samples	Proportion
A	Press reportage	44	8.8%
B	Press editorials	27	5.4%
C	Press reviews	17	3.4%
D	Religion	17	3.4%
E	Instructional writing	38	7.6%
F	Popular lore	44	8.8%
G	Biographies and essays	77	15.4%
H	Reports and official documents	30	6.0%
J	Academic prose	80	16.0%
K	General fiction	29	5.8%
L	Adventure fiction	24	4.8%
M	Science fiction	6	1.2%
N	Adventure fiction	29	5.8%
P	Romantic fiction	29	5.8%
R	Humour	9	1.8%
Total		500	100%

World Edition, hereafter referred to as BNCdemo), which contains approximately four million words of conversational English sampled between 1985 and 1994 in the UK (Aston & Burnard, 1998). For spoken Chinese, we have used the CallHome Mandarin Chinese Transcripts – XML Edition released by the Linguistic Data Consortium (McEnery & Xiao, 2008). The corpus comprises a contiguous 5- to 10-minute segment taken from each of the 120 unscripted telephone conversations between native speakers of Mandarin Chinese, totalling approximately 300,000 word tokens. While it is true that telephone calls can differ from face-to-face conversations along some dimensions, the sampling period of CallHome is roughly comparable.

All of the corpora introduced above are annotated with word-class information, for both English and Chinese texts. They are encoded in Unicode and marked up in extensible markup language (XML), a combination that not only represents the current standard of corpus creation, but has also allowed us to use the same XML-aware, Unicode-compliant corpus exploration tool Xaira (see Xiao, 2006 for a review) on all corpora to ensure a high degree of comparability in data extraction.

In the remaining sections of this chapter, we will first explore passive constructions and classifiers in English and Chinese, and then discuss the promise and challenge of undertaking such cross-linguistic contrast of genetically different languages. We will finally introduce a new model of Contrastive Corpus Linguistics as the way forward.

2.2 Passive constructions in English and Chinese

The passive in English is grammatically marked by a copular verb followed by a past participle. The structure *be* + past particle can be considered the norm for English passives. However, *be* in the structure can also be replaced by other copular verbs such as *get, become, feel, look, remain* and *seem* because the passive meaning is essentially expressed by the past participle. There are clear differences between *be* passives and these variants in their structural configuration – the latter require the auxiliary verb *do* in negations and questions, for example. In addition to such surface differences, there are further differences between the two as well (see Xiao et al., 2006). Nevertheless, we will confine our discussion to *be* and *get* passives in this study as the use of other passive constructions is limited by the lexical meanings of those semi-linking verbs.

It has been observed that some sentences in the active voice can also express a passive meaning (e.g. Kenneth, 1993). For example, it is said that *These clothes wash well* is equivalent to *These clothes are washed well*.

Nevertheless, while the two sentences express a sort of passive meaning – clothes do not wash themselves – the active form indicates the inherent property of these clothes (i.e. they can be washed well) whereas the passive form expresses a different meaning (i.e. they are washed well on a particular occasion). Given these differences, and considering that unmarked passives cannot be studied efficiently using a corpus-based approach, we will not consider notional passives in this chapter.

In relation to English, Chinese employs a wider range of devices to express passive meaning. The most important passive marker in Chinese is *bei* (被). In addition, passives in Chinese can be alternatively marked by more colloquial forms including *rang* (让), *jiao* (叫), *gei* (给), and the archaic structure *wei ... suo* (为 ... 所). However, *rang, jiao,* and *gei* have not been fully grammaticalized as passive markers because they are mainly used as lexical verbs, meaning 'allow; concede', 'call; order', and 'give' respectively while *gei* is typically used as a dative marker that introduces the recipient or beneficiary of an action. In addition to these syntactic passive markers, there are a number of lexical verbs with an inherent passive meaning including, for example, *ai* (挨) 'suffer; endure', *shou* (受) 'suffer; be subjected to', and *zao* (遭) 'suffer; meet with'. The sentences containing such intrinsically passive verbs are referred to as 'automatic passives' (Zhang, 1953). One important difference between these automatic passives and passive constructions marked by syntactic passive markers lies in that the former can take aspect markers whereas the latter cannot. This chapter focuses on syntactically marked passive constructions since lexical passives, in a strict sense, do not belong to the grammatical category of passive.

As in English notional passives, the passive in Chinese can take the unmarked form, which has the patient as the grammatical subject (e.g. *fan zuo-hao le* 'The meal is cooked'). While such sentences can express the passive meaning because of the nature of their subjects, they are nevertheless not passive constructions in a strict sense (see Tang, 2006 for a discussion of differences between the two types of sentences). As in English, such notional passives in Chinese are also excluded from our analysis.

Our study indicates that while passive constructions in English and Chinese express a basic passive meaning, they also show a range of differences in terms of overall frequencies, syntactic features and functions, semantic properties, and distributions across genres. It is important to note, however, that many of the differences discussed below are quantitative rather than qualitative, reflecting the statistical norms of using passives in English and Chinese.

2.2.1 Overall frequencies

The first obvious difference is that syntactic passives are by far more frequent in English than in Chinese. Table 2.2 shows the raw and normalized frequencies of passives in the two languages. As can be seen, with total normalized frequencies of 1,026 and 110 instances per 100,000 words in the two languages respectively, passive constructions are nearly ten times as frequent in English as in Chinese. Note that the frequency for the English data only includes passive constructions without an intervening adverbial. If occurrences with intervening adverbials are also included, the frequency for English passives would be much greater and an even more marked contrast would be expected.

A number of reasons can be forwarded which help to account for this contrast between English and Chinese. Firstly, as *be* passive originated from the predicative structure (i.e. a copular verb followed by a subject predicative), this unmarked passive form can be used for both static and dynamic situations while Chinese passives can only occur in dynamic events. Secondly, Chinese passives typically have a negative semantic prosody (i.e. negative pragmatic meaning, see further discussion below) while English passives (especially *be* passives) do not. Finally, English has a tendency to overuse passives, especially in formal writing, whereas Chinese tends to avoid syntactic passives wherever possible. It has been observed that English (official documents, scientific writing, and news reportage in particular) 'is so addicted to the passive voice that you must constantly alert yourself against its drowsy, impersonal pomp' (Baker, 1985: 121) and the excessive use of passives has been criticized by many scholars including Quirk (1968: 170). In a parallel corpus composed of 250,000 English words and over 400,000 Chinese words, only about 20% of *be* passives are translated into Chinese using syntactically marked passive constructions, with the majority being translated using so-called notional passives, subjectless sentences, sentences with

Table 2.2 Overall frequencies of passives in English and Chinese

Language	Passive form	Raw frequency	Normalized frequency
English	*be* passive	14,909	1,026
	get passive	1,374	
Chinese	*bei*	1,300	110
	wei...suo	69	
	gei	40	
	jiao	15	
	rang	4	

vague subjects (e.g. *youren* 'someone', *renmen* 'people', *dajia* 'all'), and special sentences (e.g. the disposal *ba* construction and the predicative *shi* ... *de* structure). Given that Chinese passives are much more restricted in use than their English counterparts, their low frequency is hardly surprising.

2.2.2   Long versus short passives

As the passive voice is often used as a strategy to highlight the patient and its affectedness, the agent is often optional in the right context. Following Biber et al. (1999: 935), we refer to passives with an agent as 'long passives' and to those which leave the agent unexpressed as 'short passives'. The agent in the long passive in English is introduced by *by*, which is left out together with the agent in the short passive. In Chinese the agent is introduced by *bei* in the long passive while in short passive, only the agent, but not *bei*, is omitted, because *bei* plays the double role of marking passive constructions as well as introducing the agent. It is also apparent that the agent in the long passive normally follows the passivized verb in English but occurs before the verb in Chinese.

As can be seen in Figure 2.1, short passives typically account for over 90% of total occurrences of *be/get* passives in English, a proportion slightly higher than what was observed by Quirk et al (1985: 164) – 'approximately four out of five English passive sentences have no expressed agent'. In Chinese, in contrast, three out of the five syntactic passive markers (*wei* ... *suo*, *jiao*, and *rang*) only occur in long passives. For the two remaining passive markers, *bei* and *gei*, which allow both long and short passives, the proportions of short passives (60.7% and 57.5% respectively) are significantly lower than those for English passives. Early Chinese grammarians such as Wang (1984) and Lü and Zhu (1979) noted that an agent must normally be spelt out in Chinese passive constructions, though this constraint has become more relaxed nowadays. That may explain why a vague expression such as *ren* 'person, someone' and *renmen* 'people' is often specified when it is difficult to spell out the agent. In the LCMC corpus, there are 58 instances of *ren/renmen* 'person, someone/people' as the agent without a modifier, and all of these can be optionally removed without causing loss of information. In contrast, the agents in English long passives are rarely those informationally light, vague words such as *someone, somebody*, or *people* without a post-modifier. In FLOB, for example, there are seven instances of *by people*, six of which have a post-modifier or are followed by a clause where the agent NP also functions as the subject; and of the five instances of *by somebody/someone*, three have a post-modifier.

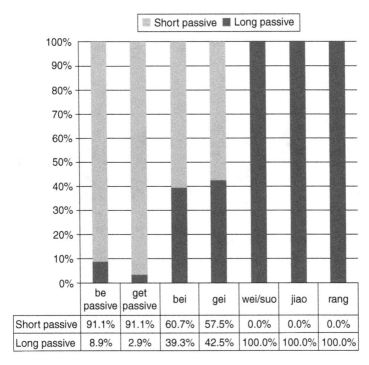

	be passive	get passive	bei	gei	wei/suo	jiao	rang
Short passive	91.1%	91.1%	60.7%	57.5%	0.0%	0.0%	0.0%
Long passive	8.9%	2.9%	39.3%	42.5%	100.0%	100.0%	100.0%

Figure 2.1 Long and short passives in English and Chinese

2.2.3 Pragmatic meanings

A major distinction between passive constructions in the two languages under consideration is that Chinese passives are more frequently used with an inflictive meaning than English passives. As can be seen in Figure 2.2, which compares the distribution of passives in different meaning categories, with the exception of the archaic form *wei ... suo*, over 50% of passive constructions marked by all syntactic passive markers in Chinese occur in adversative situations, a proportion considerably higher than that for English passives (15% for *be* passives and 37.7% for *get* passives).

The prototypical passive marker *bei* was derived from a verb with an inflictive meaning. As such, Chinese passives were used at early stages primarily for unpleasant or undesirable events. While this semantic constraint on the use of passives has become more relaxed, especially in written Chinese, under the influence of western languages, disyllabic words made up of *bei* and a single character verb as used in

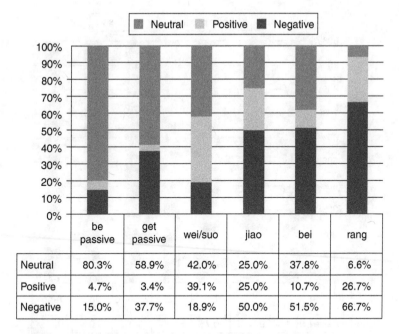

	be passive	get passive	wei/suo	jiao	bei	rang
Neutral	80.3%	58.9%	42.0%	25.0%	37.8%	6.6%
Positive	4.7%	3.4%	39.1%	25.0%	10.7%	26.7%
Negative	15.0%	37.7%	18.9%	50.0%	51.5%	66.7%

Figure 2.2 Pragmatic meanings of passives in English and Chinese

modern Chinese typically refer to something undesirable, as in *beibu* 'be arrested', *beifu* 'be captured', *beigao* 'the accused', *beihai* 'be a victim', and *beipo* 'be forced'. In this respect, the *get* passive is closer to Chinese passives than the unmarked *be* passive, because the use of *be* passives is more stylistically oriented, i.e. to make the discourse sound more impersonal, objective, formal, and technical. Marking negative semantic prosodies is not a basic feature of English passives. Hence, unsurprisingly, of the three meaning categories, the neutral use of the passive is predominant in English, followed by negative and positive categories, whereas for Chinese, the order is different: negative, neutral, and positive (cf. Li, 2004: 11). In short, positive categories of passive constructions are least frequent in both languages, while the difference consists in how much negativity is coded in passives.

2.2.4 Syntactic functions

This section compares the syntactic functions of passives in English and Chinese. English maintains the distinction between finite and non-finite verb forms. The finite form exclusively functions as a predicate in a sentence or clause while the non-finite forms (e.g. infinitive and –*ing*) can either function as other sentential constituents or co-occur with auxiliary verbs as predicates. Chinese, unlike English, does not formally differentiate between finite and non-finite forms. Hence, Chinese passive constructions can be either finite or non-finite (even though in reality finite uses, e.g. as predicates, are more common).

In addition to functioning as a predicate, a passive construction can occur in a sentence as the subject or object, or as an attributive or adverbial modifier. In English, the attributive uses of passive forms typically refer to post-modifiers of nouns while adverbial uses typically relate to the adverbial of purpose with an infinitive or the so-called absolute structure consisting of a noun followed by an –ing form. A passive form functioning as a complement, which is only found in English but not in Chinese, can be complementary to the subject, object or the predicate adjective. Both infinitival and –ing forms of passives in English are found in the object position, with the former as the object of a verb (e.g. want) and the latter as the object of a verb or preposition. Only the –ing form of the get passive was found in the subject position in the concordance samples we have examined. In Chinese, passive constructions are also likely to occur in nominal phrases such as bei boxue zhe 'the exploited', bei tongzhi jieji 'the ruled class', and bei qinhai ren 'victim', though the distinction between the nominal and attributive uses is not always clear-cut.

Table 2.3 shows the proportions of various syntactic functions of passive forms in English and Chinese. As passives are basically verb constructions, they are most frequently used as predicates in both English and Chinese. However, the proportion of passive constructions as predicates in English (over 95%) is much higher than that in Chinese (three quarters on average), though there are great variations in such proportions for different passive markers in Chinese. While passives are more frequent in the object than subject position in both languages,

Table 2.3 Syntactic functions of passives

Passive	Predicate	Attributive	Adverbial	Subject	Object	Compl.	Nominal
be passive	97.25%	0.40%	0.35%	0%	1.05%	0.95%	-
get passive	95.58%	0.66%	0.74%	0.15%	1.25%	1.55%	-
bei	74.3%	14.9%	4.5%	0.9%	2.6%	-	2.8%
wei ... suo	95.7%	4.3%	0%	0%	0%	-	0%
gei	97.5%	0%	0%	0%	2.5%	-	0%
jiao	100%	0%	0%	0%	0%	-	0%
rang	93.3%	0%	0%	0%	6.7%	-	0%

they often function as attributive modifiers in Chinese but as complements in English. In general, passive constructions in Chinese (*bei* passives in particular) are more balanced across syntactic functions than English passives.

It is also important to note that Chinese passives in the predicate position typically interact with aspect. Passive constructions with bare verbs in this position are uncommon, though they are frequent in other syntactic slots. The contexts where bare passives occur as predicates are also the same as those which encourage omission of aspect markers in Chinese discourse in general (e.g. a preceding modal auxiliary such as *hui* 'will', *neng/nenggou* 'can', *yuanyi* 'be willing to', and *keyi* 'may'; a preceding time adverbial such as *yi/yijing* 'already', *jiang* 'will', *jiuyao/ yao* 'will'; see Xiao et al., 2006 for details). In English, the interaction between passives and aspect is not as apparent as in Chinese because all English sentences and clauses are formally marked by combined tense-aspect markers.

2.2.5   Genre variations

There are clearly genre variations in the distribution of passive variants in both English and Chinese. In English *get* passives are most commonly found in informal written genres and colloquial genres, while in Chinese syntactic passives with markers other than *bei* show great variation across genres, with *wei ... suo* typically occurring in formal written genres and *jiao, rang* and *gei* in colloquial genres. This section only compares the unmarked *be* passive in English and the prototypical *bei* passive in Chinese.

Figure 2.3 illustrates the distribution of English *be* passive and Chinese *bei* passives across the 16 written and spoken genres in terms of normalized frequencies (per 100,000 words). As can be seen, in both English and Chinese, passives are more common in writing (A-R) than in speech (S). Passives in English occur more frequently in informative (A-J) than imaginative (K-R) genres. Reports/official documents (H) and academic prose (J), in particular, show very high proportions of passives. In contrast, these two genres have the lowest proportions of passives in written Chinese, where mystery/detective stories (L) and religious writing (D) show exceptionally high proportions of passives. The difference in the overall distribution of passives is closely associated with the different functions of passive constructions in the two languages. In addition to expressing a basic passive meaning, the passive is primarily used to mark an impersonal, objective, and formal style in English whereas it is typically an 'inflictive voice' in Chinese (Lian, 1993: 92). Mystery

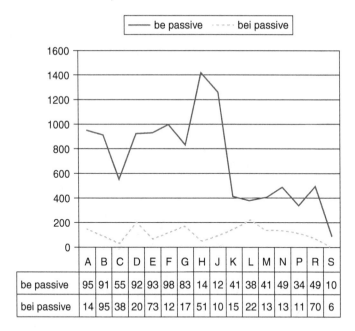

	A	B	C	D	E	F	G	H	J	K	L	M	N	P	R	S
be passive	95	91	55	92	93	98	83	14	12	41	38	41	49	34	49	10
bei passive	14	95	38	20	73	12	17	51	10	15	22	13	13	11	70	6

Figure 2.3 Distribution of English *be* passive and Chinese *bei* passives

and detective stories are often concerned with victims who suffer from various kinds of mishaps and the attentions of criminals. In Chinese religions, human beings are passive animals whose fate is controlled by some kind of supernatural force. It is thus hardly surprising to find passive constructions most frequently in these two genres in Chinese. In English, however, these genres are not obtrusive because of the overall high frequencies of passives in informative genres and low frequencies in imaginative genres.

2.2.6 Typological difference

Klaiman (1991: 23) proposes a three-way classification of voice types in his cross-linguistic study of grammatical voice: basic, derived, and pragmatic. Active/middle voice is the unmarked, basic type while passivization is the 'nonbasic', derived voice type. Pragmatic voice involves 'assignment to some sentential arguments of some special pragmatic status or salience' (Klaiman, 1991: 24). Our discussions above appear to suggest that the essential typological difference between passives in English and Chinese lies in the fact that the former is a derived voice which involves passivization, whereas the latter is a pragmatic voice. Our finding is in line with Wu (2005: 134–136), who observes three characteristics of passive constructions in Chinese: entailing no morphosyntactic alternation, involving the assignment of pragmatic salience, and (the universal *bei* passives) generally expressing a sense of adversity and highlighting the affectedness of the patient.

2.3   Classifiers in English and Chinese

Chinese is generally recognized as a 'classifier language' not only because of its large inventory of classifiers but also because the use of classifiers is mandatory in this language. As a result, classifiers are generally considered the core of quantifying constructions in Chinese. While it is difficult to give an exact number of classifiers because of the fuzzy boundaries between classifiers and nouns on the one hand and between classifiers and numerals on the other hand (Xing, 1993; Li, 2000), it has been estimated that there are 500–600 commonly used classifiers in Chinese (Guo, 1987: 10).

On the other hand, it is debatable whether English also has classifiers. Current English grammars rarely mention the term 'classifier'. Counterparts of Chinese classifiers in English are treated as a special group of nouns. Nevertheless, classifiers in English, while they may not be termed as such in grammar books, are clearly parallels of classifiers in Chinese in spite of some language-specific differences which will be discussed later in this section.

In English, while the term 'measure noun' in a narrow sense refers only to standardized measure terms like *acre* and *kilo*, it has also been used in a broad sense to refer to classifiers in general. For example, Brems (2003: 284) extends the use of the term 'measure nouns' (MNs) from 'nouns of measurement' in a narrow sense (e.g. *acre, kilo, litre*) 'to include nouns which, strictly speaking, do not designate a "measure", but display a more nebulous potential of quantification' (e.g. *bunch, heap*, and *pile*). In doing so, Brems (2003: 285) is actually using the term MNs to mean what Langacker (1991: 88) refers to as 'a diverse and open-ended class' of nouns:

> Some of these nouns still have an interpretation in which they designate a physical, spatially-continuous entity that either serves as the container for some portion of a mass (*bucket, cup, barrel, crate, jar, tub, vat, keg, box*) or else is constituted of some such portion (*bunch, pile, heap, loaf, sprig, head, stack, flock, herd*).

According to Lyons (1977: 462), such nouns 'are very similar, both syntactically, and semantically', to classifiers in classifier languages such as Chinese, as demonstrated in his examples *fifty head of cattle, three sheets of paper, that lump of iron*, where *head, sheet*, and *lump* 'serve exactly the same function – that of individuation and enumeration – as do the classifiers in Tzeltal, Chinese and Burmese'.

While English differs from a classifier language like Chinese in that English maintains a grammatical distinction between countable and non-countable nouns, the grammatical category of countability, like the grammatical category of number (i.e. singular vs. plural), is also based upon, or presupposes, 'the possibility of individuation and enumeration' (Lyons, 1977: 462). Furthermore, the plural form of countable nouns in English 'is semantically, though not formally, unmarked', because there is 'an obvious semantic parallel' between noncount nouns like *water* and collective nouns like *cattle* (ibid.); noncount nouns in English can sometimes be 'reclassified' as count nouns (Quirk et al., 1985: 248), as exemplified in *Two coffees please*. Also, there is a clear parallelism between 'enumerable quanta' (Lyons, 1977: 463) in noncount nouns (*two coffees, two cups of coffee*) and 'enumerable entities' (ibid.) in count nouns (*three tables, three table-entities*) in English, which are treated 'in much the same way' (ibid.) in a classifier language like Chinese.

If we follow Lyons (1977), it can be reasonably argued that English, like Chinese, also uses classifiers. Our argument is supported by Allan's (1977) cross-linguistic research of classifiers in general and Lehrer's (1986) study of English classifier constructions in particular. Classifiers are treated as a special group of nouns in current English grammar, for example, as 'partitive nouns' in Quirk et al. (1985: 249) and as collective nouns, unit nouns, quantifying nouns, and species nouns in Biber et al. (1999: 247–257). Interestingly, classifiers in Chinese were also treated as a special class of nouns until they became established as a separate word class in the 1950s.

The typical structure for quantifying nouns in Chinese is 'numeral + classifier + noun' while the typical quantifying constructions in English include (a) 'numeral + count noun' and (b) 'numeral + N1 + of + N2'.[1] In our study, we have used a semantic test to decide whether N1 is a classifier. If the semantic focus falls upon N2 in a noun phrase, N1 is judged as a classifier; otherwise the noun phrase has N1 as the head modified by the prepositional phrase introduced by *of* (e.g. *one word of warning*). Classifiers in English and Chinese can be grouped into eight semantic categories as shown in Table 2.4, which also includes some illustrative examples of each category.

Table 2.4 Semantic categories of classifiers in English and Chinese

Category		Illustrative examples
Unit classifiers	English	piece, bit, loaf, portion
	Chinese	个, 位, 条, 张, 名, 件, 句
Collective classifiers	English	army, band, brood, crowd, flock, gang, group, host, mob, pack, party, swarm, team
	Chinese	套, 批, 双, 系列, 副, 群, 代, 组, 对, 队
Container classifiers	English	cup, glass, bottle, coachload, lorry-load, handful, mouthful
	Chinese	杯, 碗, 盒, 袋, 桶, 瓶
Standardized measure classifiers	English	ounce, ton, litre, acre
	Chinese	元, 米, 吨, 克, 美元, 厘米, 度, 平方米, 里, 亩, 斤
Species classifiers	English	sort, kind, type
	Chinese	种, 类, 级, 样
Arrangement classifiers	English	bunch, pile, row, scattering
	Chinese	层, 堆, 团, 沓, 串, 丝, 排, 把, 滴, 束
Temporal classifiers	English	minutes, months, years
	Chinese	年, 天, 岁, 分钟, 小时, 会儿, 段
Verbal classifiers	English	times
	Chinese	次, 下, 场, 番, 下子, 阵, 趟, 回, 遍, 顿

It is important to note that some classifiers can belong to different categories, depending upon their meaning and entities being quantified. For example, *course* can be a collective classifier (e.g. *a course of skin treatments*) or a unit classifier (e.g. *a main course of grilled medallions of venison with garlic flavoured lentils and fried celeriac*); *line* can be a unit classifier (e.g. *one line of text*) or an arrangement classifier (e.g. *a line of parked cars*); *pack* can be a container classifier (e.g. *a pack of frozen peas*) or a collective classifier (e.g. *a pack of playing cards*); and *cup* can be a container classifier (e.g. *a cup of tea*) or a standardized measure term (e.g. *two cups of flour*).[2] Similarly in Chinese, depending on context, *ba* (把) can be a unit classifier (e.g. *yi ba dao* 'a knife'), an arrangement classifier (*yi ba cao* 'a bundle of straw'), or a verbal classifier (e.g. *la ta yi ba* 'give him a tug'). Ambiguous cases like these were all evaluated in context by human analysts and appropriately categorized.

The remainder of this section will compare the uses of classifiers in English and Chinese.

2.3.1 The scope and frequency of use

As noted earlier, before classifiers were established as a separate word class in Chinese in the 1950s, they were treated as a special group of nouns just as they are in English today. Indeed, classifiers and nouns are so closely interwoven that no firm line can be drawn between the two out of context. On the one hand, a large number of commonly used classifiers in Chinese nowadays are temporary borrowings from nouns which function as classifiers on an *ad hoc* basis; on the other hand, some classifiers can be used in a way similar to nouns. Even in context, it is not always possible to make a clear distinction between classifiers and nouns (see Li, 2000). In spite of the interwoven relationships, classifiers were nevertheless separated from nouns to become a word class of their own in Chinese because of their mandatory grammatical status, whereas their counterparts in English are conventionally not considered as a separate word class because they are only required for noncount nouns. In other words, they are optional for count nouns even though they can affect meaning (e.g. *an orange* vs. *a piece of orange*). By contrast, Chinese is a language that does not make a morphological distinction between single and plural nouns, or between count and noncount nouns at all, which means that an appropriate classifier is required for all nouns in Chinese, with a few exceptions, for example, in formulaic expressions handed down from classical Chinese (e.g. *jiu niu er hu zhi li* 'the strength of nine bulls and two tigers – tremendous effort'), in parallel structures (e.g. *san tou liu bi* 'three heads and six arms – superhuman power'), and in some compact forms (*liu guo yuyan* 'languages of six countries'). But these are exceptions rather than the norm for classifier use in Chinese.

It is clear that the most obvious difference in quantifying constructions in English and Chinese relates to the different scopes of mandatory use of classifiers. That is, classifiers are obligatorily used in quantification of all nouns in Chinese whereas they are required only for noncount nouns in English. This cross-linguistic difference is closely associated with the presence or absence of morphological inflection for plurality in nouns in English and Chinese. As classifiers have a much wider scope of use in Chinese than in English, it is hardly surprising that classifiers are 29 times as common in Chinese as in English in their overall frequency of use (2,251 and 88 instances per 100,000 words respectively).

2.3.2 Semantic categories of classifiers

English and Chinese have the same eight semantic categories of classifiers, but as can be seen in Figure 2.4, which shows their proportions in terms of tokens, unit classifiers are predominant in Chinese whereas container classifiers and collective classifiers are significantly more common in English. While unit classifiers are also the most frequent

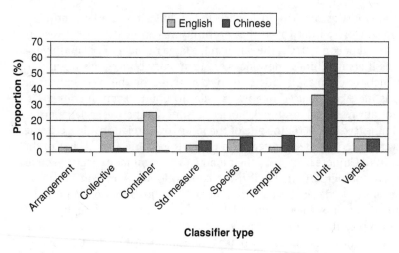

Figure 2.4 Proportions of eight categories of classifiers in terms of tokens

category in English, their normalized frequency (42 instances per 100,000 tokens) is much lower than that in Chinese (1,866 instances per 100,000 tokens). In terms of types, Chinese has a greater number of unit classifiers, standardized measure classifiers, arrangement classifiers and verbal classifiers whereas English uses more collective classifiers and container classifiers (see Figure 2.5).

In spite of the quantitative differences in the types and tokens of classifiers used, English and Chinese do not differ much qualitatively in their use of classifiers. Of the eight categories of classifiers, the most noticeable difference lies in unit classifiers, because their individuation is mandatory for all nouns in Chinese whereas they are only required for noncount nouns in English. Other categories of classifiers are qualitatively more similar than different in the two languages. They have full lexical meanings and can find their counterparts in the other language even though they are likely to be known by different terms. It is interesting to note that some Chinese nouns that denote parts of the human body or an enclosed area, e.g. *lian* (脸) 'face', *zui* (嘴) 'mouth', *tou* (头) 'head', *duzi* (肚子) 'belly', and *zhuozi* (桌子) 'tableful' are sometimes used as temporary classifiers. A peculiarity of classifiers of this kind is that they are more descriptive than quantifying, as the preceding numeral is typically restricted to *yi* 'one', which is equivalent to *man* 'full'. An interesting coincidence is that such temporary borrowings are parallel to container classifiers ending with the suffix *–ful* in English

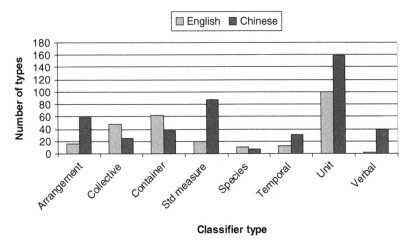

Figure 2.5 Numbers of eight categories of classifiers in terms of types

(e.g. *handful, fistful, armful, mouthful, eyeful, earful, lungful*), except that such English classifiers are not restricted to singular forms (e.g. *armfuls of wet blankets and clothes*, FLOB: N).

On the other hand, there is an important difference in the way actions and events are quantified in the two languages. In Chinese, there are some fully-fledged verbal classifiers and a large number of *ad hoc* verbal classifiers which are borrowed from nouns denoting parts of the human body and instruments or media (e.g. *sheng* (声) 'sound, voice', *yan* (眼) 'eye', *kou* (口) 'mouth', *dao* (刀) 'knife', and *jiao* (脚) 'foot'), whereas in English, the verbal classifier *times* and adverbs *once* and *twice* are used to indicate the count of actions or events. In addition, English relies heavily upon light verb constructions, which consist of a light verb and a verbal action noun (e.g. *have a look, give the car a push*), to approximate the quantifying function of temporarily borrowed verbal classifiers in Chinese. While there are some variations in frequencies of use of standardized measure terms, species classifiers and temporal classifiers in English and Chinese, these categories do not differ much in their behaviour in the two languages.

2.3.3 Motivation for noun-classifier co-selection

The co-selection of nouns and classifiers is motivated cognitively, pragmatically as well as conventionally in both English and Chinese. For example, in both English and Chinese, arrangement classifiers and unit classifiers are largely motivated by the cognitive basis of shape, as exemplified by unit classifiers *kuai* (块), *tiao* (条), and *zhang* (张) in Chinese, and arrangement classifiers *bunch*, *pile*, and *row* in English. While unit classifiers are largely related to the shapes of the individual items they quantify, arrangement classifiers indicate constellational arrangements. The two categories of classifiers differ in that the shapes associated with unit classifiers are natural or inherent in the objects being quantified, i.e. 'entities that belong to natural kinds' (Lyons, 1977: 465), whereas arrangement classifiers indicate the arranged or perceived shapes.

Some classifiers are also motivated pragmatically. For example, English classifiers like *gang*, *mob*, and *pack* usually refer to a group of people the speaker does not approve of, which differentiates them from more neutral collective classifiers such as *crowd* and *group*. Similarly, in Chinese, collective classifiers like *huo* (伙) are habitually negative in evaluation; and so are verbal classifiers like *tong* (通), whereas unit classifiers such as *wei* (位) can only be used for respectable people. Co-selection by conventions is another important criterion for use of classifiers in both languages. Sometimes, the choice of a classifier has to be interpreted by following long-term linguistic conventions because it is not always possible to track the grammaticalization path of a classifier to ascertain the relationship between its original lexical meaning with the entities being quantified.

2.3.4 Syntactic behaviour

There are a number of language-specific syntactic differences in the use of classifiers in English and Chinese. Firstly, English classifiers as a special group of nouns have singular and plural forms (e.g. *a piece of cake* vs. *two pieces of cake*), while their counterparts in Chinese do not. Secondly, the majority of monosyllabic classifiers in Chinese can be reduplicated, whereas classifiers in English cannot. Monosyllabic classifiers in Chinese are reduplicated to express a general grammatical meaning, i.e. co-existence or repetition of entities or events, which can have different situational variants such as 'all around', 'many', 'one by one', and 'continuous' (Guo, 1999). Thirdly, the numeral *yi* 'one' in quantifying constructions can be omitted in Chinese if they function as objects (e.g. *xie (yi-)feng xin* 'write a letter' and *wo hai you (yi-)ge wenti* 'I have another question'), but quantifying determiners and numerals in English cannot.

Fourthly, inverted quantifying constructions are found in Chinese but not in English. The inverted quantifier construction occurs typically at the end of a clause so that the end focus falls upon the quantifier. The quantifier is taken into focus in this context mainly for two reasons. One reason is that there is a contrast in enumeration of various items (*ganlanyou 20 haosheng, qu ke jidan yi zhi* '20 ml of olive oil, and one peeled egg', LCMC: E). This pattern is most common in instructional writing (E) and reports/official documents (H). The other reason is that the quantifier is topicalized in a conjoined clause (e.g. *anpai zhili xiangmu 1789 ge, jungong xiangmu 1491 ge, jungong lü da 88.2%* 'Of 1,789 [pollution] control projects which were initiated, 1,491 were completed, accounting for 88.2%', LCMC: H). This pattern typically occurs in reports/official documents (H) and news reportage (A). The focus on quantifiers makes these genres appear more authoritative while the archaic flavour of inverted quantifier constructions is compatible with their formal style. Inverted quantifier constructions are also found in a very different context, though much less frequently, where the numeral is restricted to *yi* 'one', and the noun is highly evaluative – usually deriding or negative – and becomes the focus while the quantifier functions to instantiate a member of the evaluated class (cf. Chu, 2001), e.g. *huobao yi ge* 'A funny fellow'. This pattern typically appears in speech or literary texts.

Finally, while they do not regularly take a modifier in both languages, classifiers take a considerably greater variety of modifiers in English than in Chinese. Classifier modifiers in Chinese are largely classifier intensifiers, which emphasize the large or small quantity or amount, e.g. *da* 'big, large', *xiao* 'small', *man* 'full', *zheng* 'whole', *chang* 'long', *hou* 'thick', and *bao* 'thin'. There are two major types of classifier modifiers in English, namely classifier intensifiers like their counterparts in Chinese (e.g. *full, great, huge, large, little, small, whole*) and evaluative qualifiers relocated from the nouns being quantified (e.g. *a late-night cup of coffee, an old piece of machinery, a fucking pint of beer*). However, when a modifier of N2 does not have an evaluative meaning, it cannot be relocated (e.g. *a glass of red wine; a handful of German scholars*); neither can a modifier be relocated from N2 to N1 if N1 already has a premodifier (e.g. *a large mug of strong tea, a strong cup of tea* vs. **a large strong cup of tea*). Similarly, a modifier preceding a classifier is not necessarily relocated from N2 (e.g. *an earthen pitcher of clean water*). However, modifier relocation is largely pragmatically motivated and cannot be predicted systematically (Brems, 2003: 300). No such relocation is found to occur with classifier modifiers in Chinese.

2.3.5 Genre variations

Classifiers show similar distribution patterns across genres in English and Chinese (see Figure 2.6), with noticeable exceptions in conversations (S) and news reportage (A), which have greater proportions of

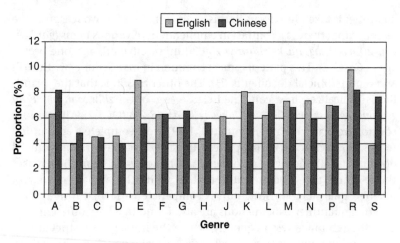

Figure 2.6   Proportions of classifiers across genres

classifiers in Chinese, and in instructional writing (E) and humour (R), which have higher proportions of classifiers in English. Classifiers are considerably more common in conversations and news reportage in Chinese than in English largely because of the overwhelming proportion of unit classifiers in Chinese, and in the case of news reportage, also because of the frequent use of standardized measure terms. Classifiers are much more common in instructional writing (E) and humour (R) in English simply because these two are the text categories that make the most frequent use of classifiers among all of the 16 English genres covered in our corpora. With regard to classifier types, container classifiers are very common in conversations and imaginative writing in English but are rare in all genres in Chinese.

The discussions in this section suggest that even though Chinese is recognized as a classifier language while English is not, the two languages show striking similarities in their classifier systems in spite of the different terms used and some quantitative differences in addition to some language-specific syntactic behaviour.

2.4   Wide-angle contrastive analysis: promise and challenge

Our research suggests that there are both similarities and differences in such a genetically distinct different language pair as English and Chinese. Compared with typologically-related languages, the cross-linguistic contrast of such genetically distinct languages as English and Chinese is more challenging, yet promising. Many of the features uncovered in our research, e.g. the role of word order in research of time-expressions and negation, and the interaction between aspect and other grammatical categories (see Xiao & McEnery, 2010), would possibly be overlooked in contrastive analysis of more closely related languages such as English and French.

Theories based on closely related language pairs are likely to suffer from limited generalizability, as conclusions that seem certain when studying such languages can be problematized in the face of compelling evidence from distinctly different languages. This has been a problem for so-called 'translation universal' research until recently (see Xiao, 2010a). Our cross-linguistic contrast of two genetically unrelated languages, then, exemplifies the promise of stretching the boundaries of linguistic possibility, so to speak: it can help us to gain a better appreciation of the scale of variability in the human language system.

While the 'wide-angle', corpus-based contrastive studies as exemplified in this chapter are certainly desirable, coupled with the promise they hold is the challenge they face, which is both theoretical and methodological. Theoretically, the challenge relates to terminological confusion: the same phenomenon is referred to by different terms or the same term is used to refer to different phenomena. Human languages with a written form normally have their own system of descriptions; and different languages often use their own conventional technical terms in these descriptions. While similar linguistic features in closely related languages are usually described using similar terms, this may not be true in distinctly different languages.

As noted in Section 2.3, for example, classifiers in English and Chinese are described using different terms (as a special group of nouns and as a separate word class respectively), even though they are clearly parallel in the two languages. It is important, therefore, to ensure that the phenomena being contrasted are either the same or similar in their respective languages, no matter whether or not they are known by the same term. On the other hand, it should be noted that a term in one language and its translation in another language may not necessarily refer to the same phenomenon in those languages.[3] So knowing what has been said about respective languages, often in the context of distinct traditions of linguistic analysis, presents a substantial challenge to the linguist embarking on such a contrastive study.

The methodological challenge faced by 'wide-angle', corpus-based contrastive studies largely relates to the difficulty encountered in creating genuinely comparable corpora of widely different languages because different languages may not have exactly the same genres, and the amounts of text created in different languages may also vary markedly across genres. Such differences can be a practical issue in building comparable corpora for use in contrastive analysis. For example, at noted in Section 2.1, the Lancaster Corpus of Mandarin Chinese (LCMC) was designed as a Chinese match for the FLOB corpus of British English. Text category N in the English corpus is 'western fiction'. However, there is simply no western fiction of a similar nature in Chinese. On the other hand, an important type of fiction in Chinese, martial arts fiction, can hardly find an equivalent in any other language. Martial arts fiction is conventionally written in a style of vernacular Chinese with a flavour of classical Chinese fitting in well with the settings of those tales. Given the importance of martial arts fiction as a genre in present-day Chinese and its concerns, similar to that of western adventure fiction in English, martial arts fiction is collected in category N in the LCMC corpus (McEnery et al., 2003). But still, as our contrastive studies have shown, text category N is a special genre which tends to stand out in analysis because of its pseudo-classical style. However, because we were aware of this peculiarity of category N when we analysed our data, this knowledge was particularly useful in helping to account for what we observed in our contrastive analysis. In short, not only is it the case that the comparability of any two corpora in a contrastive analysis needs to be considered, it also needs to be considered that there may be limits placed upon the comparability of the languages concerned because of very real differences in the genres that should be used to credibly produce a balanced and representative corpus of those languages.

2.5   Contrastive Corpus Linguistics: the way forward

To demonstrate the promise and potential value of corpus-based contrastive studies as exemplified in this chapter, we will propose a model of Contrastive Corpus Linguistics as a starting point for the way forward.

Corpus linguistics is inherently comparative in nature. On the one hand, corpora have 'always been pre-eminently suited for comparative studies' (Aarts, 1998). For example, the corpora of the Brown family (e.g. Brown, LOB, Frown, FLOB) have been created with the explicit purposes of the synchronic and diachronic comparisons of written

British and American English as used in the early 1960s and the early 1990s; even a balanced corpus such as the BNC, which is designed to represent modern British English, provides a useful basis for various intra-lingual comparisons, e.g. between spoken and written English, between monologue and dialogue, and between language uses by different social groups. On the other hand, corpus analysis techniques are also comparative in essence. For example, keyword analysis compares the frequencies of lexical items in a target corpus and a so-called reference corpus; collocation analysis compares the frequency of a word co-occurring with the node word and its overall distribution in the corpus; and interlanguage analysis compares learner data with native speaker data, or compares data produced by learners of different mother tongues.

While corpus linguistics has benefited greatly from the comparative approach, contrastive linguistics is in turn indebted to corpus linguistics. As illustrated in Figure 2.7 (the middle part of the figure), Contrastive Corpus Linguistics brings together the strengths of contrastive analysis and corpus analysis. This synergy has not only revived contrastive analysis (Salki, 2002), but has also expanded the fields of corpus linguistics, translation studies, and second language acquisition research. Our model of Contrastive Corpus Linguistics provides a bridge that links all of these research areas. On the one hand, Contrastive Corpus Linguistics is concerned with cross-linguistic contrast of two (or more) native languages (SNL1 ... SNLn vs. TNL1 ... TNLn; NL1 vs. TL2). The results of such contrastive analysis can be used to inform translation studies as well as interlanguage research (e.g. Xiao, 2007, 2010a).

As can be seen in the lower part of Figure 2.7, interlanguage can be compared with the learner's native language (NL1) to evaluate the level of L1 transfer, and compared with the target language (TL2) to determine the extent of under- or overuse of particular linguistic features in the learner's interlanguage in relation to the native variety of the language being learned. The interlanguages of learners from different mother tongue backgrounds (IL1, IL2, IL3 ... ILn) can also be compared with each other to identify the common features of the second-language acquisition process by discarding the influence of L1 transfer of specific native languages.

On the other hand, Contrastive Corpus Linguistics can be very useful in translation studies. The corpus-based approach has developed into 'a coherent, composite and rich paradigm that addresses a variety of issues pertaining to theory, description, and the practice of translation'

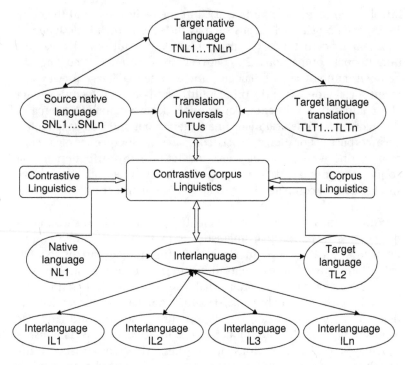

Figure 2.7   A model of Contrastive Corpus Linguistics

(Laviosa, 1998b: 474). It has been observed that 'Corpus Translation Studies is central to the way that Translation Studies as a discipline will remain vital and move forward' (Tymoczko, 1998: 652). Corpora have imparted even more vigour to Descriptive Translation Studies (DTS; see Toury, 1995). The corpus-based approach, as 'a common way forward for contrastive linguistics and translation studies' (Granger, 2003: 17), has brought contrastive linguists and translation researchers closer to each other in a relationship of mutual cooperation (Laviosa, 1998b; Malmkjær, 1998), as the two research areas are interconnected (cf. Ramon Garcia, 2002).

As illustrated in the triangle in the upper part of Figure 2.7, cross-linguistic contrast of the source native language (SNL1 ... SNLn) and the target native language (TNL1 ... TNLn) on the basis of multilingual comparable corpora can shed new light on differences among human languages (as demonstrated in this chapter), which can in turn be useful in translation studies. Contrastive studies of the source native language

(SNL1 ... SNLn) and the target language translation (TLT1 ... TLTn) on the basis of monolingual comparable corpora can help to uncover the features of translations (e.g. Laviosa, 1998a and Xiao, 2010a; see Xiao & Yue, 2009 for an overview). Some of these features may simply be due to the effect of the source language shining through (Teich, 2001, 2003), which can be identified by comparing the target language translation (TLT1 ... TLTn) with the target native language (TNL1 ... TNLn) on the basis of parallel corpora, while others may be common features of translational language irrespective of language pairs in translations. These common features are conventionally referred to as 'translation universals', which make translational language a 'third code' different from both the source language and the target native language (Frawley, 1984). Translation universals, which have become a focus of translation studies nowadays, can only be studied reliably on the basis of comparable and parallel corpora.

In conclusion, the above elaboration has clearly demonstrated the great potential of Contrastive Corpus Linguistics. In this connection, the work presented in this chapter might as well be regarded as a first small step towards realizing our new model of contrastive language studies.

Notes

1. The term *numeral* here should be understood in a broad sense as including cardinal numbers and indefinite articles *a/an*. For easy manipulation of data, quantifying determiners such as *a great deal* and *a lot of* are excluded from our analysis. Instances of *sort of* and *kind of* used as hedges are also excluded through human analysis.
2. As a standardized measure term, one cup equals eight ounces in the US or 10 ounces in the British Commonwealth countries (cf. Lehrer, 1986: 120).
3. For example, the term *idiom* in English and *chengyu* 'idiom' in Chinese are not the same concept (see Xiao, 2010b).

References

Aarts, J. (1998) 'Introduction'. In S. Johansson and S. Oksefjell (eds) *Corpora and Cross-Linguistic Research*, ix–xiv. Amsterdam: Rodopi.

Allan, K. (1977) 'Classifiers'. *Language* 53, 281–311.

Aston, G. and Burnard, L. (1998) *The BNC Handbook*. Edinburgh: Edinburgh University Press.

Baker, S. (1985) *The Practical Stylist* [6th ed.]. New York: Harper & Row.

Biber, D., Johansson S., Leech G., Conrad S. and Finegan, E. (1999) *Longman Grammar of Spoken and Written English*. London: Longman.

Brems, L. (2003) 'Measure noun constructions: An instance of semantically-driven grammaticalisation'. *International Journal of Corpus Linguistics* 8(2), 283–312.

Chu, Z. (2001) '"Ming + shuliang" yuxu yu zhuyi jiaodian' (The word order 'noun + numeral-classifier' and the focus of attention). *Chinese Language* 2001(5), 411–417.

Frawley, W. (1984) 'Prolegomenon to a theory of translation'. In W. Frawley (ed.) *Translation: Literary, Linguistic and Philosophical Perspectives*, 159–175. London: Associated University Press.

Granger, S. (2003) 'The corpus approach: A common way forward for Contrastive Linguistics and Translation Studies'. In S. Granger, J. Lerot and S. Petch-Tyson (eds) *Corpus-based Approaches to Contrastive Linguistics and Translation Studies*, 17–29. Amsterdam: Rodopi.

Guo, J. (1999) 'Zai tan liangci chongdie de yufa yiyi' (Reanalysis of grammatical meaning of classifier reduplications). *Chinese Language Learning* 1999(4), 4–9.

Guo, X. (1987) *Xiandai Hanyu Liangci Shouce (A Handbook of Classifiers in Modern Chinese)*. Beijing: Peace Press of China.

Hundt, M., Sand, A. and Siemund, R. (1998) *Manual of Information to Accompany the Freiburg-LOB Corpus of British English*. Freiburg: University of Freiburg.

Johansson, S., Leech, G. and Goodluck, H. (1978) *Manual of Information to Accompany the Lancaster-Oslo/Bergen Corpus of British English, for Use with Digital Computers*. Oslo: University of Oslo.

Kenneth, W. (1993) *The Columbia Guide to Standard American English*. New York: Columbia University Press.

Klaiman, M. (1991) *Grammatical Voice*. Cambridge: Cambridge University Press.

Langacker, R. (1991) *Foundations of Cognitive Grammar* [Volume 2]. Stanford: Stanford University Press.

Laviosa, S. (1998a) 'Core patterns of lexical use in a comparable corpus of English narrative prose'. *Meta* 43(4), 557–570.

Laviosa, S. (1998b) 'The corpus-based approach: A new paradigm in translation studies'. *Meta* 43(4), 474–479.

Lehrer, A. (1986) 'English classifier constructions'. *Lingua* 68, 109–148.

Li, Y. (2000) 'Liangci yu shuci, mingci de niujie' (Fuzzy boundaries of classifiers with numerals and nouns). *Language Teaching and Linguistic Studies* 2000(3), 50–58.

Li, Z. (2004) 'Hanyu beidongju de yuyi tezheng jiqi renzhi jieshi' (The semantic property of Chinese passives and its cognitive explanation). *Journal of PLA University of Foreign Languages* 27(6), 7–11.

Lian, S. (1993) *Ying Han Duibi Yanjiu (Contrastive Studies of English and Chinese)*. Beijing: High Education Press.

Lü, S. and Zhu, D. (1979) *Yufa Xiuci Jianghua (Talks on Grammar and Rhetoric)*. Beijing: Chinese Youth Press.

Lyons, J. (1977) *Semantics*. Cambridge: Cambridge University Press.

Malmkjær, K. (1998) 'Love thy neighbour: Will parallel corpora endear linguists to translators?'. *Meta* 43(4), 534–541.

McEnery, T. and Xiao, R. (2007) 'Parallel and comparable corpora: What are they up to?' In G. James and G. Anderman (eds) *Incorporating Corpora: Translation and the Linguist*, 18–32. Clevedon: Multilingual Matters.

McEnery, T. and Xiao, R. (2008) *CallHome Mandarin Chinese Transcripts—XML Version*. Pennsylvania: Linguistic Data Consortium.

McEnery, T., Xiao, R. and Mo, L. (2003) 'Aspect marking in English and Chinese: Using the Lancaster Corpus of Mandarin Chinese for contrastive language study'. *Literary and Linguistic Computing* 18(4), 361–378.

McEnery, T., Xiao, R. and Tono, Y. (2006) *Corpus-Based Language Studies: An Advanced Resource Book*. London: Routledge.

Quirk, R. (1968) *The Use of English* [2nd ed.]. London: Longman.

Quirk, R., Svartvik, J., Leech, G. and Greenbaum, S. (1985) *A Comprehensive Grammar of the English Language*. London: Longman.

Ramon Garcia, N. (2002) 'Contrastive linguistics and translation studies interconnected: The corpus-based approach'. *Linguistica Antverpiensia* 1, 393–406.

Salkie, R. (2002) 'How can linguists profit from parallel corpora?'. In L. Borin (ed.) *Parallel Corpora, Parallel Worlds*, 93–109. Amsterdam: Rodopi.

Tang, S. (2006) 'Hanyu beidongju de san-ge jufa wenti' (Three syntactic issues of Chinese passives). In F. Xing (ed.) *Hanyu Beidong Biaoshu Wenti Yanjiu Xin Tuozhan (New Developments in the Issues on Passive Expressions in Chinese)*, 92–99. Wuhan: Huazhong Normal University Press.

Teich, E. (2001) 'Towards a model for the description of cross-linguistic divergence and commonality in translation'. In E. Steiner and C. Yallop (eds) *Exploring Translation and Multilingual Text Production: Beyond Content*, 191–227. Berlin: Mouton de Gruyter.

Teich, E. (2003) *Cross-Linguistic Variation in System and Text: A Methodology for the Investigation of Translations and Comparable Texts*. Berlin: Mouton de Gruyter.

Toury, G. (1995) *Descriptive Translation Studies and Beyond*. Amsterdam: John Benjamins.

Tymoczko, M. (1998) 'Computerised corpora and the future of translation studies'. *Meta* 43(4), 652–60.

Wang, L. (1984) *Zhongguo Yufa Lilun (Theory of Chinese Grammar)*. Jinan: Shandong Education Press.

Wu, Y. (2005) *The Dynamic Syntax of Left and Right Dislocation: A Study with Special Reference to Chinese*. PhD thesis, the University of Edinburgh.

Xiao, R. (2006) 'Review of Xaira: An XML Aware Indexing and Retrieval Architecture'. *Corpora* 1(1), 99–103.

Xiao, R. (2007) 'What can SLA learn from contrastive corpus linguistics? The case of passive constructions in Chinese learner English'. *Indonesian Journal of English Language Teaching* 3(2), 1–19.

Xiao, R. (2009) 'Theory-driven corpus research: Using corpora to inform aspect theory'. In A. Lüdeling and M. Kyto (eds) *Corpus Linguistics: An International Handbook* (Vol. 2), 987–1007. Berlin: Mouton de Gruyter.

Xiao, R. (2010a) 'How different is translated Chinese from native Chinese'. *International Journal of Corpus Linguistics* 15(1), 5–35.

Xiao, R. (2010b) 'Idioms, word clusters, and reformulation markers in translational Chinese: Can "translation universals" survive in Mandarin?'. In R. Xiao (ed.) *Proceedings of the 2010 Conference of Using Corpora in Contrastive and Translation Studies*. Edge Hill University, 27–29 July 2010.

Xiao, R. and McEnery, T. (2010) *Corpus-Based Contrastive Studies of English and Chinese*. London and New York: Routledge.

Xiao, R., McEnery, T., and Qian, Y. (2006) 'Passive constructions in English and Chinese: A corpus-based contrastive study'. *Languages in Contrast* 6(1), 109–149.

Xiao, R. and Yue, M. (2009) 'Using corpora in Translation Studies: The state of the art'. In P. Baker (ed.) *Contemporary Corpus Linguistics*, 237–262. London: Continuum.

Xing, F. (1993) 'Xiandai Hanyu shuliangci xitong zhong de "ban" and "shuang"' ('Half' and 'double' in the numeral-classifier system of modern Chinese). *Language Teaching and Linguistic Studies* 1993(4), 36–56.

Zhang, Z. (1953) *Hanyu Yufa Changshi (Elementary Knowledge of Chinese Grammar)*. Beijing: Chinese Youth Publishing House.

3
Learning Chinese with the Sketch Engine

Adam Kilgarriff, Nicole Keng, and Simon Smith

3.1 Introduction

For the last 20 years, the world of English language teaching has come to realize the value of corpora and has worked out how to use them in the preparation of teaching materials, dictionary-making, syllabus design, and in the classroom. In the last few years, the teaching of Chinese has grown rapidly. Thus it is desirable to transfer the expertise across, so Chinese teaching benefits from the experience of corpus use in English teaching.

Two central components of corpus-based language learning are: (1) the corpus itself; (2) corpus analysis software. The Sketch Engine (Kilgarriff et al., 2004) provides both. Chinese Gigaword is a very large corpus of Chinese journalism (and there is also zhTenTen, a large Chinese web corpus, available). The software offers a wide range of functions for learning from corpora. In this chapter we introduce the Sketch Engine and its core functions, with examples drawn from Chinese.

3.2 The Sketch Engine

The Sketch Engine is designed for anyone wanting to research how words behave, including lexicographers, linguists, and language teachers and learners. It is a Corpus Query System incorporating concordancing, word sketches, and a distributional thesaurus. In this chapter, the key features of the Sketch Engine will be introduced, as well as some useful tasks for teachers and learners of Chinese.

3.3 Basic concordance

A concordance is a list of every occurrence of a given word in the corpus. The concordance shows the word itself in a different colour, then the parts of the sentence right before and after the keyword.

Figure 3.1 shows that after logging in on the Sketch Engine website, it is easy to find various corpora (with more than 42 different languages covered). Figure 3.2 shows the Sketch Engine's concordance input form.

Any keyword (single or multiple character) keyword can be input at this interface. Figure 3.3 shows the first of four pages of occurrences of the keyword 公车 in a general web corpus of 10 million words. 公车 has three distinct meanings: in standard Mandarin, it refers to an *official or government vehicle*, while informally, especially in Taiwan (and apparently in Xi'an) it is used to mean simply *bus*; and there is a historical meaning 'selecting politicians to be officials', as in the second instance below.

A glance at the KWIC (KeyWord In Context) concordance output of Figure 3.3 brings out the two meanings of the word quite clearly for the learner, and even gives them a rough idea of the distribution. In many cases, though, the difference between usages is not so clear cut: a term, especially an abstract term, may have several senses, difficult to pick

Corpora	Corpora			
Create corpus				
WebBootCaT	Corpus name	Language	Tokens	Words
Compare corpora	Chinese GigaWord 2 Corpus: Mainland, simplified	Chinese, Simplified	280,124,230	205,031,379
Configuration templates	Internet-ZH	Chinese, Simplified	277,931,664	198,205,344
Sketch grammars	zhTenTen (10M)	Chinese, Simplified	11,028,308	9,012,125
Subcorpus definitions	British Academic Spoken English Corpus (BASE)	English	1,252,256	1,186,290
User groups	enTenTen08	English	3,268,798,627	2,759,340,513
Admin	enTenTen12	English	12,968,375,937	11,191,860,036
Local administration	FinnishWaC	Finnish	144,972,820	112,389,123
	esTenTen11 (Eu+Am, Freeling)	Spanish	9,797,406,054	8,380,202,011
Support				Show b
Help	Corpus name	Language	Tokens	Words
Support	Arabic_web_corpus	Arabic	174,239,600	407,005
	arTenTen	Arabic	6,637,387,738	5,794,161,583
	CHILDES Afrikaans Corpus	Arabic	33,134	26,020
	BasqueWaC	Basque	123,856,183	99,719,584
	BengaliWaC	Bengali	13,719,158	11,761,881
	BulgarianNC	Bulgarian	26,518,884	20,974,953
	BulgarianNC2 nonweb	Bulgarian	27,721,533	22,398,409
	BulgarianNC2 web	Bulgarian	545,637,740	419,509,472
	BulgarianNC2 web 10M	Bulgarian	9,478,549	7,693,929
	CHILDES Catalan Corpus	Catalan	277,816	209,525
	Internet-ZH (10M)	Chinese, Simplified	9,431,058	6,229,745
	zhTenTen	Chinese, Simplified	2,106,661,021	1,729,867,455
	Chinese GigaWord 2 Corpus: Taiwan, traditional	Chinese, Traditional	455,526,209	382,600,557
	ChineseTaiwanWaC	Chinese, Traditional	349,198,060	259,156,002
	ChineseTaiwanWaC (Universal Sketch Grammar)	Chinese, Traditional	349,198,060	259,156,002
	CHILDES Croatian Corpus	Croatian	389,674	286,765

Figure 3.1   Start page

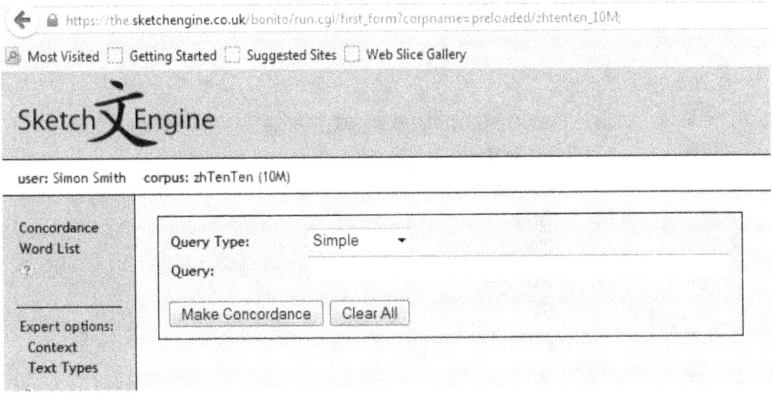

https://the.sketchengine.co.uk/bonito/run.cgi/first_form?corpname=preloaded/zhtenten_10M;

Most Visited   Getting Started   Suggested Sites   Web Slice Gallery

Sketch 文 Engine

user: Simon Smith   corpus: zhTenTen (10M)

Concordance
Word List
?

Expert options:
Context
Text Types

Query Type: Simple   ▾

Query:

Make Concordance   Clear All

Figure 3.2 Concordance form

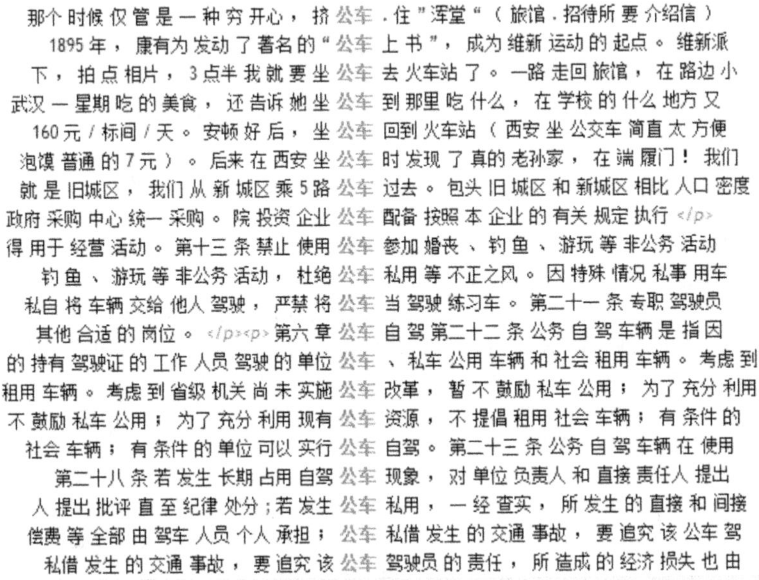

那个 时候 仅 管 是 一 种 穷 开心，挤 公车 . 住 " 浑堂 "（ 旅馆 . 招待所 要 介绍信 ）
1895 年，康有为 发动 了 著名 的 " 公车 上书 "，成为 维新 运动 的 起点。维新派
下，拍点 相片，3 点半 我 就要 坐 公车 去 火车站 了。一路 走回 旅馆，在 路边 小
武汉 一 星期 吃 的 美食，还 告诉 她 坐 公车 到 那里 吃 什么，在 学校 的 什么 地方 又
160 元 / 标间 / 天。安顿 好后，坐 公车 回到 火车站（ 西安 坐 公交车 简直 太 方便
泡馍 普通 的 7 元）。后来 在 西安 坐 公车 时 发现 了 真的 老孙家，在 端 履门 ！ 我们
就是 旧城区，我们 从 新城区 乘 5 路 公车 过去。包头 旧城区 和 新城区 相比 人口 密度
政府 采购 中心 统一 采购。院 投资 企业 公车 配备 按照 本 企业 的 有关 规定 执行 </p>
得 用于 经营 活动。第十三 条 禁止 使用 公车 参加 婚丧、钓鱼、游玩 等 非公务 活动
钓鱼、游玩 等 非公务 活动，杜绝 公车 私用 等 不正之风。因 特殊 情况 私事 用车
私自 将 车辆 交给 他人 驾驶，严禁 将 公车 当 驾驶 练习车。第二十一 条 专职 驾驶员
其他 合适 的 岗位。</p><p>第六 章 公车 自驾 第二十二 条 公务 自驾 车辆 是 指 因
的 持有 驾驶证 的 工作 人员 驾驶 的 单位 公车、私车 公用 车辆 和 社会 租用 车辆。考虑 到
租用 车辆。考虑 到 省级 机关 尚 未 实施 公车 改革，暂 不 鼓励 私车 公用；为了 充分 利用
不 鼓励 私车 公用；为了 充分 利用 现有 公车 资源，不 提倡 租用 社会 车辆；有 条件 的
社会 车辆；有 条件 的 单位 可以 实行 公车 自驾。第二十三 条 公务 自驾 车辆 在 使用
第二十八 条 若 发生 长期 占用 自驾 公车 现象，对 单位 负责人 和 直接 责任人 提出
人 提出 批评 直至 纪律 处分；若 发生 公车 私用，一经 查实，所 发生 的 直接 和 间接
偿费 等 全部 由 驾车 人员 个人 承担；公车 私借 发生 的 交通 事故，要 追究 该 公车 驾
私借 发生 的 交通 事故，要 追究 该 公车 驾驶员 的 责任，所 造成 的 经济 损失 也 由

Figure 3.3 Concordance for 公车

out by scanning concordance lines. Inexperienced corpus users such as language learners typically do have difficulty with this task: there may be many thousands of pages of concordance output, rather than a mere four, and it is the higher frequency words which typically have many nuances of meaning. To capture these nuances, we need to explore the collocational behaviour of keywords and their distribution across the corpus; the Sketch Engine provides a number of tools to allow just that.

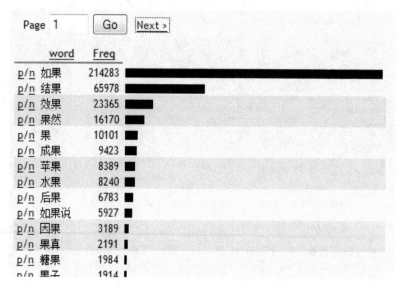

	word	Freq
p/n	如果	214283
p/n	结果	65978
p/n	效果	23365
p/n	果然	16170
p/n	果	10101
p/n	成果	9423
p/n	苹果	8389
p/n	水果	8240
p/n	后果	6783
p/n	如果说	5927
p/n	因果	3189
p/n	果真	2191
p/n	糖果	1984
p/n	果子	1914

Figure 3.4   Frequency list of all words including the character 果

3.4   Character search

Students of Chinese need to acquire vocabulary *and* learn the characters
that make up the new words: this is one of the features of the language
that make it tough to learn. An effective and popular strategy for inter-
nalizing newly-learned characters is to look up other words which share
one of the characters of a recently learned item of lexis. In the Sketch
Engine, it is possible to get a concordance and frequency lists for all
words which incorporate a particular character, such as the 果 in 结果
(*result*). A student learning 结果 for the first time would very likely be
interested to know what other words incorporate the character 果, and
he or she can use the Sketch Engine to find out which are the most
common in a given corpus. As usual with the Sketch Engine, clicking
on a hyperlink calls up a concordance of examples of that word in use.

We can see from Figure 3.4 that 如果 (*if*) is far and away the most common word that includes 果. Following that is 结果 itself, and after that
效果 (*effect*, similar in meaning to *result*). There are several other 'result'
related words in the list, including 成果, used to refer to a positive outcome, and 后果, which signals a negative consequence of some action.
The student will be interested (and even entertained, perhaps) to learn
that the words for *fruit* (水果) and *apple* (苹果) are also related.

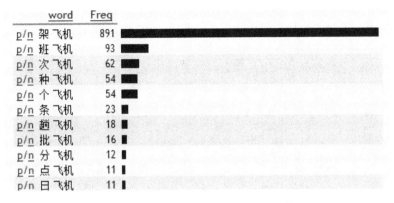

Figure 3.5 Frequency of measure words associated with 飞机

3.5 Measure words

Chinese measure words (量词, also known as classifiers, discussed by Xiao, this volume) are used alongside nouns when the latter are qualified by numerals or determiners. The most common measure word, used with the majority of nouns, is 个 (as in 一个人, *a person*). However, a substantial minority of nouns are associated with a different measure word, which in the case of concrete nouns often reflects the object's shape. But there are no easy rules, and measure words have to be learned and memorized by students. The Sketch Engine allows the student to see quickly which measure word collocates with a given noun, as shown in Figure 3.5, and as usual to click on the links to see concordance examples of the measure word + noun collocations. The measure word associated with 飞机 (*plane*) is indeed 架. The motivated student may wish to investigate what has prompted use of the other measure words in the display. The second-ranking measure word 班, for example, is used in combination with 飞机 (*plane*) to mean *flight*, as in *the next flight to London*.

3.6 Word Sketch

The Word Sketch is a distinctive feature of the Sketch Engine. It shows, in a convenient and learner-friendly one-page summary, a list of words that commonly collocate with the keyword.

Figure 3.6 shows the most frequent collocations in which 说 (*speak/say*) occurs, in Chinese Gigaword, a 200 million-word newswire corpus.

说 Chinese GigaWord 2 Corpus: Mainland, simplified freq = 736823 (2945.8 per million)

Subject	609585	8.4	Modifier	82540	3.3	Object	5366	0.1	Modifies	719	0.0
他	139180	11.86	来	18717	11.16	实话	174	9.98	心里话	13	8.21
她	13831	9.3	还	13168	10.39	空话	88	8.98	话	220	8.17
记者	19637	8.92	可以	4416	9.99	话	425	8.87			
声明	8983	8.8	激动	1938	9.52	心里话	73	8.62	**PP_向**	**667**	**0.8**
报告	9488	8.76	高兴	2212	9.39	普通话	64	7.8	报界	38	9.46
报导	7330	8.5	感慨	1463	9.11	句	82	7.64	新闻界	95	8.28
发言人	7094	8.44	着	1726	8.92	真话	33	7.61	群	11	5.88
官员	6627	8.29	应该	1119	8.53	新闻界	80	7.48	报告	69	4.37
公报	6089	8.28	此间	1064	8.5	报界	29	7.2	媒体	12	3.57
李鹏	6192	8.25	动情	921	8.48	老实话	24	7.19	记者	151	2.79
江泽民	6047	8.16	兴奋	876	8.4	遍	29	7.14			
负责人	4996	7.87	自豪	779	8.24	英语	54	7.13	**PP_把**	**133**	**0.3**
消息	4764	7.83	都	1736	8.09	假话	21	6.98	道理	9	6.63
人士	4605	7.66	却	859	8.06	实在话	17	6.69			
文章	3613	7.55	常	712	8.05	汉语	33	6.61	**PP_在**	**85**	**0.1**
代表	4819	7.43	所	1150	8.02	脏话	14	6.38	嘴	10	6.68
钱其琛	2910	7.23	接着	665	8.01	话题	23	6.26			
他们	3745	7.14	再	969	7.88	坏话	10	5.92			
谈话	2722	7.14	又	1205	7.82	滋味	12	5.9			
专家	3003	6.99	曾	822	7.76	中国话	10	5.88			
人	4258	6.94	则	661	7.61	笑话	10	5.84			
评论	2261	6.9	没	581	7.45	相声	11	5.81			
社论	2198	6.87	不能	569	7.32	声	18	5.8			
我	2129	6.55	别	401	7.22	藏语	10	5.7			
教授	1869	6.53	连声	339	7.06	事	78	5.62			

Figure 3.6   Word Sketch output for 说

It also presents the grammatical relationship with the keyword. Not unexpectedly, the most frequent subject collocating with 说 is 他 (*he*). The next is 她 (*she*). There are also subjects like 记者 (*journalist*), 申明 (*declamation*), 报告 (*report*), or even 发言人 (*spokesperson*), which reflect the language of news articles. The most frequent object collocation is 说话, which means *say a few words* in most of the example sentences. The second most frequent object collocation is 说实话 (*to be honest; truth to tell*). Other objects include languages such as 普通话 (*Mandarin*), along with lower-ranking near-synonyms 汉语 and 中国话, as well as 藏语 (*Tibetan*) and 英语 (*English*). The object can also convey a genre or type of speech, as in 脏话 (*bad language*), 笑话 (*joke*) or 相声 (*xiangsheng*, a traditional type of Chinese humorous dialogue).

The most common modifier used with 说 is 来, which is not really related to its literal translation *come*. It is used in the sentence to represent 'For ...'. For example, 对伊拉克来说 (*For Iraq*) or 就全国来说 (*For the whole country*). The second word 还 is used in a similar sense as 来 to represent 'also'. The other common words are adverbs like 激动 (*thrilled*), 高兴 (*happy*), 感慨 (*rueful*), 动情 (*moved*), 兴奋 (*excited*), and 自豪 (*proud*). These typical patterns of collocation are not generally available in dictionaries, and are of great value to learners.

After clicking on the number next to the word 心里话 (the collocation frequency – 13 in this example), we see a concordance for the collocation (see Figure 3.7). The HTML-like formatting here shows paragraph boundaries.

也 反映：人民 代表 为 群众 说 心里话，威信 更 高 了。 </p> 我国 完成 服装
知道 你 干 的 是 县委 书记。 说 心里话，瞧 你 那 打扮，一件 油渍 麻花 的
这次 会议 大家 畅所欲言，说 了 心里话，只要 心 合 在一块，一切 都 好
晓平 办事 又 公道 又 热心，说 句 心里话，不看 国家 就 看 他 这个 人
生活，演 农民 身边 事，说 农民 心里话，生活 气息 浓郁，形式 多样
许多 在 学校、在 家里 不 敢 说 或 顾 不 上 说 的 心里话，在 孩子们 的 节日
向 省委、省政府 领导 同志 说 心里话，反映 基层 实际 情况 创造 了 良好
的 朋友。他 说，人们 开始 说 心里话 时，这 世界 会 十分 美丽。 </p> 四川
和 真 办 实事 的 好 市长 多 说 点 心里话，可 又 不 知 说 什么 好，只是
都 认 他 做 朋友，也 跟 他 说 心里话。 </p><p> 转眼 暮霭 降临，老农林
为 同胞 救死扶伤 的 医生，说 句 心里话，还是 共产党 好 啊！"</p> 求医
我 都 是 四川人，你 对 我 说 心里话，上 三峡 工程 到底 是 好 还是 不 好
厂长 陈励君 言词 诚恳："说 心里话，看到 西泠厂 这 几 个 月 的 飞速 发
这 也 是 一 种 激励。不过 说 心里话，只有 我 能 夺 冠军，因为 我 想 这
认识到 了 军人 的 伟大。说 句 心里话，他们 图 的 什么，还不是 各 族
划桨"。有的 农民 对 记者 说 了 心里话，"现在 各 种 各样 的 服务，除
直播室，既 侃 天下 事，也 说 心里话，再 热 的 话题，也 不惧 直面 现实
是 伴 着着 吉他 同唱 一 曲 "说 句 心里话，我 也 想家 ……" 但 他们 耐住
芝英 共 图 大业。 </p><p> " 说 心里话，娶 女 大学生 为 妻，绝不 是 为了
献 良策，提 合理化 建议；说 句 心里话，为 母校 留言；植 一 片 绿茵

Figure 3.7   Concordance for 说 ... 心里话

3.7   Thesaurus

The thesaurus is another function which allows the learner to explore words which are related to the keyword specified (see Figure 3.8). It represents the words that share most collocates with the keyword and looks at distributions to show words that occur in the same contexts as the keyword. Usually these are words which are close to the keyword in meaning.

The word 表示 (*indicate; state*) in Figure 3.8 is the most common word sharing a meaning with 说 in the journalism corpus. 认为 (*think; consider*) is another formal word with the same meaning as 说. Typically, students will input a high frequency, default word, and this may lead to the discovery of similar but rarer terms, teaching the learner about differences in register. The actual usage of the new words found can of course be checked by clicking on the concordance link, as a safeguard against the inappropriate use of a hitherto unknown word.

When clicking the first word '表示', which is a more formal term for 'say', the differing usages of the two words are revealed (see Figure 3.9). It can be seen that these two words share many subject collocates, for example, 他们 (*they*), 负责人 (*person in charge*), 官员 (*official*), and 发言人 (*spokesperson*). The difference is that 表示, being more formal, is usually used in more formal contexts, for example with 遗憾 (*regret*), 敬意 (*respect*), 谢意 (*thanks*), and 忧虑 (*worry*). This is the function in the Sketch Engine called 'Sketch Diff', which displays the similarities and differences between similar words. The next section will describe this function.

说   Chinese GigaWord 2 Corpus: Mainland, simplified freq = 736823

Lemma	Score	Freq
表示	0.562	222142
指出	0.547	117059
强调	0.494	80782
认为	0.488	178028
宣布	0.405	90484
发表	0.392	88600
谈	0.391	14844
介绍	0.386	124870
接受	0.371	67910

Figure 3.8   Thesaurus output for 说

说 / 表示 Chinese GigaWord 2 Corpus: Mainland, simplified freqs = 736823/222142

| 说 | 6.0 | 4.0 | 2.0 | 0 | -2.0 | -4.0 | -6.0 | 表示 |

Object	5366	7491	0.1	0.3	Subject	609585	158379	8.4	7.7
遗憾	0	1129	0.0	11.5	立场	0	1036	0.0	7.4
歉意	0	646	0.0	11.0	成就	0	895	0.0	7.2
谢意	0	336	0.0	10.3	上述	138	4390	2.8	9.5
忧虑	0	437	0.0	10.3	双方	126	2652	2.5	8.3
歉意	0	224	0.0	9.8	家属	48	700	1.3	7.0
兴趣	0	246	0.0	8.7	领导人	317	1212	3.8	7.2
异议	0	91	0.0	8.4	他们	3745	2277	7.1	7.5
意向	0	74	0.0	7.8	负责人	4996	2076	7.9	8.1
看法	0	142	0.0	7.8	人士	4605	1478	7.7	7.4
心意	0	40	0.0	7.3	官员	6627	1497	8.3	7.7
诚意	0	41	0.0	6.9	发言人	7094	1296	8.4	7.6
新闻界	80	405	7.5	9.6	钱其琛	2910	449	7.2	6.3
报界	29	35	7.2	7.1	代表	4819	1046	7.4	6.2
话	425	17	8.9	4.1	声明	8983	877	8.8	7.1
实在话	17	0	6.7	0.0	李鹏	6192	607	8.3	6.5
假话	21	0	7.0	0.0	她	13831	1575	9.3	7.6
英语	54	0	7.1	0.0	江泽民	6047	638	8.2	6.4
遍	29	0	7.1	0.0	谈话	2722	201	7.1	5.2
老实话	24	0	7.2	0.0	他	139180	21132	11.9	9.8
真话	33	0	7.6	0.0	公报	6089	201	8.3	5.1
句	82	0	7.6	0.0	记者	19637	978	8.9	5.2
普通话	64	0	7.8	0.0	文章	3613	70	7.6	3.7
心里话	73	0	8.6	0.0	报告	9488	124	8.8	3.9
空话	88	0	9.0	0.0	消息	4764	16	7.8	1.2
实话	174	0	10.0	0.0	报导	7330	17	8.5	1.4

Figure 3.9 Sketch Diff for 说 and 表示

3.8 Sketch Diff

In Chinese, as in all languages, many words share the same meaning. The use of the word depends strongly on its context. It is usually difficult for learners of Chinese to decide which is the most appropriate in a certain context. Sketch Differences (also known as Sketch Diff) is a unique function in the Sketch Engine to help learners understand how similar words differ in order to help with the choice of the right words.

Figure 3.10 shows the Sketch Diff for two similar words: 成立 and 建立, which could be translated into English as *establish*. The words shown in light grey (green in the Sketch Diff interface, in the lower part of the table) are

成立 / 建立   Chinese GigaWord 2 Corpus: Mainland, simplified freqs = 99674/154021

| 成立 | 6.0 | 4.0 | 2.0 | 0 | -2.0 | -4.0 | -6.0 | 建立 |

Object	50167	104311	3.5	4.4		Subject	41495	43159	3.4	2.2
现代企业制度	0	2466	0.0	9.5		领土	11	268	2.3	6.9
关系	0	7206	0.0	9.0		主张	9	143	2.4	6.3
机制	0	1295	0.0	7.9		城市	96	670	3.8	6.6
制度	7	1742	0.2	7.8		省	70	412	3.8	6.3
档案	0	683	0.0	7.6		企业	418	2036	4.3	6.6
长期	0	1002	0.0	7.6		地	280	1134	6.0	8.0
责任制	0	527	0.0	7.2		单位	203	737	5.0	6.8
套	0	506	0.0	7.0		基础	230	770	5.0	6.8
基地	7	1032	0.7	7.4		双方	374	754	6.2	7.2
体系	7	929	0.9	7.4		他们	421	833	5.5	6.5
基础	38	1231	2.4	7.1		政府	1961	833	6.5	5.3
自由贸易区	39	923	4.5	8.1		共同体	136	49	6.4	4.8
基金	72	611	4.4	6.9		集团	1257	372	7.6	5.9
巴勒斯坦国	102	747	6.0	7.8		联盟	484	114	6.7	4.6
支	131	661	5.5	7.2		小组	275	36	6.4	3.4
合资企业	88	522	5.6	7.2		共和国	2680	337	9.2	6.2
个	2247	4841	6.0	7.1		股份	258	25	6.7	3.3
委员会	1118	253	7.4	4.9		共产党	1394	98	8.9	5.1
小组	661	161	7.5	4.9		理事会	156	11	6.3	2.5
年	2548	321	8.0	4.8		新政府	271	16	7.4	3.2
际	535	27	8.1	2.9		联合会	339	13	7.2	2.5
周年	5294	139	11.0	5.0		行政区	772	17	8.8	3.3
前夕	228	0	7.0	0.0		联谊会	119	0	6.4	0.0
仪式	513	0	7.4	0.0		署名	212	0	7.3	0.0
大会	1853	12	8.5	0.8		研究会	383	0	8.0	0.0

Figure 3.10   Sketch Diff for 成立 and 建立

more likely to collocate with 成立, while the dark grey ones (originally green, in the upper part of each table) are more likely to collocate with 建立. The white ones collocate equally with both. From the examples in Figure 3.10, we can see that 成立 is usually used with words related to social organization based on people's decision making, like 大会 (*meeting*), 仪式 (*ceremony*), 小组 (*team*), or 委员会 (*committee*). 建立 is usually used in the context of establishing something intangible, such as 关系 (*relationship*), 制度 (*regulatory system*), 责任制 (responsibility), 体系 (*organizational system*), or 基础 (*foundation*).

When learners click on the number next to the objects, they see the example sentences. Figure 3.11 shows the examples of 建立关系 (*establish relationship*). For instance, the first sentence shows 英国政府正谋求同中国政府成立更好的工作关系 ('The British government is trying to establish a better work relationship with the Chinese government'.)

说，英国政府正谋求同中国政府 建立 更好的工作关系。他指出，这不
关系"，同捷克斯洛伐克和匈牙利 建立 伙伴关系的政策。他强调同西欧
他强调同西欧、特别是同法国 建立 友好关系的重要性。他认为，同
人士、旅游业同行来深观光考察， 建立 合作关系；另一方面调整发展战略
赛格集团已和一批国际知名的厂商 建立 良好的合作关系，5 年来引进
国际形势下，日中两国携起手来 建立 坚如磐石的友好关系比任何时候
目的首先在于通过访问，同南朝鲜" 建立 面向未来的合作关系"。日本过去
贸易发展。1965年日本同南朝鲜 建立 外交关系后，双方一直没有解决
汉城举行的第二轮会谈中，就双方 建立 伙伴关系的原则达成了协议
进行交流、合作，增进理解，以 建立 真正的伙伴关系；为亚太地区的
工商联的帮助下，与26家企业 建立 了长期的业务关系，生意越做越
世界一流同类专业的院校都和他们 建立 了各种形式的合作关系。</p>南
加工出口，同90多个国家和地区 建立 了正式贸易关系，使一向没有多少
个省(市)、130多个地、市 建立 了比较固定的贸易关系，一些省
与中国人民银行和中国银行都已 建立 了正常的业务关系。</p><p>代表团
临时代办顾思聪，对中、马正式 建立 外交关系表示高兴。</p><p>卡布阿
威士兰王国两国政府2月1日决定 建立 大使级外交关系。据罗新社报导
于同年7月1日促成了中泰两国 建立 正式外交关系。</p>快讯：王秀兰
与美、德、日、苏等11个国家 建立 了良好的交流合作关系。目前
银行去年还与27家国外金融机构 建立 了代理行关系，将国外代理行增加

Figure 3.11 Example sentences for 建立关系

3.9 Conclusion

After many years of corpus work to support English Language Teaching,
there is a substantial body of knowledge on how corpora can be put
to good use in language education. Much of this will transfer to the
teaching and learning of other languages, for example Chinese. A
crucial component is the corpus query tool. In this chapter we have
introduced one leading corpus tool, the Sketch Engine, which is available via the Internet, and we have shown how it can be used, together
with a corpus of Chinese which is already loaded into it, by learners of
Chinese. We have introduced its core functions: concordances, character search, Word Sketches, thesaurus, and Sketch Differences. We believe
the Sketch Engine is a useful tool for learners to explore the structure,
grammar, and collocations of Chinese words and phrases.

Reference

Adam Kilgarriff, Pavel Rychly, Pavel Smrz, David Tugwell. 2004. *The Sketch
Engine*. Proc EURALEX, Lorient, France; pp. 105–116.

4
Patterned Distribution of Phraseologies within Text: The Case of Research Articles

Maocheng Liang

4.1 Introduction

Studies on phraseology originated from Sinclair's (1991) 'idiom principle', which holds that 'a language user has available to him or her a large number of semi-preconstructed phrases that constitute single choices, even though they might appear to be analysable into segments' (Sinclair, 1991: 110). In this view, the phraseological tendency of language is such that words 'go together and make meanings by their combinations' (Sinclair, 2004: 29). It is not difficult to see the link between this view and Firth's theory of *meaning by collocation*, which holds that 'one of the meanings of *night* is its collocability with *dark*, and of *dark*, of course, collocation with *night*' (Firth, 1957: 196). Sinclair's theory was further developed into what is often called corpus-driven linguistics, of which Lexical Priming (Hoey, 2005), Pattern Grammar (Hunston & Francis, 2000), and Semantic Prosody (Louw, 1993) are often thought of as the most important strands.

With a research background in discourse analysis, Sinclair believes that the integrity of each text within a corpus must be respected, and that 'a corpus built up of whole documents is open to a wider range of linguistic studies than a collection of short samples' (Sinclair, 1991: 19). He strongly disapproves of sample corpora (such as Brown and LOB, which constitute a number of texts of equal size), and holds that 'the use of samples of a constant size gains only a spurious air of scientific method' (Sinclair, 1996: 9). However, constrained by limitations of corpus analysis software, Sinclair and his followers hardly did any large-scale corpus analysis of discourse structure. In fact, there is to date no such tool that can effectively analyse phraseologies across different sections of corpus texts, such as the introduction, the body, or the end. As McEnery and Hardie (2012: 153) put it:

> The fact is that although a corpus of whole texts offers the *theoretical* prospect of examining the entire discourse structure of each individual text, in *practice* the techniques of analysis on which corpus linguistics is founded typically either are extremely local in scope – such as concordances and collocation – or else abstract away from the textual data, ignoring the sequential features of the discourse and merging together the results for different texts – such as frequency lists and keywords.

With this in mind, this chapter introduces a new research approach to discourse structure. The chapter begins by arguing that linguistic features, including phraseologies, vary across different sections of the same text. This is followed by a discussion of the need for a new functionality in corpus analysis tools. The author then introduces a new corpus analysis tool, TextSmith Tools, designed and developed at Beijing Foreign Studies University. To illustrate how this tool can be used to enhance the study of phraseologies across different sections of the text, it is then used to analyse the phraseologies in different sections of the texts in a corpus of English research articles in the field of Applied Linguistics.

4.2   Linguistic features across different sections of the text

In this section, I argue that linguistic features often vary across different sections of the text. In other words, each section of any text is often characterized by its own unique style, choice of words, and phraseologies, so that you just cannot write the beginning of a text the way you draw your conclusion. Nor can you begin a story the way you develop the story. To illustrate this point, the discourse patterns of two types of ancient Chinese texts are discussed. This is followed by a discussion of previous research on different sections of research articles in the academic genre.

4.2.1   Discourse patterns in text: past to present

As one of the oldest civilizations in the world, China has a long history, most of which has largely been reconstructed with unearthed relics and preserved writings of various kinds. The oracle-bone inscriptions, dated from the 14th century BC to the 11th century BC and first discovered at the end of the 19th century, are believed to be the earliest system of writing in China. These inscriptions provide the first glimpse of the Chinese language and of Chinese characters.

According to Keightley (1978) and a number of other reports, in the Shang Dynasty (1600 BC–1046 BC), when members of the royal families felt unsure whether or not to take some important actions, such as a military operation or crop planting, they went for divination. They got pieces of turtle shells or ox bones, and carefully sawed, scraped, and polished them. Then, a series of hollows was bored or chiselled into the back or inner surface of the bone or shell. At the moment of divination, heat was applied to these hollows in the back. The application of heat scorched and charred the bone or shell with the result that a crack formed in the front. After this, the crack was interpreted, as either auspicious or inauspicious, and an engraver then cut a record of the divination into the scapula or plastron.

The engravings lay under the earth for thousands of years before they were discovered. Each of the inscriptions (more than 155,000 of them) (Wilkinson, 2000), as they were found, is an authentic text, recording what really happened at the divination. Together, these inscriptions make up a big corpus of oracle-bone texts.

Several scholars have studied the discourse features of the oracle-bone inscriptions. Keightley (1978) carefully examined what was written there, and was able to find some interesting discourse patterns in them. He regards the record as consisting of 'a preface (and postface), charge, crack number, crack notation, prognostication, and verification, though these elements were not all present in every case' (Keightley, 1978: 28). Pletcher (2011) observes roughly the same elements in the inscriptions. Wilkinson (2000) also reports his categorization of the discourse structure found in the oracle-bone inscriptions. The main elements, he reports, include 'the time of the divination and the name of the diviner; the question inquired about; and the judgment of the oracle and in some cases the outcome of the action' (Wilkinson, 2000: 393).

Evidence from the oracle-bone inscriptions, which date back to more than 3,000 years ago, seems to indicate that even the oldest writings in history have their unique discourse patterns. Discourse patterns seem to be intrinsic to human writing, and they are probably linked to the way people think about what they do, as well as the way they do what they do.

The case of oracle-bone inscriptions is an example of discourse patterns found in texts engraved on turtle shells or ox bones. These inscriptions also recorded the worries of and the actions taken by the early superstitious people. About 3,000 years later, in the Ming and Qing dynasties, officials in the royal court were worried about something different. They were eager to recruit the right personnel as royal officials. At the time, there was widespread interest in becoming an official among the people who hoped to help manage the huge empire. To find the best personnel, national civil service exams were organized annually, in which participants went through intense scholarly competitions. In the civil service exams, all participants were given the same essay prompt, usually an extract from the classics. Each of the participants was required to write an essay to further develop the statement given in the prompt. The chief emphasis of the task, as reported in Kracke (1953, cited in Kirkpatrick & Xu, 2012: 77), was placed on 'the study of the older writings as a guide to present conduct'. What is worthy of special attention is that the essay was meant to follow a regulated format called the *Baguwen*, the 'eight-legged essay', with each 'leg' performing a unique function. The first leg, for example, would always open the topic. Though very often viewed negatively for its rigid structure of writing, the *Baguwen* is thought of by some as the 'crystallization' of Chinese literature. Usually, the top prize-winners produced arguments that were philosophical, insightful, and coherent. Many of these winners are still remembered today.

The rigidly regulated format of the *Baguwen* is not the only type of writing with regular discursive patterns. Swearingen (2013) observes that the sequence of steps the *Baguwen* follows are, 'after all, mirrored to a greater or lesser extent in "free" discursive essays from all over the world' (Swearingen, 2013: 117). Citing Teng (1943), Swearingen (2013: 117) argues that 'the use of a standardized canon of literary touchstones was borrowed by the English from the Chinese, as a basis for the administrative exams that credentialed many provincials for service in the British empire'. Some scholars even maintain that the *Baguwen* is an effective way to train logical thinking.

Whether or not the *Baguwen* is good writing is not an issue in this chapter. What can be observed from earlier writings is that whole texts are not simply chunks of integrity, and that different sections of a text often serve different purposes. While it is not illogical to retrieve any relevant fragment from any text when the description of a language is at issue (as is often the case with corpus-driven descriptions of English), different sections of the same text might show different features in language use, and the study of such features might also be interesting. After all, while it is perfectly normal to begin an argument by saying 'to begin with', and equally normal to end up an argument by saying 'to sum up', it is less likely that we will ever begin an argument by saying 'to sum up', or end up an argument by saying 'to begin with'. It seems that some phraseologies, bound by their unique discourse functions, tend to be used only in certain sections of the text.

4.2.2   Discourse patterns in research articles

In the last 40 years or so, academic writing has attracted the attention of numerous researchers, particularly in ESP (English for Specific Purposes) settings.

A number of studies are concerned with the overall organization of texts in academic writing, especially research articles (RAs). Among these, the most influential approach is probably the *structural moves analysis* developed from Swales (1981, 1990), who identifies the research article as normally comprising Introduction, Methods, Results, and Discussion (hence the IMRD model). Based on this framework, researchers have concerned themselves with the overall organization of and the moves in various sections of the research article, such as the abstract (Stotesbury, 2003; Lorés, 2004; Cross & Oppenheim, 2006; Duncan, 2008), the introduction (Swales, 1981, 1990; Swales & Najjar, 1987; Dudley-Evans & Henderson, 1990; Samraj, 2002, 2005), the literature review (Kwan, 2006; Ridley, 2008; Thompson, 2009), the methods sections (Lim, 2006); the results sections (Thompson, 1993; Brett, 1994), the discussions (Hopkins & Dudley-Evans, 1988; Holmes, 1997; Skelton & Edwards, 2000; Ruiying & Allison, 2003), and even the abstracts (Salager-Meyer, 1992; Melander et al., 1998; Samraj, 2005). The standard method for classifying moves, as suggested by Dudley-Evans (1994) and Holmes (1997, 2001), is the four-step procedure:

(1) look for organization and patterns; identify moves and boundaries
(2) use sentence-level analysis
(3) assign all sentences to a move
(4) authenticate the classification by using two independent raters

With this model, and with careful manual work and adequate expertise, researchers can effectively identify and classify the moves in each section of research articles. While the move-analysis model does provide useful information about academic text structure, thus offering valuable pedagogical advice on ESP instruction, it fails to describe the academic genre in terms of phraseology across different sections of the text. This is at least in part due to its heavy reliance on manual work. It is easy to imagine that such a method is unlikely to be done on a large scale. In his seminal study, Swales (1981) was only able to investigate 48 research article introductions, from which he derives the famous CARS (Create A Research Space) model.

In recent years, with the growth in corpus linguistics, studies on academic writing have been greatly enhanced with the use of large corpora and sophisticated corpus-processing techniques. Nesi and Gardner (2012), for example, examine the social functions of university student writing on the basis of the British Academic Written English corpus (BAWE). Gardner and Holmes (2009, 2010) conduct corpus analysis on section headings in assessed university student writing. Besides, there has been an increasing interest in the research on phraseology in academic English. Ädel and Erman (2012) compare recurrent word combinations in academic writing by native and non-native speakers of English. Hyland (2008) examines the lexical bundles in academic English across several disciplines. Liu (2011) makes use of the academic writing sub-corpora of the Corpus of Contemporary American English and the British National Corpus to identify the most frequently used multi-word constructions. Nesi and Basturkmen (2006) investigate lexical bundles and discourse signalling in academic lectures. Simpson-Vlach and Ellis (2010) use corpus methods to produce an academic formula list.

The tendency to analyse multi-word units (or lexical bundles) is obvious, but somehow previous studies are often interested either in the use of multi-word units in academic writing in general or in the use of multi-word units across disciplines. This study takes a different perspective. The major aim of this study is to explore the differences between the multi-word units employed in different sections of research articles.

4.3   In search of a new functionality for corpus processing

Several decades ago, Yule (1944) proposed the Chi-Square test, a statistical goodness-of-fit test, to measure frequency differences in samples. As corpus researchers found that the relative frequency of a word in two corpora can often reveal the unique features of the texts in a corpus, the Chi-Square test came to be used to compare word frequencies across two corpora (e.g., Rayson et al., 1997). Later researchers (e.g., Rayson & Garside, 2000) found that the Chi-Square statistic is not always reliable, especially when the frequency count of a word is less than five. As a result, the log-likelihood test was proposed.

In today's corpus-based research, a common way to find unique features of a certain type of text is the keyword method (Scott, 2004; Scott & Tribble, 2006), which involves the comparison of two word lists derived from two corpora, yielding a log-likelihood value or a

Chi-Square value for each word in the corpora. The corpus under study is often called the observed corpus, while the one against which the observed corpus is compared is often called the reference corpus. Thanks to corpus analysis tools such as WordSmith Tools (Scott, 2004), which implements the keyword analysis functionality, the keyword analysis has now been established as a standard way to compare word frequencies in corpora.

One of the prerequisites for corpus-based comparison is the availability of two corpora. Without the reference corpus, the corpus under study can be of very little value. Besides, if the researcher's interest is in a particular section of the corpus texts, it becomes difficult to apply the keyword method. Therefore, there is a need for a new functionality in corpus analysis tools, a functionality which enables the researcher to compare one section of the corpus texts with other sections. For example, if the researcher would like to identify the unique features (such as the phraseologies) in the literature review sections of research articles, one way to achieve this goal would be to compare a corpus of literature review with a whole-text corpus of research articles. To date, however, we do not yet know of any software tool which has this functionality.

4.4 TextSmith Tools

Based on our analysis of the research needs, we have designed and developed a special corpus analysis tool called TextSmith Tools[1] (after Mike Scott's WordSmith Tools). This is not a tool as sophisticated as WordSmith Tools, which is capable of several types of analyses, but it can satisfy the research needs discussed in earlier sections of this chapter.

4.4.1 Working principle

To illustrate how TextSmith Tools works, let us again take the *Baguwen* case as an example.

The *Baguwen* essays are extremely rigid in format, often to the extent of how many sentences should be written in each of the sections. Suppose we have a corpus of the *Baguwen* essays. We now decide we are interested in finding out what text features are characteristic of the *Poti* section. This is the opening section, taking up about 5% of the total length of the essay. TextSmith Tools can then read the whole corpus, splitting each of the essays into, say, 20 segments of equal lengths. The program then puts together the first segment of each essay, so that a corpus (let's call it *leg 1 corpus*) is built. This corpus is special in the sense that it contains and only contains the opening sections of the essays.

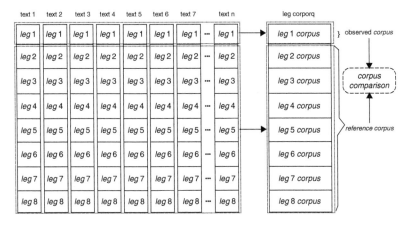

Figure 4.1 Text segmentation and merging

As the corpus contains exactly that portion of the text we would like to explore, we now take it as the observed corpus. As you have probably realized, the remaining 95% of each of the essays are also put together to make the reference corpus. In this way, an intra-text corpus comparison can be conducted. (See Figure 4.1)

Corpus comparison with TextSmith Tools is not very different from that with other corpus analysis tools. Frequencies of each of the words or multi-word combinations in both corpora are counted, so that two-word lists or multi-word lists are derived. With these two lists, the software goes on to do keyword analysis, using the log-likelihood algorithm or the Chi-Square algorithm. Keyness values are then generated for each word or multi-word combination. With these values, researchers can easily identify those text features which are unique to the text section being investigated.

4.4.2 Functions of TextSmith Tools

TextSmith Tools has a few simple functions, each of which is activated by a separate tab.

The first function is text segmentation, activated by a tab called *File Segmenter*. With this function, the researcher can choose the number of segments he or she would like to split each file into. It is worth mentioning, however, that the best number of segments often has to be explored, though you can arbitrarily choose any number between one and 100.

No.	Keyword	Freq1	Freq1%	Freq2	Freq2%	Keyness	Signifi
1	second language acquisition	51	0.09%	85	0.01%	131.543396272	0.0000
2	of second language	28	0.05%	67	0.01%	57.960370826	0.0000
3	it is argued	14	0.03%	8	0.00%	55.043131616	0.0000
4	a second language	30	0.06%	90	0.01%	52.500353617	0.0000
5	is argued that	12	0.02%	6	0.00%	48.895653903	0.0000
6	this paper examines	10	0.02%	2	0.00%	48.710919152	0.0000
7	the field of	24	0.04%	60	0.01%	48.189079231	0.0000
8	of applied linguistics	19	0.04%	35	0.00%	46.350223419	0.0000
9	and second language	19	0.04%	38	0.00%	44.152254867	0.0000
10	the study of	36	0.07%	159	0.02%	43.804075352	0.0000
11	this paper presents	7	0.01%	0	0.00%	41.518944651	0.0000
12	introduction this paper	7	0.01%	0	0.00%	41.518944651	0.0000
13	paper argues that	8	0.01%	1	0.00%	41.277049779	0.0000
14	in the field	21	0.04%	81	0.01%	37.705538999	0.0000
15	university of hong	6	0.01%	0	0.00%	35.587666844	0.0000
16	city university of	6	0.01%	0	0.00%	35.587666844	0.0000
17	paper explores the	6	0.01%	0	0.00%	35.587666844	0.0000
18	paper examines the	6	0.01%	0	0.00%	35.587666844	0.0000
19	second language learning	19	0.04%	58	0.01%	32.785006451	0.0000

Figure 4.2   Keywords analysis in TextSmith Tools

The second function of TextSmith Tools is *Keywords*. After splitting corpus texts into a number of segments, these segments are listed in the upper left-hand box (See Figure 4.2). The researcher can now choose one or more segments and click the 'Select' button to confirm his or her choice. Say we would like to explore the beginning of texts for possible linguistic features: we can then choose the first segment or the first segments. If, instead, the concluding part of the texts is what we are interested in, we can choose the last segment or the last few segments. Choosing a segment means putting it into the observed corpus. Those segments which have not been chosen will make up the reference corpus.

Another interesting feature in the *Keywords* function is the choice of cluster length. In recent years, there has been considerable scholarly interest in the so-called key-clusters (Scott & Tribble, 2006; Bondi & Scott, 2010), multi-word combinations whose frequencies in the observed corpus are significantly higher or lower than those in the reference corpus. TextSmith Tools allows the user to choose from a dropdown menu any cluster length from 1 to 10. If 1 is chosen, a simple keyword analysis is conducted. Otherwise, a key-clusters analysis is conducted. After cluster length is defined and the 'GO' button clicked, all keywords or key-clusters will be listed, along with their respective keyness values. Clicking any of the items in the keyword list will bring the *Cluster Distribution* function alive, and concordance lines of the clicked item will be displayed at the same time (Figure 4.3).

No.	Left	Node	Right
1	ifferent language contact phenomena —specifically ,	second language acquisition	and codeswitching —are sought in order to further
2	ecognize the need to examine a wide variety of SLA (	second language acquisition	) variables and to recognize the influence of learnin
3	te the many and individualized aspects of successful	second language acquisition	. Brown suggests an SLA theory which includes 'as
4	considered when examining individual differences in	second language acquisition	. Carrell et al . review recent research indicating th
5	, and on the other , accounts of formal instruction in	Second Language Acquisition	(SLA) research . One effect of this parallel is to ca
6	i related to the impact of instruction and feedback on	second language acquisition	(SLA) in the classroom . Early in the term , the stu
7	ie necessary and sufficient conditions for successful	second language acquisition	are , and , in this regard , the notion of input and int
8	ised . INTRODUCTION The psycholinguistic study of	second language acquisition	has three interrelated aspects : the study of repres
9	juisition , and the study of processing . Any theory of	second language acquisition	is incomplete without a representation component .
10	me one of the hottest areas of applied linguistics and	second language acquisition	, we are still short of a conceptual framework withir
11	nd with a summary of their presumed broad effect on	second language acquisition	. It then provides a review of typological and syntac
12	?Unequal Election of Morphemes in Adult	Second Language Acquisition	LONGXING WEI Montclair State University Morphe
13	acy and acquisition order is a frequent subject in the	Second Language Acquisition	research literature (Bailey et al . 1974 ; Krashen 1!
14	roaches to interlanguage pragmatics as a subfield of	Second Language Acquisition	. A first approach locates the development of pragn
15	vriting may provide important insights for the study of	second language acquisition	and socialization , researchers should approach lar

Distribution of "second language acquisition" across 20 segments

		2	3	4	5	6	7	8	9	10	11	12	13	14	15	16	17	18	19	20
Total 139	51	16	15	7	4	2	4	3	2	2	3	1	3	1	1	1	3	3	4	13
%	36.69%	11.51%	10.79%	5.04%	2.88%	1.44%	2.88%	2.16%	1.44%	1.44%	2.16%	0.72%	2.16%	0.72%	0.72%	0.72%	2.16%	2.16%	2.88%	9.35%

Figure 4.3 Cluster Distribution in TextSmith Tools

The *Cluster Distribution* function is usually activated by clicking an item in the keyword list, but it can also be activated by a manual search (See Figure 4.3). What is most important is that under this tab, the distribution of a keyword list item or a searched item across all the segments will be displayed, so that the researcher can see the possible difference in the distribution of the item. Figure 4.3 is a screenshot of an analysis conducted on a corpus of research articles in applied linguistics. It can be seen that 51 (out of 139) instances of 'second language acquisition' (36.69%) occur in the first segment (beginning of text). Therefore, it is a key-cluster when the beginning of the text is being examined. Further, as can be seen in the figure, this three-word combination also occurs relatively more frequently in segments two and three (11.51% and 10.79% respectively). Put together, 58.99% of the occurrences of the three-word combination are found in the first three segments, though these three segments only take up 15% of the total text length. Careful readers might have also noticed that 9.35% of the occurrences are found in the last segment. Therefore, in a vast majority of cases, the phrase 'second language acquisition' occurs in the beginning and the end of the articles. While the theoretical construct is important in applied linguistics, much of the discussion in the research article goes into details, focussing on methods and data. It is only at the beginning and the end of the article that the theoretical construct is referred to.

The last function of TextSmith Tools is *Case Analysis*. This function allows the researcher to spot, in the whole corpus, the file with the most

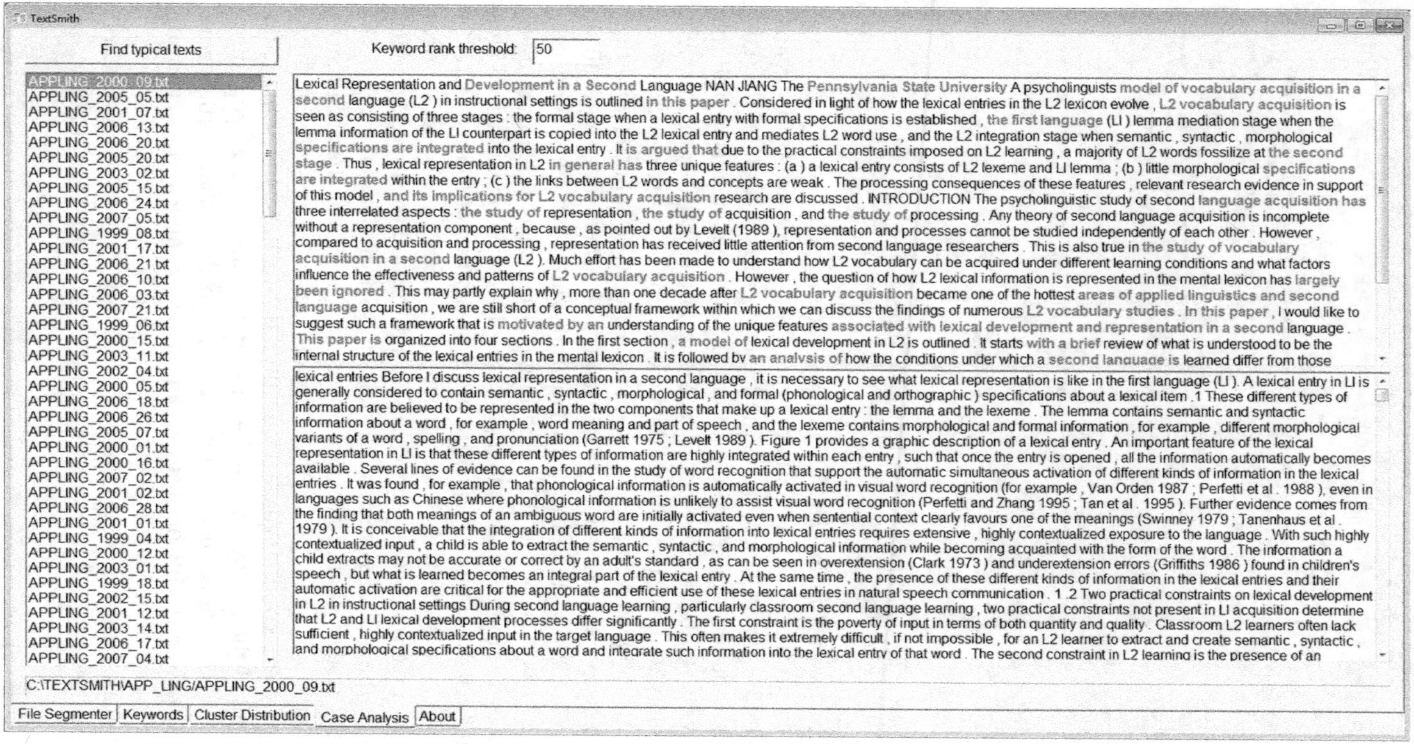

Figure 4.4 Case analysis in TextSmith Tools

typical set of phraseologies in the segment (See Figure 4.4). In this func-tion, the left-hand box lists all the names of the files in the corpus, in the order of typicality of the files. Figure 4.4 shows that, when the first segment (5%) is under investigation, the first file in the list is the most typical, in the sense that the first 5% of text in the file includes a set of phraseologies which best characterize the segment. This segment does not simply contain the most key-clusters, but when the keyness of each cluster is added up, this text has the highest total. Upon clicking the file name, the contents of the file will be displayed, with key-clusters highlighted, so that the researcher gets to know which features make this file typical in terms of its beginning.

4.4.3 Strengths and weaknesses of TextSmith Tools

TextSmith Tools is a specialized corpus analysis tool. To date, it is the only corpus tool that we know of which is capable of analysing the rhetorical structure of a large quantity of texts. As it is based on intra-text comparison, it does not resort to external texts as a refer-ence corpus.

However, as TextSmith Tools is only a specialized tool for corpus analysis, it cannot be expected to do intertext analysis, which involves the comparison of two or more corpora. Neither can TextSmith Tools perform word list analysis. For such functionalities, researchers are advised to use WordSmith Tools or other similar corpus analysis tools, which can perform a wide range of tasks.

Besides, TextSmith Tools works best when analysing homogeneous texts – texts in the same genre with identifiable features in terms of rhetorical structure. It may not make any sense to use TextSmith Tools to analyse texts from different genres.

4.5 Phraseologies in research articles

In this section, we report the results of a study conducted with TextSmith Tools on a corpus of research articles in Applied Linguistics. Different from those studies reviewed earlier in this chapter, this study attempts to explore the phraseologies used in different sections of these academic texts.

4.5.1 The corpus and text segmentation

The corpus used in this study is a small collection of research arti-cles published in *Applied Linguistics*, an academic journal published by Oxford University Press. It is claimed that the journal 'publishes research into language with relevance to real-world problems' (Applied Linguistics, 2015). Our collection comprises 170 research articles published between 1999 and 2007, as summarized in Table 4.1.

As research articles in *Applied Linguistics* are generally fairly long in terms of the number of tokens (each with more than 8,000 words not including references), we decided to split the texts into 20 segments. Splitting the texts into more segments could have resulted in too many short fragments, while splitting them into fewer segments could have caused different sections of the articles to be jumbled together, in which case it would have become hard to identify text features unique to each section.

Cluster size was set to three in this study, though smaller and greater values also turned out some interesting results. Due to limitations of space, we will only report the results obtained when cluster size was set to three.

4.5.2   Results and discussion

Results of our analysis show that each of the sections of the research articles features unique phraseology.

4.5.2.1   *The title and abstract section*

It was found that the title and abstract put together take up about 5% of the total length of the article. When this section was compared to the rest of the text, 1,875 three-word combinations stood out as key-clusters. The top 50 are given in Table 4.2.

It can be seen in Table 4.2 that the three-word combinations roughly fall into three categories: introductory expressions, background-related expressions, and content-related expressions.

The function of the first category, introductory expressions, is to inform the reader what the article is about. Such phrases include *this paper is, paper is a, it is argued, is argued that, paper argues that, it argues that, this paper argues, this paper examines, paper examines the, paper explores the, this paper explores, study explores the, this paper presents, this paper considers, paper considers the, this paper investigates, this paper discusses, paper reports on,* etc. Needless to say, one of the things that have to be stated in the abstract is the aim of the study.

The function of the second category, background-related expressions, is to introduce the need for the study. Such phrases include *the field of, in the field, in recent years, there has been, the origin of, has long been, field of second, field of applied,* etc.

The function of the third category, content-related expressions, is to give information on the aboutness of the paper.[2] Such phrases include

Table 4.1 Corpus statistics

Year	Texts	Tokens
1999	19	160835
2000	18	165173
2001	18	153430
2002	16	132714
2003	16	133712
2004	18	153693
2005	20	160850
2006	23	195272
2007	22	165714
Total	170	1421393

Table 4.2 Phraseologies in the abstract

No.	Three-word combinations	No.	Three-word combinations
1	second language acquisition	26	field of second
2	of second language	27	the implications of
3	it is argued	28	second language teaching
4	a second language	29	second language learners
5	is argued that	30	in applied linguistics
6	this paper examines	31	the origin of
7	the field of	32	this paper considers
8	of applied linguistics	33	prosody of near
9	and second language	34	this paper investigates
10	the study of	35	for comprehension and
11	this paper presents	36	paper considers the
12	paper argues that	37	this paper discusses
13	in the field	38	paper reports on
14	paper explores the	39	5 million word
15	paper examines the	40	study explores the
16	second language learning	41	this paper is
17	in recent years	42	has long been
18	in second language	43	in academic writing
19	language acquisition and	44	in a second
20	this paper explores	45	paper is a
21	vocabulary acquisition in	46	protracted vocabulary growth
22	it argues that	47	for the study
23	there has been	48	applied linguistics as
24	deep vocabulary knowledge	49	and semantic prosody
25	this paper argues	50	field of applied

second language acquisition, of second language, a second language, and second language, the study of, second language learning, in second language, language acquisition and, vocabulary acquisition in, deep vocabulary knowledge, field of second, the implications of, second language teaching, second language learners, in applied linguistics, prosody of near, for comprehension and, 5 million word, in academic writing, in a second, protracted vocabulary growth, applied linguistics as, and semantic prosody, etc. It can be seen that, though the journal claims to publish 'research into language with relevance to real-world problems', a major concern is in fact second language teaching and learning.

The purpose of the abstract, according to Bhatia (1993: 78ff.), is 'a description or factual summary' of the much longer article, meant to 'give the reader an exact and concise knowledge of the full article', and to present 'a faithful and accurate summary, which is representative of the whole article'. In other words, an abstract helps the reader quickly ascertain the writer's intention as to the purpose and scope of a research article. It seems that abstracts in *Applied Linguistics* are doing exactly that.

4.5.2.2   The literature review section

It was found that the literature review section takes up about 20% of the total length of the research article. When this section was compared to the rest of the text, the software identified 915 three-word combinations as key-clusters. The top 50 are given in Table 4.3.

It can be seen in Table 4.3 that the three-word combinations in the literature review section are a bit difficult to categorize, but at least three types of phrases can be easily identified: citation references, theories and concepts, and reporting phrases.

The first type of cluster, citation references, are simply authors' names and/or publication year. These include *lakoff and johnson, berkenkotter and huckin, schmidt and frota, nelson et al, and frota 1986, and newton 1997, nation and newton, gass and varonis, bardovi-harlig and dornyei's, and de graaff, and huckin 1995,* etc. It is interesting to note who are among the most frequently cited authors in *Applied Linguistics.*

The second type of cluster, theories and concepts, are most probably the key concepts in the research article. These include *the third move, incidental focus on, literal and figurative, the grammatical feature, the learner's attention, of vocabulary in, motivation as a, literary reading tasks, background knowledge on, distinction between literal, the bilingual mind, notion of multicompetence, language and speech, less marked codas, two low-rising contours, a given node, the frye standard,* etc. These phrases also give some clue to what the journal is more interested in. When these clusters are compared with the second category of clusters in the abstract section, it

Table 4.3 Phraseologies in the literature review

No.	Three-word combinations	No.	Three-word combinations
1	lakoff and johnson	26	that language play
2	berkenkotter and huckin	27	of vocabulary in
3	the degree to	28	in the 1980s
4	degree to which	29	in the late
5	in this paper	30	between the input
6	the third move	31	motivation as a
7	schmidt and frota	32	bardovi-harlig and dornyei's
8	have focused on	33	and de graaff
9	nelson et al	34	found that mandarin
10	are referring to	35	literary reading tasks
11	and frota 1986	36	background knowledge on
12	incidental focus on	37	distinction between literal
13	literal and figurative	38	the bilingual mind
14	and newton 1997	39	notion of multicompetence
15	nation and newton	40	literature in the
16	as proposed by	41	language and speech
17	the grammatical feature	42	stems from the
18	the 95 per	43	less marked codas
19	present study is	44	two low-rising contours
20	this article is	45	a given node
21	95 per cent	46	the frye standard
22	the learner's attention	47	in the fields
23	he suggests that	48	to the study
24	from information science	49	the present paper
25	gass and varonis	50	and huckin 1995

can found that clusters in this category are often related to less conceptual, yet more operational constructs.

The third type, reporting phrases, are phrases which the author uses to report what has been done in the reviewed literature. These include *have focused on, are referring to, as proposed by, he suggests that, found that mandarin*, etc.

There are some other word combinations which are difficult to categorize, but obviously, they may also be useful phrases for writing a literature review.

4.5.2.3 *The methods section*

It was found that the methods section takes up about 20% of the total length of the research article. When this section was compared to the rest of the text, the software identified 870 three-word combinations as key-clusters. The top 50 are given in Table 4.4.

Table 4.4 Phraseologies in the methods section

No.	Three-word combinations	No.	Three-word combinations
1	base list 1	26	of an interpretive
2	per million words	27	the coding system
3	times per million	28	based on the
4	increase in their	29	the situations were
5	of the participants	30	the central executive
6	the factory floor	31	in comprehension processes
7	meara and bell	32	no attempt was
8	of rare words	33	may have on
9	interested in it	34	x thematic role
10	at event c	35	like to have
11	did detect it	36	the prior turn
12	their english proficiency	37	and the researcher
13	a previously stated	38	which of the
14	an oral narrative	39	an interpretive hypothesis
15	table of the	40	exposure to english
16	cite resource difficulty	41	see appendix a
17	specific content-related matters	42	the following sections
18	in the program	43	level of directness
19	the preparatory consultation	44	yip and matthews
20	utterance in which	45	of the video
21	we had to	46	the mssr activity
22	grade point average	47	types of reading
23	of internal consistency	48	second type of
24	the second type	49	of reading materials
25	in our analysis	50	of the interview

Word combinations in the methods section fall into varied types. A better categorization of these word combinations may require the observation of a list longer than the top 50. However, a few things seem fairly clear.

First, corpora seem to have been used much more than other types of data. Phrases such as *base list 1, per million words, times per million,* and *of rare words* all rank high in the list. As the titles of these research articles indicate, these articles themselves may not really have focused on a corpus linguistic problem, but more often than not, corpora are being used simply as data sources, though some other sources of data (as indicated by phrases such as *of the participants, an oral narrative, the coding system, of the video,* and *of the interview*) have also been used.

Some word combinations are clearly related to research instruments, or the theoretical basis for the research instruments. Examples are *at event c, their english proficiency, the preparatory consultation, utterance in which, grade point average, of internal consistency, the second type, x thematic role, the prior turn, an interpretive hypothesis, level of directness, the mssr activity, second type of, of reading materials, meara and bell, yip and matthews,* etc.

Another point noticeable from these word combinations is that the methods section uses the past tense much more, as it is often necessary to describe the process of data collection and data analysis, which happened before the article is written. These phrases include *did detect it, we had to, the situations were,* etc.

4.5.2.4 The results section

It was found that the results section is the longest section, taking up about 45% of the total length of the research article. When this section was compared to the rest of the text, the software identified 1,055 three-word combinations as key-clusters. The top 50 are given in Table 4.5.

Table 4.5 Phraseologies in the results section

No.	Three-word combinations	No.	Three-word combinations
1	per cent of	26	the np group
2	the complex version	27	in table 2
3	5 per cent	28	receptive knowledge of
4	the target structure	29	known information questions
5	of the poem	30	per cent and
6	difference between the	31	to be statistically
7	in table 5	32	productive knowledge of
8	the difference in	33	and standard deviations
9	the basic stage	34	produced on day
10	in the previous	35	the whole sample
11	in table 6	36	that the difference
12	in table 4	37	in correctly producing
13	beginning of the	38	stage japanese learners
14	narratives and expositories	39	of topical co-constructions
15	scores for the	40	in stage ii
16	g and f	41	between the two
17	types in the	42	the game card
18	analysis of variance	43	table 3 shows
19	east asian students	44	in the student
20	stage chinese learners	45	4 per cent
21	appears to be	46	the previous section
22	as can be	47	the naturalistic data
23	there was a	48	the original version
24	cent of the	49	the untimed gjt
25	7 per cent	50	the narrative and

Empirical research is now dominant in the field of Applied Linguistics. Therefore, in the results sections of the research articles, many key-clusters seem to be related to statistical analysis. These include *per cent of, 5 per cent, difference between the, in table 5, the difference in, in table 6, in table 4, scores for the, analysis of variance, cent of the, 7 per cent, in table 2, per cent and, to be statistically, and standard deviations, the whole sample, that the difference, between the two, table 3 shows, 4 per cent,* etc.

There are also some key-clusters which are related to the concepts mentioned earlier in the methods section, as statistics will often have to be discussed with reference to theoretical concepts, and the purpose of statistics is often to test a theoretical hypothesis. These clusters include *the complex version, the target structure, narratives and expositories, g and f, the np group, receptive knowledge of, known information questions, productive knowledge of, of topical co-constructions, the untimed gjt,* etc.

Other word combinations seem to be related to the subjects in the experiment, the research instrument, or the experimental process. These include *of the poem, the basic stage, in the previous, beginning of the, east asian students, stage chinese learners, produced on day, in correctly producing, stage japanese learners, in stage ii, the game card, in the student,* etc.

It is also worth noting that some word combinations, such as *appears to be* and *as can be,* are lexico-grammatical devices used for discussing results.

4.5.2.5   The conclusion section

It was found that the conclusion section takes up about 10% of the total length of the research article. When this section was compared to the rest of the text, 2,179 three-word combinations were identified as key-clusters – more than any other section. This shows that many of the things mentioned in this section, such as limitations for the study and suggested future work, have not been mentioned at all in earlier sections of the articles. The top 50 are given in Table 4.6.

As seen in Table 4.6, what stands out in the conclusion section of the research articles is the use of lexico-grammatical devices to summarize findings. These devices include *this paper has, this study has, study suggests that, of this study, in this paper, i have also, the present findings, discussed in this, this study suggest, in this article, the present study, this exploratory study, studies like this, this study suggests, study suggest that, the current study,* etc. It is worth noting that the present perfect tense is often used to fulfil this function.

Table 4.6   Phraseologies in the conclusion section

No.	Three-word combinations	No.	Three-word combinations
1	this paper has	26	differences in lexical
2	this study has	27	in production accuracy
3	study suggests that	28	their technical knowledge
4	of this study	29	in this exploratory
5	an understanding of	30	and reliance on
6	in this paper	31	of classroom teaching
7	be made aware	32	for literacy and
8	limitations of this	33	his participation in
9	of inclusive and	34	closed compound nouns
10	i have also	35	studies like this
11	future research on	36	hope that this
12	the present findings	37	literacy and vocabulary
13	and exclusive pronouns	38	will need to
14	discussed in this	39	this study suggests
15	remains to be	40	future research should
16	this study suggest	41	is difficult for
17	for the formative	42	inclusive and exclusive
18	research is needed	43	limitations of the
19	in this article	44	the findings in
20	remote pro-form resolution	45	study suggest that
21	the present study	46	further research is
22	at odds with	47	for future research
23	i hope that	48	the current study
24	this exploratory study	49	needs to be
25	should continue to	50	aware of the

To be theoretically useful, the conclusion section also seems to frequently mention some theoretical constructs, as indicated by phrases such as *of inclusive and, and exclusive pronouns, for the formative, remote pro-form resolution, differences in lexical, in production accuracy, their technical knowledge, of classroom teaching, for literacy and, closed compound nouns, literacy and vocabulary,* and *inclusive and exclusive.* It might be interesting to compare these theoretical constructs with those found in other sections of the article.

Not surprisingly, the conclusion section employs quite some lexico-grammatical devices to talk about limitations of the study and to suggest some future work, as indicated by phrases such as *be made aware, limitations of this, future research on, remains to be, research is needed, i hope that, should continue to, studies like this, hope that this, will need to, future research should, limitations of the, further research is, for future research, needs to be,* and *aware of the.*

4.6   Conclusion

In this chapter, I have argued that texts in the same genre are often similarly structured, so that it is possible and necessary to explore the linguistic features in each section of the text; but research in corpus linguistics and genre analysis has not been able to adequately address this issue. I then introduced a new corpus analysis tool called TextSmith Tools, which has been specially developed to enable research on this issue. In the latter half of the chapter, I have demonstrated how TextSmith Tools was used to examine the lexico-grammatical features of each section of some research articles published in *Applied Linguistics*. Some typical phraseologies in each section were extracted, and brief discussions were undertaken on the categorization of these word combinations.

This is only an exploratory study, and there is much work to be done in the future. Most important of all, as we have observed from our data set, the distribution of phraseologies across the texts in the corpus has to be considered when the software extracts key-clusters. This probably implies that a different or improved algorithm will be needed. In addition, even the most homogeneous texts will vary in the lengths of different sections. This will inevitably cause the segmenter to include text which should not have been there and/or miss text which does not belong there. As a result, the findings in this study only show the central tendency. Finally, in future studies, research articles in more journals and more disciplines could be explored for their phraseological patterns.

Notes

This study is supported by (1) the MOE Project of Key Research Institute of Humanities and Social Sciences at Universities (11JJD740011); (2) National Social Science Fund (09BYY033).

1. TextSmith Tools is a freeware program. It is downloadable from http://www.bfsu-corpus.org/static/BFSUTools/TextSmith.exe.
2. In this study, the titles of the research articles have not been separated from the abstracts. Therefore, the first segment includes the abstract as well as the title. As a result, some of the three-word clusters listed in Table 4.2 (especially the content-related ones) are frequent clusters in the titles.

References

Ädel, A. & Erman, B. 2012. Recurrent word combinations in academic writing by native and non-native speakers of English: A lexical bundles approach. *English for Specific Purposes* 31(2): 81–92.

Applied Linguistics, (2015). Oxford Journals | Arts & Humanities | Applied Linguistics. [online] Available at: http://applij.oxfordjournals.org/ [Accessed 12 May 2015].

Bhatia, V. K. 1993. *Analyzing Genre: Language Use in Professional Settings*. New York: Longman Publishing.

Bondi, M. & Scott, M. (eds). 2010. *Keyness in Texts*. Amsterdam & New York: John Benjamins.

Brett, P. 1994. A genre analysis of the results section of sociology articles. *English for Specific Purposes* 13(1): 47–59.

Cross, C., & Oppenheim, C. 2006. A genre analysis of scientific abstracts. *Journal of Documentation* 62(4): 428–446.

Duncan, B. R. 2008. *A computational linguistic analysis of biomedical abstracts: Differences between native and Korean speakers of English* (Doctoral dissertation, University of Memphis). ProQuest Digital Dissertations, AAT 3328191.

Dudley-Evans, T. 1994. Genre analysis: An approach to text analysis for ESP. In M. Coulthard (ed.) *Advances in Written Text Analysis*, 219–228. London: Routledge.

Dudley-Evans, A. & Henderson, W. 1990. The organisation of article introductions: evidence of change in economics writing. In A. Dudley-Evans and W. Henderson (eds) *The Language of Economics: the Analysis of Economics Discourse. ELT Documents 134*, 67–78. London: Modern English Publications and The British Council.

Firth, J. R. 1957. Modes of meaning. In J. R. Firth (ed.) *Papers in. Linguistics*, 190–215. London: Oxford University Press.

Gardner, S. & Holmes, J. 2009. Can I use headings in my essay? Section headings, macrostructures and genre families in the BAWE corpus of student writing. In M. Charles, S. Hunston & D. Pecorari (eds) *Academic Writing: At the Interface of Corpus and Discourse*, 251–271. London: Continuum.

Gardner, S. & Holmes, J. 2010. 'From section headings to assignment macrostructure in undergraduate student writing'. In E. Swain (ed.). *Thresholds and Potentialities of Systemic Functional Linguistics*, 254–276. Trieste: Edizioni Universitarie Trieste.

Hoey, M. 2005. *Lexical Priming: A New Theory of Words and Language*. London: Routledge.

Holmes, R. 1997. Genre analysis and the social sciences: An investigation of the structure of research article discussion sections in three disciplines. *English for Specific Purposes* 16(4): 321–337.

Holmes, R. 2001. Variation and text structure: the discussion section in economic research articles. *ITL Review of Applied Linguistics* 131–132: 107–135.

Hopkins, A. & Dudley-Evans, T. 1988. A genre-based investigation of the discussion sections in articles and dissertations. *English for Specific Purposes* 7(2): 113–122.

Hunston, S. & Francis, G. 2000. *Pattern Grammar: A Corpus-Driven Approach to the Lexical. Grammar of English*. Amsterdam: John Benjamins.

Hyland, K. 2008. As can be seen: Lexical bundles and disciplinary variation. *English for Specific Purposes* 27(1): 4–21.

Keightley, D. N. 1978. *Sources of Shang History: The Oracle-Bone Inscriptions of Bronze Age China*. Berkeley: University of California Press.

Kirkpatrick, A. & Xu, Z. 2012. *Chinese Rhetoric and Writing: An Introduction for Language Teachers*. Fort Collins, Colorado & Anderson, South Carolina: the WAC Clearinghouse and Parlor Press.

Kracke, E. A. 1953. *Civil Service in Early Sung China, 960–1067. Vol. 13*. Cambridge: Harvard University Press.

Kwan, B. 2006. The Schematic Structure of Literature Reviews in Doctoral Theses of Applied Linguistics. *English for Specific Purposes* 15(1): 30–55.

Lim, J. M. H. 2006. Method sections of management research articles: A pedagogically motivated qualitative study. *English for Specific Purposes* 25(3): 282–309.

Liu, D. 2012. The most frequently-used multi-word constructions in academic written English: a multi-corpus study. *English for Specific Purposes* 31(1): 25–35.

Lorés, R. 2004. On RA abstracts: From rhetorical structure to thematic Organization. *English for Specific Purposes* 23(3): 280–302.

Louw, B. 1993. Irony in the text or insincerity in the writer? The diagnostic potential of semantic prosodies. In M. Baker, G. Francis. & E. Tognini-Bonelli (eds) *Text and Technology: In honour of John Sinclair*, 157–176. Philadelphia/Amsterdam: John Benjamins.

McEnery, T. & Hardie, A. 2012. *Corpus Linguistics: Method, Theory and Practice*. Cambridge: Cambridge University Press.

Melander, B., Swales, J., & Fredrickson, K. M. 1988. Journal abstracts from the academic fields in the United States and Sweden: National or disciplinary? In A. Duszak (ed.) *Intellectual Styles and Cross-Cultural Communication*, 251–272. Amsterdam: Mounton de Gruyter.

Nesi, H. & Gardner, S. 2012. *Genres across the Disciplines: Student writing in Higher Education*. Cambridge: Cambridge University Press.

Nesi, H. & Basturkmen, H. 2006. Lexical bundles and discourse signalling in academic lectures. *International Journal of Corpus Linguistics* 11(3): 283–304.

Pletcher, K. (ed.). 2011. *The History of China (Britannica Educational Publishing)*. New York: the Rosen Publishing Group.

Rayson, P. and Garside, R. 2000. Comparing corpora using frequency profiling. In *Proceedings of the Workshop on Comparing Corpora, held in conjunction with the 38th annual meeting of the Association for Computational Linguistics (ACL 2000)*, 1–6. Hong Kong.

Rayson, P., Leech, G. & Hodges, M. 1997. Social differentiation in the use of English vocabulary: some analyses of the conversational component of the British National Corpus. *International Journal of Corpus Linguistics* 2(1): 133–152.

Ridley, D. 2008. *The Literature Review: A Step-by-Step Guide for Students*. London: Sage Publications.

Ruiying, Y. & Allison, D. 2003. Research articles in applied linguistics: moving from results to conclusions. *English for Specific Purposes* 22(4): 365–385.

Salager-Merer, F. 1992. A text-type and move analysis study of verb tense and modality distribution in medical English abstracts. *English for Specific Purposes* 11(1): 279–305.

Samraj, B. 2002. Disciplinary variation in abstracts: The case of wildlife behavior and conservation biology. In J. Flowerdew (ed.) *Academic Discourse*, 105–120. New York: Longman.

Samraj, B. 2005. An exploration of a genre set: Research article abstracts and introductions in two disciplines. *English for Specific Purposes* 24(2): 141–156.

Scott, M. & Tribble, C. 2006. *Textual Patterns: Keyword and Corpus Analysis in Language Education*. Amsterdam: Benjamins.

Scott, M. 2004. *WordSmith Tools Version 4*. Oxford: Oxford University Press.

Simpson-Vlach, R. & Ellis, N. 2010. An academic formulas list: new methods in phraseology research. *Applied Linguistics* 31(4): 487–512.

Sinclair, J. 1991. *Corpus, Concordance, Collocation*. Oxford: Oxford University Press.

Sinclair, J. 1996. *Preliminary Recommendations on Corpus Typology, Expert Advisory Group on Language Engineering Standards (EAGLES)*. Available online at: www.ilc. cnr.it/EAGLES/pub/eagles/corpora/corpustyp.ps.gz (Accessed August 22 2013).

Sinclair, J. 2004. *Trust the Text.* London: Routledge.

Skelton, J. & Edwards, S. 2000. The function of the discussion section in academic medical writing. *British Medical Journal* 320: 1269–1270.

Stotesbury, H. 2003. Evaluation in Research Article Abstracts in the Narrative and Hard Sciences. *Journal of English for Academic Purposes* 2(4): 327–341.

Swales, J. 1981. *Aspects of Article Introductions.* Birmingham: University of Aston.

Swales, J. 1990. *Genre Analysis: English in academic and research settings.* Cambridge: Cambridge University Press.

Swales, J. & Najjar. 1987. The writing of research article introduction. *Written Communication* 4(2): 175–191.

Swearingen, J. 2013. Rhetoric in cross-cultural perspectives. In P. Simonson, J. Peck, R. T. Craig, & J. Jackson, Jr. (eds) *The Handbook of Communication History,* 109–121. New York: Routledge.

Thompson, D. K. 1993. Arguing for Experimental 'Facts' in Science. *Written Communication* 10(1): 106–128.

Thompson, P. 2009. Literature reviews in applied PhD theses: evidence and problems. In K. Hyland & G. Diani (eds) *Academic Evaluation: Review Genres in University Settings,* 50–67. Basingstoke: Palgrave Macmillan.

Wilkinson, E. 2000. *Chinese History: A Manual (2nd edition).* Cambridge (Massachusetts) & London: Harvard University Press.

Yule, G. 1944. *The Statistical Study of Literary Vocabulary.* Cambridge: Cambridge University Press.

5

Corpus Pedagogic Processing of Phraseology for EFL Teaching: A Case of Implementation

Anping He

5.1 Introduction

Corpus pedagogic processing (or pedagogic mediation) is a current issue in applying corpus linguistics to classroom teaching. It is based on some scholars' questioning of the direct use of corpora in EFL classes. For example, Widdowson (2004) questions the decontextualized nature of corpus data, and points out that the data are merely a sample of language rather than an example of authentic language use and thus may not meet the standard required of pedagogic materials. Braun (2005) is also concerned about the clash between currently existing general corpora and pedagogic requirements, particularly in terms of content, size, format, and annotation (see also Aston, 1995; Cook, 1998; Flowerdew, 2008). To address these problems, a pedagogic processing is needed to 'transfer corpus findings into pedagogically accepted materials and means, ... [which] should be realized at the level of corpus content and design as well as at the level of corpus exploitation by learners and teachers' (Braun, 2005: 55). Some empirical studies have been conducted to implement the idea of corpus pedagogic processing. An early example is Braun's (2005) multimedia learning platform of ELISA, which consists of a corpus engine, an authentic interview transcription, videos, communicative tasks and language exercises. Other examples include Milton's (2006) software that provides didactic written hints to help students become independent writers; Vannestål and Lindquist's (2007) experiment of using concordances in a university grammar course; and Pérez-Paredes and Alcatraz's (2008) SACODEYL, which serves as a pedagogical mediator based on pedagogic corpora in seven European languages. Flowerdew (2008) has advocated the incorporation of student group discussion activities to authenticate corpus data for teaching university students' contextual writing and raising their consciousness for register phraseology. Furuta (2012) has taken a corpus-driven approach to examine patterns, variations, and functions of the English expressions based on the comparison, *not so much A as/ but B*, and related the findings to pedagogical use.

Enlightened by the studies cited above, the current study tries to implement corpus pedagogic processing in two ways. Firstly, it builds a link between two English as a Foreign Language (EFL) courses in South China Normal University,[1] namely, the courses of 'Corpus Application to Foreign Language Education' and 'Multimedia techniques for EFL Teaching'. One objective of both courses is to enable university students (mostly pre-service EFL teachers) to develop corpus-aided multimedia courseware for EFL teaching in middle schools. Secondly it joins two research projects that have hitherto been separately carried out in a university and a middle school. One is the 'Corpus Phraseology Theory and Pedagogic Processing', which was funded by a national grant and carried out by teachers at SCNU; the other is the 'Rolling Blocks Lexical Chunk Teaching', which was provincially funded and carried out by middle school EFL teachers in Zhuhai, Guangdong, China. These will henceforth be referred to as the SCNU Team and the Zhuhai Team, respectively. One objective of both projects is to improve the 'Technological Pedagogical Content Knowledge (TPCK)'[2] of pre- and in-service EFL teachers.

Apart from the issue of pedagogic processing referred to above, another issue is phraseology in EFL teaching, which is challenging the traditional notion of teaching the single word as basic unit of meaning. From the perspective of corpus linguistics, 'phraseology is due to become central in the description of English' because 'units of meaning are expected to be largely phrasal' (Sinclair, 2004: 30) and 'the central notion of a phrase entails co-selection, the simultaneous selection from both grammar and lexis' (Sinclair, 2008: 407). This implies that the main focus of teaching and learning English should be on '(a) the commonest word forms in the language; (b) their central patterns of usage; and (c) the combinations which they typically form' (Sinclair & Renouf, 1988: 150). However, the application of corpus phraseology in EFL education is, as pointed out by Granger and Meunier (2008: 240), falling far short of 'empirical evidence of the actual impact of a phraseological approach to teaching and learning, the types of phrase that are worth teaching as wholes, the optimal length (if any) of such phrases, or the effects on short and long term retention'. There is an urgent need to 'create ready-made and user-friendly interfaces to enable learners and teachers to access multiword units' and to 'train pre- and in-service teachers to be aware of the phraseological view of language and of the exercises and tools' (ibid., 253). To meet this need, the current study tries to use corpus means to identify pedagogically relevant phrasal units and their typical patterns and subsequently transfer them to multimedia EFL courseware. It is then implemented in the aforementioned university courses and projects.

The current study addresses two problems: (a) how to identify, sequence, and highlight phrases as teaching targets, and (b) how to expose phrases to students in their preferred ways. The study is divided into three phases, as elaborated below. The first two phases tackle the first problem, while the third phase tackles the second problem.

5.2   Phase One: Identifying phrases as teaching targets

This phase is a corpus-based search for verb phrases with pedagogic motivation. A phrase is defined as a meaningful chunk which consists of an occurrence of a verb with its co-selection of lexical collocates, grammatical patterns, and semantic preference (Sinclair, 2008: 407). The university students who took the first course actually took part in building a pedagogic corpus named 'EFL Textbook Corpus' (Textbook Corpus hereafter). By 2014 it contained 9.19 million words in total, with 227 English textbooks at both primary and secondary school levels. It is also attached to a reference corpus that consists of classical literature for children from native English-speaking countries (so far including 21 novels with about 1.2 million words in total). As a pedagogic corpus has 'all the language that a learner has been exposed to in the classroom – mainly the texts and exercises that the teacher has used' (Hunston, 2002: 187), a Textbook Corpus is more relevant to current curriculum objectives, more coherent in topic content and sequencing, and makes it easier for teachers and students to interpret concordances from such known texts (see also Hunston, 2002: 187; Braun, 2005: 54; O'Keeffe & McCarthy, 2010: 360). Based on the corpus, target phrases were selected according to two criteria, namely, being pedagogically relevant and linguistically essential.

In order to meet the criterion of pedagogical relevance, the target phrases had to contain verbs included in the phrasal lists[3] of current middle schools' textbooks and the *English Curriculum Standards* (China Education Ministry, 2001), both of which have prescribed the lists as explicit teaching targets. Moreover they also had to be included in 'trouble-point lists' made by middle school teachers, which indicate that they have either easily caused confusion for or often been misused by students (see Appendix for an example). To meet the criterion of linguistic essentialness, the target verbs should be included in at least three basic 2,500-word lists retrieved from three international English corpora[4] so as to ensure that they can be regarded as basic knowledge of English and thus taken as essential and typical teaching targets.

The two criteria above indicate that corpus-aided phraseology teaching is highly selective with both general and specific pedagogic consideration. The corpus-aided phraseology teaching is general in terms of its essentialness coming from large native English speakers' corpora; it is specific in terms of its special demanding by EFL curriculum, course books, and teaching practice in a Chinese context. The Zhuhai Team provided a 'trouble-point list' which was collected from local teachers, and the SCNU Team taught students to check that list via corpus means so as to find out what verb phrases needed to be taught as a priority. The joint effort answered the call that 'a shift is needed in the relationship between teachers, academics and publishers, from the teacher seen as consumer to the teacher as participant in the corpus revolution' (McCarthy, 2008: 563). It also addressed the need that 'it's time to ask what a corpus could do for a language teacher instead of what a language teacher can do with a corpus' (Frankenberg-Garcia, 2010: 3).

5.3   Phase Two: Analysing phrase distribution and phrasal patterns

This was a phase of corpus-driven analysis by the SCNU Team, and was implemented in the course 'Corpus Linguistics and Foreign Language Education'. The SCNU students were required to do phraseology analysis of those target verbs found in Phase One as one of their course assignments. In order to decide what phrases were to be taught and when, four criteria were developed by the SCNU Team as follows.

1. Frequency from high to low. This referred to the frequency of phrases distributed in a certain level of textbooks. The assumption was that 'frequency would reveal centrality and typicality' (Hunston, 2002: 42) and 'the more frequent a word in language use, the more likely it is to be useful to the learner' (Leech, 2011: 12).
2. Knowledge from concrete to abstract. This referred to four levels of phrasal knowledge to teach. According to Sinclair's (2004: 142) model of lexical item analysis, the most concrete level was lexical

collocation, which was then upgraded to more abstract levels such as colligation, semantic preference, and semantic prosody.
3. Patterns from simple to complex. The longer the pattern the more structure transformation would be needed and thus the pattern would become more complex (Collins et al., 2009: 339). For example, 'wh-question' as the object of a preposition, which involves seven steps of transformations, is more complex than the simple past tense in English, which involves just one step (ibid.). Moreover, phrasal patterns' identification, classification, and sequencing also refer to Thornbury's (2004) book of *Natural Grammar,* which provides typical grammar patterns, collocations and set phrases of 100 most frequent words used in a 100 million-word corpus named BNC.[5]
4. Contexts from 'familiar' to 'extended'. Here familiarity means the contexts embedded in the concordances of a phrase are closely related to students' life experience and common knowledge, for 'it is much easier to interpret concordances when they come from known texts' (Gavioli, 1997, cited by Braun, 2005: 54). This demand is mostly met with the help of the Textbook Corpus and the reference corpus.

To take COME[6] as an example, its grammar patterns and core meanings are shown in Thornbury's book (2004: 43) as follows:

1: COME | + adverbial → to talk about people or things moving towards the speaker
2: COME | + to-infinitive → to talk about the reason for the movement towards the speaker
3: COME | + and | + verb → to talk about two closely related actions, where the second is the reason for the first
4: COME | + -ing → to describe actions that are often fast and sudden

The course students would investigate all these patterns in the Textbook Corpus so as to find their frequencies and possible teaching sequences. Tables 5.1 and 5.2, and Figures 5.1 and 5.2 demonstrate some results.

Table 5.1 shows that the most frequent collocates with COME were quite different at three levels of EFL course books, thus indicating that different teaching focus of COME could be highlighted at each level (see Table 5.2). At the Primary school level, the top frequent phrases were 'Come on' and 'Come from (some place)', showing an orientation of spoken English. At the Junior Middle school level, there were more varieties of adverbs following COME, and some were more complex,

Table 5.1 Collocates of COME at three levels

1R collocates of COME (T-score ≥ 2)

Primary	Junior	Senior	
on	to	to	before
from	from	from	down
to	back	out	over
and	on	back	off
in	up	into	round
back	down and	up and	for
	out	in	at
	home	a	I
	with	on	first
	here	true	but
	in	across with	along
	I	home	towards
	or	the	through
			again

Table 5.2 Teaching focus of COME at three levels

Primary	* Come on/in * COME + to/from + s.place (94%) * COME + and + Verb (.09%)
Junior	* COME + Adv. (e.g., up/down/out) * COME + to + Verb (15%, e.g., eat/ live/ stay/ see/ visit
Senior	* COME + to + (various) Verb (30%) * COME + to + Noun (with 25% abstract nouns) * COME + Verb-ing (1%, e.g., Come dashing / scrambling / crowding

including 'COME up with' (see Figure 5.1). Yet the majority of the cases were still 'COME to/from (some place)' with only 15% cases of 'COME + to + Verb'. At the Senior Middle school level, the frequency of 'COME + to + Verb' was doubled (30%) with a much more variety of verbs. And the noun (phrase) after 'COME to' was not merely related to 'some place', such as 'come to school', as they were in the former two levels. Instead, they appear to be abstract concepts or situations such as 'come to a conclusion' or 'came to life' (see Figure 5.2). Moreover, there was a more complicated pattern of 'COME + -ing', such as 'came dashing through the door'. All this shows a gradually increasing tendency of complexity in structure and abstractness in meaning. This kind of corpus-based

```
1  . Hey, we're coming up with a lot of good ideas
2  . We need to come up with a plan. 2. We can't _
3  : We need to come up with a plan.  B: Let's have
4  w we need to come up with a plan to tell people
5   His Work He came up with an idea for hybridizii
6   after        come up with  give out            1
7  t you always come up with good solutions to peop
8  ng lessons / came up with ideas for making money
9  a row wins.] Come up with Put off Write down Pu1
10  We need to come up with some ideas.
11 h. I need to come up with some way of getting me
12 blish, start Come up with:  We need to come up
13 gies that he came up with worked out fine. He ne
```

Figure 5.1   COME + adverb at junior level concordance

```
1  hare your ideas. Come to a conclusion and
2  s 6 The murderer comes to a sticky end.
3  he situation and come to an agreement.]
4   it difficult to come to an agreement Af·
5  ious (= keen) to come to an agreement as
6   quarrel finally came to an end. 8 It see
7  r but his career came to an end when he d
8  th  be ready to  come to life make ... d
9  kes 2 The statue comes to life;- This mea
10 ng only when you come to new information
11 fore the Emperor came to power,  _____
12 n for  bring up  come to power  earn one
13 now the question comes to their minds, ⅅ
```

Figure 5.2   COME + abstract nouns at senior level concordance

investigation could help pre-service teachers to make pedagogic decisions such as identifying, specifying, and sequencing teaching focus at different levels of course books.

Another course assignment was phrasal pattern analysis. The course students, after learning 'lexico-grammar' theory (Sinclair, 2004: 131–148)

wear a belt, jewellery	put on her shoes. Sh	dressed as a man (3) .. .. ..
wears a big hat£¬large t	put on his clothes q	dressed in expensive clothes
wearing a black pearl ne	put on my jacket and	dressed in green looks very s
wearing a black suit is		
wearing a black T-shirt	put on my school __	dressed quickly. He and Danny
wearing a blouse today.	put on my sweater...	dressed up for formal occasio
wearing a blue and white	put on your clothes .	
wearing a blue dress? A	Put on your shoe.	dressing yourself properly?

Figure 5.3 Concordances of 'WEAR', 'PUT on' and 'DRESS' from the Textbook Corpus

in constructing a meaningful phrasal unit, were guided to work out lexical, structural, and semantic co-occurring features of target verbs with the help of the Textbook Corpus and other resources. Below is a case demonstrating a process of distinguishing WEAR, DRESS, and PUT ON. The three verbs shared a meaning of 穿 (put on) in Chinese, yet their English phrasal patterns were not the same. Quite a number of concordances were retrieved from a 0.66 million-word Textbook Corpus at Junior School level, including 139 cases of WEAR, 40 cases of DRESS, and 41 cases of PUT ON. It was found that each of the three verbs was accompanied with different types of collocates, from which two colligation patterns could emerge, i.e., 'WEAR / PUT on + Noun (phrase)' and 'DRESS + Prep. (Phrase)' (see Figure 5.3 below).

Figure 5.3 demonstrates that 'WEAR' and 'PUT on' tended to be followed by nouns relating to substitute clothing such as 'suits, T-shirt, blue dress' and also clothing accessories such as 'belt', 'hat', and 'shoe'. By contrast 'DRESS' was followed by adverbial phrases relating to styles or ways of dressing, such as 'dressed as a man', 'in expensive clothes', and 'in green'.

As a result, a large number of concordances of target verbs were collected, not only with contextual information familiar to middle school students but also typical phrasal patterns for teaching. They could serve as a rich database for 'rolling block' courseware development in the next phase.

5.4 Phase Three: Transferring corpus findings to multimedia courseware

The third phase was concerned with 'pedagogic enrichment', which was 'crucial in helping learners make the move from the text materials presented in the corpus to a real discourse situation' (Braun, 2005: 55). Pedagogic enrichment in this study was implemented in another course named 'Multimedia Techniques and EFL Teaching', in which SCNU students undertook a course assignment to transfer corpus findings in Phase Two into multimedia courseware. In this course the Zhuhai Team's courseware of 'rolling blocks lexical chunks' served as an initial model, because of its colourful and reflective format as well as popularity in the EFL classes of local schools in Zhuhai. The initial model was in need of improvement because the language examples of the courseware were mostly contrived on the basis of the local teachers' intuition instead of being based on typical patterns in contexts that were familiar to middle school students. As Warschauer (1996: 7–8) points out, 'most classroom teachers lack the training or the time to make even simple programs, let alone more complex and sophisticated ones', while 'the commercial developers often fail to base their programs on sound pedagogical principles', hence a need for 'integrating meaningful and authentic communication into all aspects of the language learning'. Accordingly, this is an area where the SCNU Team and its university students can join forces with the Zhuhai Team to improve the quality of the courseware and to save the time of in-service teachers who would otherwise have to implement the improvements by themselves.

The designing phase was guided, first of all, by Chapelle's (1998: 23–25) language learning courseware designing principles, namely, (a) highlighting linguistic characteristics of target input, (b) helping learners to comprehend semantic and syntactic aspects of linguistic input, (c) providing tasks to engage learners in meaningful interaction, and (d) offering opportunity for learners to produce, notice, and modify their output. Secondly, the process was guided by the assumption that both **co-text** and **context** are essential for EFL teaching and learning. Specifically, co-text was provided by verbal versions such as concordances of target verbs to reveal phrasal patterns, whereas context was provided by other media such as picture, video, and sound versions to help students comprehend language input. As a course assignment, the students were required to browse websites or other resources to find pictures and video episodes to match situations depicted in the concordances of target verbs and then include such resources in their multimedia-courseware designing. For example, based on the concordances demonstrated in Figure 5.3 above, some course students made 'rolling blocks' of 'DRESS', 'WEAR', and 'PUT on' in a PowerPoint version courseware, part of which is illustrated in Figure 5.4.

In Figure 5.4, the PowerPoint pages could be 'rolled out' step by step with pictures and phrasal 'blocks' to create both contexts and co-texts in

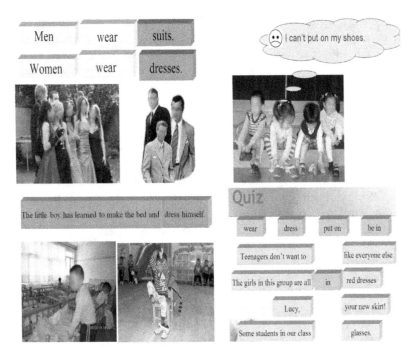

Figure 5.4   'WEAR', 'PUT on', and 'DRESS' relating to clothing

joining a car club?   3 In t
join a clean-up campaign. I
join a club. International I
Join a club or a sports team
joined a group of friends an
join a sports or hobby club
joined a theatre company. He
join an English language clu
join as many clubs as they :
join at least one.jxbzb1-6wl
joining CCTVs Around The Wor
joined Chinese Air Force and
join English sounds or even
join "environment clubs." In

taking part in a project to help pe
take part in after-school clubs. Ae
take part in Paralympics, and at tl
take part in recycling programmes.
took part in the Gamesf¬with a larc
took part in the Olympic Games?   :
take part in the Olympics.   c)Te
took part in the Piano Competition
take part in the sports meeting la:
Take part in your class talk. Thinl

Figure 5.5   Junior Text book Concordances for 'JOIN' and 'TAKE Part in'

classes. The colourful blocks highlight each verb phrase in 'blocks' and then end up with a Quiz as a check. Another example refers to 'JOIN' and 'TAKE part in'. Both verbs shared the Chinese meaning of 参加 (participate), but could be distinguished by different semantic preferences in terms of phrasal patterns (see Figure 5.5).

Figure 5.5 show that both verbs (phrase) were followed by nouns or noun phrases but the nouns denoted different semantic preference. Nouns after JOIN tended to relate to a human group or an organization such as a 'club', 'company', or 'Air Force'; whereas those after 'TAKE part in' were more often related to activities such as 'project', 'games', and 'class talk'. These extracts might have been presented directly in classes, but it was found that middle school students actually preferred the 'enriched version' as demonstrated in Figures 5.6 and 5.7 below.

Figure 5.6 shows several features of an improved 'rolling block' courseware. It contextualized the concordances in Figure 5.5, in which both pictures and blocks could be 'rolled out' by the courseware device. It thus provided students with visual and verbal help to perceive different types of nouns collocating with the two verbs and then guided students to perform some drilling exercises as the pictures changed. Figure 5.7 demonstrates a 'hands on' exercise that asked students to select the right word to fill in the empty block, for which they were provided with prompt feedbacks through a sound device in the courseware.

Figure 5.8 below shows one more example, which involves a video episode in the courseware to make it more attractive. A few seconds of the video 'Mr. Bean', as demonstrated on the right hand side of Figure 5.8, could be activated as an authentic situation where students were required to reorder the 'phrasal blocks' into a correct sequence, such as 'Mr. Bean has difficulty keeping awake'. This is a 'drag and drop' task to learn the phrasal chunk of 'have difficulty doing something'.

Figure 5.6   Courseware demo 1

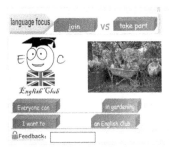

Figure 5.7 Courseware demo 2

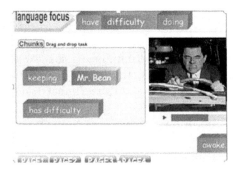

Figure 5.8 Courseware with a video episode

With hundreds of university students regularly taking the two courses in SCNU every year, the corpus-aided multimedia courseware has continued to develop through trials in EFL classes by either pre-service teachers in their teaching practicum or by in-service teachers of Zhuhai and other local middle schools. Very positive feedback has been obtained from both.[7] This research-and-development exercise demonstrates that 'no teaching method can become an important innovation, whatever it is potential, if it does not make its way to the normal classroom where teachers and students can use it as part of their everyday routines, with not too much extra hassle' (Mauranen, 2004: 99).

5.5 Summary

The corpus pedagogic processing of this study, which went through three phases, may be summarized in four steps of pedagogic enrichment:

1. Check potential target verbs in the Textbook Corpus and other pedagogic resources to provide EFL teachers with a reasonable selection for teaching focus;
2. Provide EFL teachers with many examples relevant to middle school students' knowledge;
3. Carry out corpus research to reveal typical patterns of target verbs and then demonstrate them by means of 'rolling blocks';
4. Enrich previous 'rolling block' courseware with multimedia resources such as audio and video materials.

The research, which was a cooperation between two project teams, turned out to benefit both. The SCNU Team integrated ideas and techniques of corpus linguistics and multimedia courseware development into university courses and thus introduced corpus concepts and skills to middle school EFL teaching. And the Zhuhai Team upgraded and enriched the quality and quantity of their courseware in a joint effort with the SCNU Team. It also became a virtuous circle of education at two levels. At the university level, a coherent link between courses has been built to apply theory to practice. As Leech (1998: 3) points out, 'teaching is a natural extension of research'. Students who studied basic concepts and skills of corpus linguistics in one course moved on to study multimedia courseware development in another course. What they learnt in both courses was applied to their teaching practicum in local schools and tackled practical problems there. The new learning experience not only helped students develop their abilities in conducting corpus research but also informed university educators what middle school teachers needed from this new pedagogic technology. At the middle school level, the research enhanced in-service teachers' language awareness and enthusiasm in doing research and trying out modern information technology. All this can be regarded as a part of 'Technological Pedagogical Content Knowledge' (TPCK), which, as Mishra and Koehler (2006: 1029) point out, 'is central to teachers' work with technology' and 'is a good basis for teaching'.

Appendix

Extract from 'Trouble-point list in teaching vocabulary and grammar (offered by middle school EFL teachers of Zhuhai)'

- must & have to
- may & might
- maybe & may be
- will & would
- as noise & sound & voice
- say & speak & talk & tell
- so...that & such...that
- as & like
- either & neither
- both & all
- none & no one
- hope & wish
- each & every
- besides & except & but
- also & too & either
- join & take part in
- too much & much too
- everyone & every one
- noise & sound & voice
- say & speak & talk & tell
- so...that & such...that

- across & through & cross
- Adj + enough & enough + Noun
- cost & take & pay & spend
- have sth. & there be sth.
- look & see & read & watch
- Noun + called & Noun + named
- dress & put on & wear & be in
- used to do sth. & be used for doing sth.
- after s/time & s/time later & in s/time
- bring & take & fetch & get & carry
- a number of & the number of
- at the end & in the end & by the end of
- in front & in front of & in the front of
- how often & how long & how soon
- have been to & have been in & have gone to
- sth. cost+ (money) & sth is worth + (money)
- another & other & others & the other & the others
- sometimes & sometime & some times & some time

Notes

The work described in this chapter was substantially supported by a grant from the Research Grants of China's National Planning Office of Philosophy and Social Science (Project No: 09BYY067) with the title of 'Corpus' Phraseology Theory and its Pedagogic Processing', led by He Anping, the author of this chapter. It is also supported by a grant from the Science & Technology Bureau of Zhuhai (Project No: 2005–21) with the title of 'Rolling Blocks & Word Chunk Teaching', led by Huang Aihong and Liu Dongfang.

1. A teacher training and education university in Guangzhou, China.
2. For detail see Mishra and Koehler (2006).
3. The phrasal lists usually appear as a part of vocabulary list at the end of textbooks and curriculum.
4. They are word-lists from BNC, *Longman Corpus Network* and *COBUILD corpus*.
5. For details, see http://corpus.byu.edu/bnc/.
6. A fully capitalized word in this chapter means a word lemma, including its word types, e.g., COME, including 'come, comes, coming, and came'. The words after 'à' explain the meaning of the pattern before them.
7. A recent thesis (Huang Yingying 2012) in SCNU has found that 100% of the course students used one or more following words in their course comments: 'useful', 'practical', 'helpful', 'great', 'important'. Further detailed feedback from middle school students and teachers can be seen in a journal paper by Liu Dongfang and He Anping (2011: 32–38).

References

Aston, G. (1997) Enriching the Learning Environment: corpora in EFL. In Wichmann, A., Fligelstone, S., McEnery, T. and Knowles, G. (eds) *Teaching and Language Corpora*, 51–64. London/New York: Longman.

Braun, S. (2005) From pedagogically relevant corpora to authentic language learning contents. *ReCall*. 17(1): 47–64.

Chapelle, C. (1998) Multimedia CALL: lessons to be learned from research on instructed SLA. *Language Learning & Technology*. 2(1): 22–34.

China Education Ministry. (2001) *English Curriculum Standard* (a tried version for secondary education in mainland China), Beijing: Beijing Normal University Press.

Collins, L., Trofimovich, P., White, J., Cardoso, W. and Horst, M. (2009) Some input on the easy/difficult grammar question: an empirical study. *Modern Language Journal*. 93(3): 336–353.

Flowerdew, L. (2008) The pedagogic value of corpora: a critical evaluation. In *Proceedings of 8th Teaching and Language Corpora Conference (TALC 8)*. 3rd-6th July 2008, Lisbon, Portugal.

Framlemberg-Garcia, A. (2010) Hands-on/hands-off: varying approaches in data-driven learning. In *Proceedings of 9th Teaching and Language Corpora Conference (TALC 9)*. 30th June-3rd July 2010, Brno, Czech Republic.

Furuta, Y. (2012) A corpus-driven approach to English expressions based on comparison: not so much A as B and not so much A but B. *International Journal of Computer-Assisted Language Learning and Teaching*. 2(1): 24–34.

Gavioli, L. (1997) Exploring Text through the Concordancer: guiding the Learners. In Wichmann, A., Fligelstone, S., McEnery, T and Knowles, G. (eds) *Teaching and Language Corpora*, 83–99. London: Longman.

Huang, Y. (2012) *On learners' evaluation of corpus linguistic course*. Unpublished BA thesis of South China Normal University, Guangzhou, China.

Hunston, S. (2002) *Corpora in Applied Linguistics*. Cambridge: Cambridge University Press.

Leech, G. (1998) Preface. In S. Granger (ed.) *Learner English on Computer*. London: Longman.

Leech, G. (2011) Frequency, Corpora and Language Learning. In Meunier, F., S. De Cock, G. Gilquin and M. Paquot (eds) *A Taste for Corpora –in honor of Sylviane Granger*, 7–32. Amsterdam/Philadelphia: Benjamins.

Liu Dongfang and He Anping (2011) Creation and application of 'Rolling Blocks' Lexical Teaching. *Foreign Language Education in China*. 4(3): 32–38.

Mauranen, A. (2004) Spoken Corpus for an Ordinary Learner. In Sinclair, J. (ed.) *How to Use Corpora in Language Teaching*, 89–105. Amsterdam/Philadelphia: Benjamins.

McCarthy, M. (2008) Accessing and interpreting corpus information in the teacher education context. *Language Teaching*. 41(4): 563–572.

Milton, J. (2006) Resources-Rich Web-Based Feedback: helping Learners Become Independent Writers. In Hyland, K. and Hyland, F. (eds) *Feedback in Second Language Writing*, 123–139. Cambridge: Cambridge University Press.

Mishra, P. and Koehler, M. J. (2006) Technological pedagogical content knowledge: a framework for teacher knowledge. *Teachers College Record*. 108(6): 1017–1054.

O'Keeffe, A. and M. McCarthy (eds) (2010) *The Routledge Handbook of Corpus Linguistics*. London: Routledge.

Pérez-Paredes, P. and Alcaraz, J. (2008) Annotating pedagogy: implementing language teaching and learning-oriented annotation on corpora. In *Proceedings of 8th Teaching and Language Corpora Conference (TALC 8)*. 3rd–6th July 2008, Lisbon, Portugal.

Thornbury, S. (2004) *Natural Grammar*. Oxford: Oxford University Press.

Sinclair, J. (2008) Envoi [A]. In Granger, S and Meunier, F. (eds) *Phraseology: an Interdisciplinary Perspective*, 407–410. Amsterdam/Philadelphia: Benjamins.

Sinclair, J. (2004) *Trust the Text*. London: Routledge.

Sinclair, J. and Renouf, A. (1988) A Lexical Syllabus for Language Learning. In Carter, R. and McCarthy, M. (eds) *Vocabulary and Language Teaching*, 140–160. London: Longman.

Vannestål, M. and Lindquist, H. (2007) Learning English grammar with a corpus: experimenting with concordancing in a university grammar course. *ReCall*. 19(3): 329–350.

Warschauer, M. (1996) Computer Assisted Language Learning: an Introduction. In Fotos S. (ed.) *Multimedia Language Teaching*, 3–20. Tokyo: Logos International.

6

A Corpus Analysis of Chinese Students' (Mis-)Use of Nouns at XJTLU

Wangheng Peng

6.1 Introduction

Corpus linguistics is the study of language based on real-life language use. It draws on evidence from large databases of electronically encoded texts. Corpus analysis could offer insights into some common but often ignored features of language use (Hyland, 2009). Discussing language teaching and learning, Hoey (2009) assumes that:

> Native speakers have acquired a large corpus of examples of the words of English in their typical contexts, and from this they learn how the words are used. By contrast, non-native speakers have typically heard (or read) relatively few examples of even the more common words in natural use and have therefore had less opportunity to learn the way these words typically occur.

Therefore, the starting point of this chapter is the hypothesis that non-native English speaker (NNS) learners tend to make more mistakes in the use of the language than the native English speakers. Corpus studies may help TEFL teachers to focus on the specific areas that cause problems for their students, whereas students can be made more aware of the areas of language use that they may find difficult and thus pay more attention to the areas.

It is found from corpus research that academic writing relies heavily on nouns (Reppen, 2010). In the students' writing, a common problem is the use of countable/uncountable nouns. Many students are not clear about the construct of countability in English grammar, perhaps influenced by Chinese, as their first language. One common mistake is demonstrated by uncountable nouns used in the plural form. This is what Baldwin and Bond (2003) describe as 'the noun's countability preference', which is the lexical property that determines the uses of a noun. Baldwin and Bond reiterate that 'Knowledge of countability preferences is important both for the analysis and generation of English' (2003, p. 263). It is therefore important to make the students aware of this lexical property and improve the use of nouns in their writing.

This chapter aims to demonstrate the importance of corpus studies in TEFL by analysing data in the use of some nouns collected from the Language Centre (LC) of Xi'an Jiao Tong Liverpool University (XJTLU), which is a university jointly run by Xi'an Jiao Tong University in China and Liverpool University in the UK. The LC curriculum is basically task-driven. For example, in Semester 1 of the first year, students are required to write at least three academic essays progressively from 350–450 words, 500–600 words, up to 1,000–1,500 words in length, on various topics related to their life and study. During the process of writing, their work would be peer-reviewed and self-corrected on the basis of repeated teacher feedback. In Semester 2 of the first year, students are required to conduct two research projects and write research reports of 1200–1600 words and 1,400–1,800 words respectively. The research projects are carried out as group projects to enhance the team working spirit but both of the reports are written individually.

TEFL at XJTLU is aimed at raising students' English proficiency, especially in the academic environment. Student feedback shows that what they need most in their English study are skills in vocabulary building. Therefore, vocabulary building is of central importance in the teaching. The students are expected to acquire knowledge in academic vocabulary, so as to enable them to cope with their subject courses at XJTLU and possibly in their future studies abroad. The students' levels in vocabulary are not simply measured by the number of words they could recognize or translate into Chinese, but more importantly by their ability to use the words appropriately to communicate with native English speakers in the genuine academic environment in English.

The present study is based on preliminary research using the XJTLU learner's corpus built so far, in conjunction with three other corpora, which will be described in the next section.

6.2 Corpora used in this study

The present study employs four corpora, consisting of two corpora from Chinese university students and two corpora from British students and published material. For ease of comparison, the two corpora from Chinese university assignments will be categorized as non-native

English speaker (NNS) corpora, while the two corpora from British sources will be categorized as native English speaker (NS) corpora. Of the two NNS corpora, the one under focus is the XJTLU Written English Corpus (XWEC) at its preliminary stage. The other Chinese corpus is the Spoken and Written English Corpus of Chinese Learners (SWECCL), collected from nine other Chinese universities. Two NS corpora are used for a fuller profile of the vocabulary items in question. One is the British National Corpus (BNC) and the other is the British Academic Written English Corpus (BAWE).

The Language Centre at XJTLU is one of the largest EAP units of its kind in the world. Since all students at XJTLU use English as the medium for learning and examinations in the university, there is the potential for an extraordinary collection of academic writing in different disciplines. At present, however, the samples are mainly collected from coursework of the first-year undergraduates. This study is an initial attempt in analysing the learner corpus. With the growth of the corpus in the coming years, more representative samples will be collected for future studies. In the 2011–12 academic year, the intake of students at XJTLU amounted to nearly 2,000. From the first month after they entered XJTLU, students began uploading their assignments on ICE, an intranet system based on online Moodle. To collect students' writing to build the corpus it was necessary to get the consent form signed by the students. As the corpus project only started running in May 2012, only 270 consent forms have been collected so far, and thus only samples from the writing of those students have been analysed. Nevertheless, even with this restriction, the corpus at present is already nearly 1.2 million words in size.

To compare the English levels of XJTLU students in the context of Chinese speaking communities, another NNS corpus is used, which is the Spoken and Written English Corpus of Chinese Learners (SWECCL). SWECCL covers more than 3,000 samples of writing, ranging from 200 to 800 words by undergraduates majoring in English from nine universities in China. The number of words in SWECCL is more than 1.2 million in total (Wen et al., 2009).

The two NS corpora in this study are the BNC and BAWE corpora. The BNC is a 100 million-word collection of modern British English in approximately 4,000 different text samples from an extraordinary range of sources. The written part of the BNC (90%) is claimed to comprise 96,986,707 orthographic written words, including extracts from newspapers, periodicals and journals, academic books, school and university essays, and many other kinds of text (BNC, 2007).

The BNC is freely accessible on line, thus very convenient for use in the present study.

The BAWE corpus consists of 6,506,995 words from '2,761 pieces of proficient assessed student writing, ranging in length from about 500 words to about 5,000 words' across four levels of study and representing 35 disciplines (Nesi et al., 2007). Nesi, one of the Directors of the BAWE corpus, further describes the corpus as containing texts collected from assignments with 'distinction' or 'merit' grades, with the majority written by students who identify themselves as 'native' or 'near-native' speakers of English (Nesi, 2011: 220). For the purpose of the present study, therefore, BNC and BAWE may serve as a standards for measuring writing levels of the Chinese students.

The sizes of the four corpora are summarized in Table 6.1 below:

Table 6.1 The four corpora in this study

Data from	Corpus	Tokens	Types	Type/Token ratio (TTR)
Non-Native Speakers (NNS)	XWEC	1,192,505	17,690	0.014
	SWECCL	1,255,405	19,553	0.015
Native Speakers (NS)	BNC	96,052,598	663,540	0.006
	BAWE	6,730,173	99,741	0.014

In processing the corpora, WordSmith Tools (Scott, 2010) is extensively used, especially its constituent programs of Concord, WordList, and KeyWords. Statistics of the corpora are calculated by WordSmith Tools as shown in Table 6.1 above, where the term 'token' is used instead of 'word', which explains the slight discrepancy in the corpora sizes as claimed by their compilers.

6.3   Data collection and analysis

In English grammar, subjects and verbs should agree in number (singular or plural). This often causes difficulties for the Chinese learners, mainly owing to the lack of subject/verb agreement issue in the Chinese language, and sometimes the subject/verb agreement in English is counter-intuitive or even illogical from the Chinese learner's perspective. An obstacle in the subject/verb agreement of students' academic writing lies in the concept of countability of nouns. Mistakes in using countable/uncountable nouns occur especially in those words which do not have an equivalent division in the Chinese language. Some ideas that appear to be plural to Chinese students do not have plural forms in English, whereas some ideas presented with plural forms in English appear to be a single unit in Chinese.

Corpus research is very helpful for the identification and analysis of such problems. Hyland (2009) suggests, 'Frequency is a key idea in corpus studies ... intuition and data work together to offer fresh insights on familiar, but perhaps unnoticed, features of language use' (Hyland, 2009: 28). Based on our intuition, and more specifically, on our observation from students' writings and common learners' dictionary prescriptions, we drew up a shortlist of 15 uncountable nouns which we felt students often erroneously use in the plural form in their academic writing (cf. Table 6.11).

In this section, we will examine a few nouns to illustrate our corpus analysis. The first word we choose to examine here is 'advice', which is used very frequently in academic writing. According to the Macmillan English Dictionary (Rundell, 2007), a popular learner's dictionary offering help with grammar and usage of words based on corpus data, 'advice' is an uncountable noun and never used in the plural form. Instructions on the use of the word 'advice' from the dictionary are quoted below.

Advice is an <u>uncountable</u> noun, so:
- it is never used in the plural
- it never comes after an or a number
  ✗ Naomi Wolf gave me a~~ good advice~~ in her book.
  ✓ Naomi Wolf gave me <u>some good advice</u> in her book.
  ✗ They were always there to give practical ~~advices~~.
  ✓ They were always there to give practical <u>advice</u>.

Using WordSmith to count the frequency of the plural use of this word in the four corpora, we obtained data as shown in Table 6.2, with graphic presentation in Figure 6.1 below. In Table 6.2, as well as in the remainder of this chapter, all the erroneous use of uncountable nouns are marked by a star *. At a glance, it appears as if it were not a serious problem for the NNS students in China, with fairly similar occurrences of mistakes across all the four corpora.

Table 6.2 The occurrence of '*advices' in the four corpora

	BNC	BAWE	XWEC	SWECCL
*advices	6	8	10	13

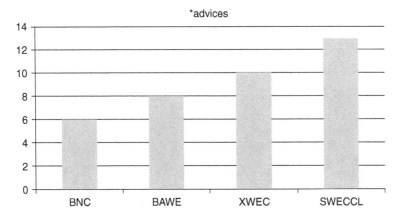

Figure 6.1 The occurrence of '*advices' in the four corpora

Table 6.3 The ratio of '*advices/advice' in the four corpora

	BNC	BAWE	XWEC	SWECCL
advice	10318	434	32	127
*advices	6	8	10	13
%	0.058	1.843	31.250	10.236

However, this does not present the true picture. Although the mistake does not appear much more frequently in the NNS corpora, it does not mean the NNS students could use the word without problems. Logically, there would not be many mistakes if the word were not used many times. To present a more revealing picture, it is better to compare the frequency of correct uses of the word in the corpora with the frequency of the erroneous uses, as in Table 6.3.

Table 6.3 makes comparison between the occurrences of correct use of the word 'advice' and the erroneous use of '*advices' in the four corpora and calculates the percentages in each case. Figure 6.2 illustrates this point graphically and more clearly.

Figure 6.2 reveals a striking picture that NNS tend to make more mistakes using the plural form of this word, whereas NS seldom if ever use 'advice' in the plural form. The ratio of incorrect/correct use in writing appears to be the highest by XJTLU students. It seems possible that this very high ratio in the XWEC corpus compared with relatively low ratio in the SWECCL corpus is because that the word is not used as much in total in the XWEC corpus as in the SWECCL corpus.

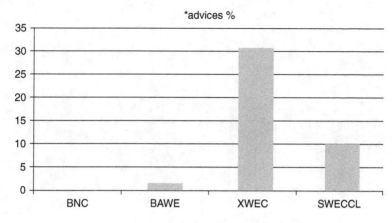

Figure 6.2   The ratio of '*advices/advice' in the four corpora

Although the analysis appears to indicate the deficiency of NNS in the use of the noun 'advice', it is still not scientifically convincing, as this phenomenon might occur by chance. Therefore, a log likelihood test is conducted to check the reliability of the analysis. Table 6.4 shows that the result of the log likelihood test supports the analysis and that the differences in the erroneous use of the word between the NNS and NS corpora are statistically significant.

The second word to be investigated here is 'evidence', which we often come across in students' academic writing. The Macmillan English Dictionary (Rundell, 2007) treats it as uncountable and gives instructions as follows:

Evidence is an <u>uncountable</u> noun, and so:
• it is never used in the plural
• it never comes after an or a number
  ✗ You need to balance ~~the evidences~~ from both sides.
  ✓ You need to balance <u>the evidence</u> from both sides.
  ✗ His response ~~is an evidence of~~ how insecure the government feels.
  ✓ His response <u>is evidence of</u> how insecure the government feels.
  ✗ This can be seen as ~~one more evidence~~ that women are in an inferior position.
  ✓ This can be seen as <u>further evidence</u> that women are in an inferior position.

Table 6.4   Log likelihood test results of '*advices' in the four corpora

NNS Freq	NNS Norm Freq %	NS Freq	NS Norm Freq %	Log Likelihood	Significance
23	4.935%	14	0.130%	98.436	0.000

Table 6.5   The occurrence of '*evidences' in the four corpora

	BNC	BAWE	XWEC	SWECCL
*evidences	38	60	13	6

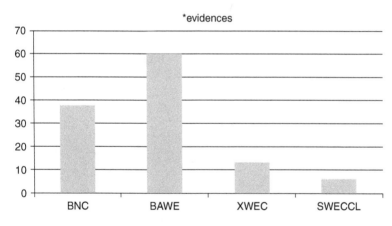

Figure 6.3   The occurrence of '*evidences' in the four corpora

Using WordSmith Tools we worked out the frequency of the wrong use of the word in the four corpora, as shown in Table 6.5 and Figure 6.3.

This appears misleadingly optimistic for the NNS. The NNS seem to make much fewer mistakes than the NS! Again, the logic 'if you don't use the word, you don't make mistakes with it' applies here. Therefore, it is necessary to compare not the actual occurrence of the mistakes, but rather the ratio of correct to incorrect use of the word. This is presented in Table 6.6 with its graphic presentation in Figure 6.4.

It is now obvious from Figure 6.4 that NNS have serious problems using this word whereas NS have almost no problem with it. To check the reliability of this statement, a log likelihood test is conducted. The result in Table 6.7 below supports the analysis and shows that the differences in the erroneous use of the word between the NNS and NS corpora are statistically significant.

Let's now turn to the word 'research', which is used very frequently in academic writing. We will examine how this word is used by NNS and NS. Below is a quote of the instructions for the use of the word 'research', provided by the Macmillan English Dictionary (Rundell, 2007).

Table 6.6 The ratio of '*evidences/evidence' in the four corpora

	BNC	BAWE	XWEC	SWECCL
evidence	21144	3343	110	31
*evidences	38	60	13	6
%	0.179	1.794	11.818	19.354

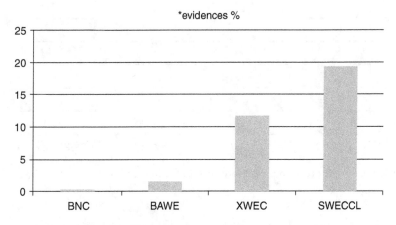

Figure 6.4 The ratio of '*evidences/evidence' in the four corpora

Table 6.7 Log likelihood test results of '*evidences' in the four corpora

NNS Freq	NNS Norm Freq %	NS Freq	NS Norm Freq %	Log Likelihood	Significance
19	13.48%	98	2.93%	26.163	0.000

> Research is an <u>uncountable</u> noun, and so:
> * it is hardly <u>ever</u> used in the plural
> * it never comes after a or a number
> ✗ Her latest work confirms the findings of earlier ~~researches~~.
> ✓ Her latest work confirms the findings of earlier <u>research</u>.
> ✗ According to ~~one recent research~~, women's earnings are still 27% lower than men's.
> ✓ According to <u>recent research</u>, women's earnings are still 27% lower than men's.

Using WordSmith to calculate the frequency of misuse of this word in the four corpora, we get a list as shown below in Table 6.8. It can be seen in Table 6.8 that next to BNC, which is nearly ten times as big as the XWEC corpus, XJTLU students make the most frequent use of the plural form of the word '*researches', with 124 occurrences, which seems unbelievably high. Strangely, BNC also has very high frequency, with 251 occurrences. This phenomenon arouses some interest and will be discussed towards the end of the present chapter. By contrast, SWECCL has only 17 occurrences. The occurrence of the plural form of the word in the four corpora is shown in Table 6.8, and graphically in Figure 6.5:

Figure 6.5 seems to show that one group of the NS (BNC) and one from the NNS (XWEC) respectively have similarly strong tendencies to use the plural form of this word, while writers of the other two corpora tend not to use the plural form of the word. However, as we mentioned before, a more sensible conclusion could be drawn from comparison of occurrences of the 'correct' use of the word with occurrences of the 'mistakes' in each corpus. The result is shown in percentages in Table 6.9 and Figure 6.6.

Figure 6.6, which is based on Table 6.8, shows that NNS use the plural form of the word far more frequently than NS in the UK. This can be explained with the fact that NS (BNC and BAWE) use the word 'research'

Table 6.8 The occurrence of '*researches' in the four corpora

	BNC	BAWE	XWEC	SWECCL
*researches	251	49	124	17

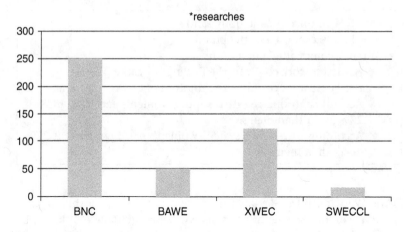

Figure 6.5 The occurrence of '*researches' in the four corpora

Table 6.9 The ratio of '*researches/research' in the four corpora

	BNC	BAWE	XWEC	SWECCL
research	26793	3851	1530	141
*researches	251	49	124	17
%	0.936	1.272	8.104	12.056

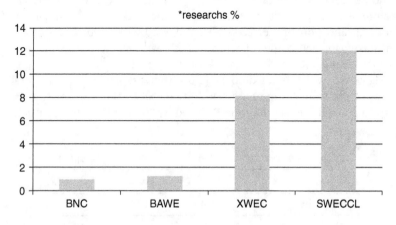

Figure 6.6 The ratio of '*researches/research' in the four corpora

Table 6.10 Log likelihood test results of '*researches' in the four corpora

NNS Freq	NNS Norm Freq %	NS Freq	NS Norm Freq %	Log Likelihood	Significance
141	8.44%	300	0.98%	314.453	0.000

far more frequently in the singular form (as uncountable noun) than the NNS in China (XWEC and SWECCL). The pattern is obvious – that NNS have problems with the use of this word while NS have nearly no problems. This analysis is supported by the log likelihood test, the result of which is shown in Table 6.10, revealing that the differences in the erroneous use of the word between the NNS and NS corpora are statistically significant.

6.4 Further analysis

Using the same method, data from the four corpora for the 15 words in the list were calculated, which are presented in Table 6.11.

Calculating the ratios of errors against correct uses of the words in Table 6.11, we calculated the ratios of the 15 words in the list, as presented in Table 6.12.

Table 6.12 reveals some interesting features. Firstly, the ratios of '*plural/singular' use in the NNS corpora are generally higher than in the NS corpora. This supports our hypothesis that NNS learners tend to make more mistakes in the use of the nouns than the NS. For example, '*softwares', ranking high in the NNS corpora, ranks very low in the NS corpora, with even a zero ratio in the NBC. However, some items have higher ratios of '*plural/singular' use in the NS corpora than in the NNS corpora. This seems to imply that NS tend to use the words erroneously more frequently than the NNS. A possible explanation for this might be that, especially as shown in the XWEC corpus, the NNS learners are made aware of the non-countability of the words and thus endeavour to use them correctly. However, further investigation needs to be undertaken on this topic, which is beyond the scope of the present study.

A log likelihood test is conducted to test the reliability of the analysis. The results are presented in Table 6.13.

It is clear in Table 6.13 that the differences in the erroneous use of most of the 15 words between the NNS and NS corpora are statistically significant. However, it should be noted that some items have negative log likelihood values, implying that NS make more mistakes than NNS in using the words, such as '*childrens', '*homeworks', '*permissions',

Table 6.11 The *plural/singular use of 15 uncountable nouns in the four corpora

Word	BNC	BAWE	XWEC	SWECCL	Word	BNC	BAWE	XWEC	SWECCL
*advices	6	8	10	13	advice	10,318	434	32	127
*childrens	105	4	0	2	children	45,724	2,447	59	5,424
*educations	14	1	0	13	education	26,113	1,319	312	5,215
*equipments	27	30	31	30	equipment	8,836	437	88	53
*evidences	38	60	13	6	evidence	21,144	3,343	110	31
*furnitures	1	0	1	0	furniture	3,458	56	35	5
*homeworks	9	0	0	2	homework	816	11	146	72
*informations	15	1	2	19	information	38,488	3,935	772	1,054
*knowledges	22	8	3	21	knowledge	14,352	2,602	563	2,020
*permissions	163	8	0	1	permission	3,166	111	23	14
*progresses	263	60	6	1	progress	8,081	737	123	246
*researches	251	49	124	17	research	26,793	3,851	1,530	141
*softwares	0	6	6	8	software	9,365	907	120	32
*staffs	227	73	20	6	staff	22,492	1,275	95	19
*vocabularies	49	12	114	5	vocabulary	1223	176	1460	82

Table 6.12 The ratios of '*plural/singular' use of 15 uncountable nouns in the four corpora

Word	BNC%	BAWE%	XWEC%	SWECCL%
*advices	0.058	1.843	31.250	10.236
*childrens	0.229	0.163	0.000	0.036
*educations	0.053	0.075	0.000	0.249
*equipments	0.305	6.865	35.227	56.603
*evidences	0.179	1.794	11.818	19.354
*furnitures	0.028	0.000	2.857	0.000
*homeworks	1.102	0.000	0.000	2.777
*informations	0.039	0.025	0.259	1.802
*knowledges	0.153	0.307	0.532	1.039
*permissions	5.148	7.207	0.000	7.142
*progresses	3.254	8.141	4.878	0.406
*researches	0.936	1.272	8.104	12.056
*softwares	0.000	0.661	5.000	25.000
*staffs	1.009	5.725	21.052	31.578
*vocabularies	4.006	6.818	7.808	6.097

Table 6.13 Log likelihood test results of the 15 uncountable nouns in the four corpora

Word	NNS Freq	NNS Norm Freq %	NS Freq	NS Norm Freq %	Log Likelihood	Significance
*advices	23	14.465%	14	0.130%	145.846	0.000
*childrens	2	0.036%	109	0.226%	−12.594	0.000
*educations	13	0.235%	15	0.054%	13.259	0.000
*equipments	61	43.262%	57	0.614%	350.818	0.000
*evidences	19	13.475%	98	0.400%	93.508	0.000
*furnitures	1	2.500%	1	0.028%	6.223	0.012
*homeworks	2	0.917%	9	1.088%	−0.049	0.824
*informations	21	1.150%	16	0.037%	84.617	0.000
*knowledges	24	0.929%	30	0.176%	31.437	0.000
*permissions	1	2.702%	171	5.218%	−0.540	0.462
*progresses	7	1.897%	323	3.663%	−3.693	0.054
*researches	141	8.438%	300	0.979%	314.453	0.000
*softwares	14	9.210%	6	0.058%	94.125	0.000
*staffs	26	22.807%	300	1.262%	99.425	0.000
*vocabularies	119	7.717%	61	4.360%	13.807	0.000

'*progresses'. One possible explanation for this phenomenon is that the test results of some items are not reliable because of very low frequencies in the NNS, such as '*childrens', '*furnitures', '*homeworks', '*permissions', each appearing only once or twice in the NNS corpora.

One interesting word is '*equipments', which has very high Log Likelihood value in Table 6.13. Comparing the data in Table 6.12, it is clear that this word has very high ratios in both NNS corpora, and it also ranks high in the BAWE corpus. Based on our assumption that NNS tend to make more mistakes than NS, it is understandable that it ranks high in the NNS corpora. But why does it also rank high in the BAWE corpus? Although the BAWE corpus was claimed to be composed of high-level students of native or near native standards, the plural use of this word should still be regarded as problematic. It is therefore necessary to check the exact samples of the plural use of this word in the NS corpora, to find out why this happens.

For this purpose, WordSmith was used to make concordance lines from the BAWE corpus, which are presented in Figure 6.7 below. The online BNC was also used to make concordance lines as presented in Figure 6.8.

Since the BAWE corpus is taken from student writings the concordance may suggest some uses of the plural form of this noun are

```
        But once HC received the    equipments   and paid to JVC the price at
      whipping of cream and so the    equipments   (bowls and beaters) should be
         lies on the residual values (  equipments   ). These residuals must be
           such as to purchase office    equipments   , computers, peripheral
           manufacturers of medical    equipments   , contribution of the top
             used for the purchase of    equipments   , fixtures and fittings, thus
      with the increasing demand of    equipments   , we could buy a new factory
        and additional $50 million on    equipments   . Selling price remains the
       high gain in the circuit. Other    equipments   : DC power supply, digital
     gas collecting and processing    equipments   and distributes propane and
        include capital, employees,    equipments   and materials to meet the cost,
       broadly way, rather than just    equipments   and plants, the effect of
         at CLK airport. Since the all    equipments   and resources had to be
       scope of T&C works for all IT    equipments   and softwares might be limited
      the way to place all facilities,    equipments   and staff in operation.
```

Figure 6.7   Concordance lines of '*equipments' from BAWE

we're down on actual stage one equipments in the month erm, we're not
a larger share of the costs of those equipments than originally planned. Okay.
and or proportionally was due to equipments themselves being more expensive
figures hmm right, yeah but all these equipments would have been selected by by
thank you very much. ask, how many equipments have still to be selected? Erm the
yet been selected. There are three equipments that have been selected where the
could decide from a menu which equipments it would fit according to their
a larger share of the cost of those equipments than originally planned. Okay, can
reached 152°F scrambling the digital equipments programming, so that Matt Bianco
made up by the host of specialised equipments that such a frigate contains. For
thousands of tons of stores and equipments internally for the RAOC for storage
delays in the deliveries of major equipments such as warships and advanced
of relatively low-cost weapons or equipments . However, herein lies the Army's
be able to provide battle-winning equipments for our own forces, but our balance
responsibility to decide what new equipments are needed, and to specify their
for the replacement of existing equipments that are likely to become
which are often devised to sell US equipments to the Western Alliance. American
needed to fly in the heavier military equipments and supplies into Amman until an

Figure 6.8   Concordance lines of '*equipments' from BNC

erroneous. Checking the concordance lines from the BAWE corpus, it may be concluded that this word was used in the plural form intentionally, not as a typo. the other hand, it is apparent from the BNC concordance lines that some of the plural use of this noun is the result of informal spoken language. Perhaps, due to the present technology of recording spoken language, the word might be spelt wrongly by the computer program. Nevertheless, the concordance lines demonstrate that it is possible for NS to use the word in the plural form legitimately, in spite of dictionary prescriptions.

'*Staffs' is another interesting noun in the list, which appears across all the four corpora, ranking very high in the NNS corpora and comparatively low in the NS corpora. Checking the 73 concordance lines from the BAWE corpus, it can be seen that some uses are actually the possessive use with an apostrophe following the letter 's' (five cases). The remaining lines are used in the sense of 'the people who work for a particular company, organization, or institution (Rundell, 2007)' and should not be used in the plural form. Limited by space, only 15 lines are presented in Figure 6.9.

	staffs	
is not the only form to reward	staffs	'creative efforts. Managers will
as the actual reward. Increasing	staffs	'monetary incomes alone doesn't
Additionally, by training	staffs	'skills and knowledge may
analysis. Obtaining organisation	staffs	'support is a key step here. Then,
conflict. For instance, the	staffs	'teamwork spirit, creative skills
as language training for exiting	staffs	, in order to communicate with
training program for excellent	staffs	, or giving them the freedom to
involve many different function	staffs	, the implementers are selected
is comprised of a mount of	staffs	, which are work independently
valuable asset of company is its	staffs	. (Slack, 1991) Organization
to provide excellent training to all	staffs	. 3.7 ProcessA good design of
enabled business involves fewer	staffs	. An ERP system offers the
of managers and collocation of	staffs	. Cell layout is self-contained, and
and reward standard and roles of	staffs	. Coupled with the layout and
up clear target and explain it to	staffs	. Furthermore, they will make high

Figure 6.9   Concordance lines of '*staffs' from BAWE

union is the Transport Salaried	Staffs	'Association (TSSA), formerly the
the general observation about	staffs	'professional identities being a
but the need for service	staffs	—that is, for people without
he broke into Keele University,	Staffs	, after taking the drug.
pigsty, had long beards and	staffs	, and went barefoot.
Bill Scragg, 74, of Sandyford,	Staffs	, caught a trophy-winning 11lb
reduced the necessity for large	staffs	, households were conscious of
subject specialist posts on their	staffs	, notably in the subject-based
to be concentrated in service	staffs	, perched rather insecurely
Gerald Tams, of Stoke,	Staffs	, said: "I didn'treally need it."
Estate, Fenton, Stoke-on-Trent,	Staffs	, ST4 2TE.
moved there from Cannock,	Staffs	, to find work.
Ron, of Gnosall,	Staffs	, who cannot work as a gardener
the school could attract to their	staffs	; and the Victorian parent still
gone, 11,000 from headquarters	staffs	alone.

Figure 6.10   Concordance lines of '*staffs' from BNC

In about 50 randomly selected concordance lines from BNC on line, it could be seen that the plural form of *'staffs'* is sometimes not a mistake; it is used not in the sense of 'people who work for a particular company, organization, or institution' (ibid.), but in other senses such as personal names, institutions, place names, or walking sticks. However, there are still numerous samples of the plural use of this noun in the main sense, which may be due to the mode of spoken English. Again, limited by space, only 15 lines are presented in Figure 6.10.

The above samples should suffice to demonstrate that language in real use is not always truly represented by dictionaries. If the use diverts from what is prescribed by the dictionaries, there might be some sound reasons for NS. However, for NNS the diversion usually results from the learner's first language interference and therefore the learners should be warned off such uses.

6.5 Conclusions

This study is a preliminary attempt to analyse NNS students' academic writing in comparison with NS corpora of students' academic writing and published writing. From the study we have achieved some insightful findings.

Firstly, learner's dictionaries are very helpful for NNS learners but they are better considered as descriptive rather than prescriptive. As language is dynamic and ever-changing, some rules for language use may be broken and changes may be accepted eventually by native English speakers. For example, although the word *'research'* is regarded by many learners' dictionaries as uncountable, numerous samples of plural use in the NS corpora suggest that, at least to a certain extent, it may be used as a countable noun in certain situations. Swales and Feak (2004) suggest that *'research* is an uncountable noun for the vast majority of native speakers; however, it is not at all inconceivable that it may someday become countable – perhaps as a result of pressure from non-native speakers'. Cambridge Dictionaries Online, (2015) supports the idea that a plural form *researches* is indeed available: *His researches in the field of disease prevention produced unexpected results.* Similarly, several uncountable nouns in the list could be used by the native English speakers as countable nouns in certain situations or with some different meanings. This poses some challenges to the EFL teachers. On the one hand, from the corpus analysis in this chapter, there is evidence that native speakers sometimes do use the word in the plural form. It is therefore recommended that the learners should keep a critical eye on dictionary explanations, and use even the best dictionaries with some caution. On the other hand, EFL teachers should approach the teaching of this word with careful consideration. It goes against authentic corpora if they teach the learners to use the word only as an uncountable noun. However, the frequency of its use as a countable noun is so low that the learners should avoid such use in the early stages of learning, and learn how it could be used in this way when they have more knowledge of the word in later stages.

Secondly, corpus research helps both the teachers and the learners to focus on what is characteristically done by native English speakers. More exposure to authentic NS material will improve NNS learners' proficiency in the use of English. EFL teachers should raise NNS students' awareness of living language in use. For the reason given by Hoey (2009), 'a non-native speaker is typically exposed to less language and to a narrower range of language'; non-native English speakers need opportunities to learn how words are used in authentic environments. Corpus study could help teachers to identify problem areas in learners' learning processes and thus focus on those areas to help the students to make improvements. If the NNS learners have access to the updated NS corpus, and exposure to real life communication with educated NS, they may acquire better knowledge of the genuine use of the language, or be properly primed to produce acceptable language in communication.

In spite of the findings, there are limitations in this research, especially in the following two aspects. Firstly, The XWEC corpus is only a very small part of the planned 45 million-word corpus, which was only collected in May 2012, from some first-year undergraduates. Nevertheless, purely judged by number of words, it is of the considerable size of one million words already. Future development of the corpus may include writings from year 2, 3 and 4 undergraduates and postgraduates, and hopefully could reveal more interesting phenomena in the students' achievements and problematic areas in their studies. In addition to the limitations in sample size, XJTLU students' assignments, submitted electronically to the University intranet system, may have already been spell-checked by word-processing software; therefore, in particular, spelling mistakes may be reduced considerably by the spell-check function. This masks the real problem to a certain extent. Teachers may not be aware of the problem if they do not see the mistakes, but in reality the students could still use the word improperly.

The next step forward is to further expand our collection of the learner corpus at XJTLU. It is planned that not only written materials but also speech transcripts will be collected into the corpus. We expect that by 2017 the corpus will be accessible on-line to the general academic community, both in China and globally, and when this happens it will be published in appropriate corpus forums. Our plan is to explore all aspects of English language learning utilizing the XWEC corpus, not only at the level of vocabulary and grammar use, but also at the level of text organization and genre. The development of corpus technology is already having an impact on English language learning at XJTLU and other institutions. The provision of corpus resources such as XWEC will ensure that many other groups of learners will be able to benefit from the corpus approach in the future.

Note

The data in the British Academic Written English (BAWE) corpus used in this study was developed at the Universities of Warwick, Reading, and Oxford Brookes under the directorship of Hilary Nesi and Sheena Gardner (formerly of the Centre for Applied Linguistics [previously CELTE], Warwick), Paul Thompson (Department of Applied Linguistics, Reading) and Paul Wickens (Westminster Institute of Education, Oxford Brookes), with funding from the ESRC (RES-000-23-0800).

References

Baldwin, T., & Bond, F. (2003). Learning the Countability of English Nouns from Corpus Data. *Proceedings of the 41st Annual Meeting of the Association for Computational Linguistics*, pp. 463–470.

BNC. (2007). *The British National Corpus.* (t. B. Consortium, Editor, & D. b. Consortium, Producer) Retrieved from http://www.natcorp.ox.ac.uk/.

Cambridge Dictionaries Online, (2015). research definition, meaning – what is research in the British English Dictionary & Thesaurus – Cambridge Dictionaries Online. [online] Available at: http://dictionary.cambridge.org/ dictionary/british/research [Accessed 12 May 2015].

Hoey, M. (2009). *Lexical priming.* Retrieved from http://www.macmillandictionaries. com/MED-Magazine/January2009/52-LA-LexicalPriming-Print.htm.

Hyland, K. (2009). *Academic Discourse: English in a Gobal Context.* London: Continuum.

Nesi, H. (2011). BAWE: An Introduction to a New Resource. In A. Frankenberg-Garcia, L. Flowerdew, G. Aston, A. Frankenberg-Garcia, L. Flowerdew, & G. Aston (eds), *New Trends in Corpora and Language Learning.* London: Continuum.

Nesi, H., Gardner, S., Thompson, P., & Wickens, P. (2007). *The British Academic Written Corpus.* Retrieved from Oxford University Computing Services: http:// ota.ahds.ac.uk/headers/2539.xml.

Reppen, R. (2010). *Using Corpora in the Language Classroom.* Cambridge: Cambridge University Press.

Rundell, M. (ed.). (2007). *McMillan English Dictionary for Advanced Lerners* (2nd ed.). Oxford: McMillan Education, a division of McMillan Publishers Limited.

Scott, M. (2010). *WordSmith Tools*, Version 5.0. Oxford: Oxford University Press.

Swales, J. M., & Feak, C. B. (2004). *Academic Writing for Graduate Students: Essential Tasks and Skills: A Course for Nonnative Speakers of English* (2nd ed.). University of Michigan Press.

Wen, Q. F., Wang, L. F. & Liang, M. C. (2009) *Spoken and Written English Corpus of Chinese Learners (SWECCL).* Beijing: Foreign Language Teaching and Research Press.

7

A Corpus-based Analysis of the Use of Conjunctions in an EAP Teaching Context at a Sino-British University in China

Bin Zou and Wangheng Peng

7.1 Introduction

Using appropriate conjunctions in writing English assignments is a crucial skill for students to achieve their academic goals at universities because of the important role played by conjunctions as logical connectors, especially in academic writing. However, according to some previous corpus studies on conjunctions, many EFL learners encounter difficulties in the use of appropriate conjunctions in their English academic writings (Granger, 1994; Granger & Tyson, 1996) and regularly use informal conjunctions or over-use and under-use some connectors (Altenberg & Tapper, 1998; Narita et al., 2004). Therefore, it is vital to teach EFL learners to use conjunctions effectively in their academic writing.

Similarly, researchers in China have found that many Chinese EFL learners at universities are likely to use informal words in their writing due to a lack of knowledge of academic styles. For example, according to Muo (2005), use of conjunctions is associated with the learners' level of writing; learners with a high level of writing skills tend to utilize more conjunctions than those with a low level of writing skills. Chinese college students are likely to use conjunctions that they are familiar with and learned in their early stages of English and that are employed in oral English and likely to be informal (He & Xu, 2003; Wen et al., 2003; Zhao, 2011). Therefore, these findings indicate that Chinese students tend to be weak in using appropriate formal conjunctions in their academic writing.

Xi'an Jiaotong-Liverpool University (XJTLU) is a joint venture between Xi'an Jiaotong University, China and the University of Liverpool, UK, offering both UK and Chinese accredited undergraduate degrees. English is the only language used in all academic departments. All teaching resources and exams should adhere to the standardization of the University of Liverpool. Students have to write essays and reports, and conduct experiments and tutorials in English. English for Academic Purposes (EAP) lessons offered by the Language Centre are compulsory for students in years one and two. Textbooks published in the UK or the US in teaching EAP courses are adopted and all handouts are created based on a variety of resources from universities in the UK. Using appropriate and formal conjunctions in academic writing is one of the key skills that students should acquire. During teaching, staff have discovered that many students tend to use informal conjunctions in their assignments and reports. Once we have exposed the informal use of conjunctions in students' essays, we produce worksheets to identify informal words used by students and provide proper formal words and suggestions. After one year of study in the Language Centre, students should have improved their use of formal conjunctions in their writings.

However, there is a lack of research investigating learners' use of conjunctions in their English writing at this Sino-British University. Thus, this study aims to explore the students' progress in the use of conjunctions and examine whether and in what ways students make progress in their writing. The researchers collected students' essays and reports in Years One and Two and utilized WordSmith Tools 5.0 (Scott, 2010) to analyse students' use of conjunctions. This data is identified as XJTLU Written English Corpus (XWEC). Moreover, we employed the corpus of British Academic Written English (BAWE) to look at whether the use of conjunctions by students in the Sino-British University is similar to British university students. In addition, it was unclear whether Chinese students at the Sino-British University had the same level of use of conjunctions as other college students in China. Hence, we employed the Spoken and Written English Corpus of Chinese Learners (SWECCL 1.0: Wen et al., 2009) at tertiary level to identify similarity and difference in the use of conjunctions with XWEC.

Corpus linguistics is one of the leading research areas in Applied Linguistics and has been broadly developed. In recent years, the development of computer technology has enhanced research of corpora and integration of corpora in language teaching and learning. Researchers have found, for example, that corpus use can improve students' language skills in grammar and vocabulary through learner corpora and web concordancing (Granger et al., 2007; Greaves & Warren, 2007). Using corpora can help EFL learners to improve their writing skills and motivate their language learning, and is more efficient than drill exercises (Huang,

2010). Language teachers can thus enhance their vocabulary teaching with a variety of corpora (He, 2004; Furuta, 2012).

Hence, this research adopted three corpora to analyse the frequency of the use of conjunctions among three groups of students in order to examine whether Chinese students at the Sino-British University and students in other nine Chinese universities use conjunctions in the same way or with similar frequency to students in British universities. The differences or similarities between the three groups of students in the use of conjunctions discovered in this study can help teachers and students in China to benefit their teaching and learning of the use of conjunctions in academic writing.

7.2   Methodology

Three corpora were selected to analyse students' use of conjunctions in writing assignments. The first is the XJTLU Written English Corpus (XWEC). Students uploaded their assignments on Moodle (the virtual learning environment in use at the institution).

Two assignments were selected for analysis, because we only wanted to investigate the learning outcomes in Year One. The first essay was written by 230 students from eight disciplines during the first month after they entered XJTLU. At this stage, their level of vocabulary-use might be same as their level in the high school. This part of the corpus consists of 300 words on average, totalling 92,183 word tokens. The essay focused on a general topic, which was the same for all 230 students. The final reports in Year One then showed students' learning outcomes after attending EAP courses for one year. Analysis of the reports might be able to demonstrate their development and progress during their English learning in Year One. This part of the corpus consists of 245 reports of 1,700 words on average, totalling 430,681 word tokens. The reports focused on various topics based on their disciplines. To comply with the ethical research policy of the University of Liverpool and XJTLU, to allow the researchers to collect and use their assignments for research purposes, all participating students signed copyright consent forms. Students were not paid to contribute their writing to XWEC.

The BAWE corpus, the second corpus used in this study, includes 1,039 undergraduate and postgraduate students' assessed essays from three UK universities (Nesi et al., 2007). BAWE contains 35 disciplines with 800 to 1,500 words for each assignment. There are more than 10 genre families with approximately 3,000 examples and 6.5 million words in total (Nesi et al., 2007; Nesi, 2011). The majority of students in this corpus were native or "near-native" English speakers and all of these essays scored above 60%, equivalent to a grade A or B (Alsop & Nesi, 2009; Nesi, 2011).

The Spoken and Written English Corpus of Chinese Learners (SWECCL 1.0, Wen et al., 2009), which was the third corpus, covers students' essays ranging from 200 to 800 words from nine Chinese universities. All the students from Years One to Four were English majors and the 16 genre families covered more than 3,000 examples of writing. The total number of words in this corpus is in excess of 1.2 million (Wen et al., 2009). Similarly, we selected essays from Years One, Two and Four to analyse students' development and progress in the use of academic vocabulary in their study. Table 7.1 below shows a summary of the three corpora used in this paper.

Some differences were noted in terms of the constitution of the corpora. All BAWE texts are good passes, up to and including Masters' degrees, and students in BAWE come from different disciplines where appropriate connector use may be very different; XWEC seems to include all levels for only first-year undergraduates, including presumably failed papers; and the SWECCL students are all English majors. Despite this, it is still interesting to compare the use of connectors among the three corpora to explore similarities and differences.

First, the researchers analysed the XWEC data to identify the development of students' writing in the Sino-British university context. Then, the investigators compared XWEC with BAWE to examine whether the writing level of students at XJTLU was close to students in the UK. Next, the researchers compared XWEC with SWECCL to find out the similarity and difference between the two contexts in China.

Table 7.1 The three corpora used in the analysis

Corpora	Tokens	Sub-corpora	Tokens
BAWE	6,730,173		6,730,173
XWEC	522,864		
		XWEC-Y1 1st	92,183
		XWEC-Y1 final	430,681
SWECCL	1,255,405		
		SWECCL 1.0-Y1	355,367
		SWECCL 1.0-Y2	402,090
		SWECCL 1.0-Y3	444,605
		SWECCL 1.0-Y4	53,343
Total	8,508,442		8,508,442

Finally, the three types of corpora were compared together to recognize similarities and differences. Conjunctions discussed in this study are adopted from Halliday & Hasan (1976), Quirk et al. (1985), and Celce-Murcia and Larsen-Freeman (1999) including causal conjunctions, additive conjunctions, contrastive and concession conjunctions, temporal conjunctions, preposition conjunctions, and conjunctions of summary. Since BAWE covers three universities in the UK, it could be regarded as a comprehensive model of academic writing. SWECCL includes texts from nine universities in China; it could also represent a model of Chinese universities, to some extent. Although students who are native speakers in BAWE may also use conjunctions inappropriately, their scores are above 60, which may be considered a positive model. If Chinese students receive more than 60 in their assignments in a British context, then they achieve good passes in their English writing. This is possibly an ideal and positive outcome in academic writing for L2 learners and it is also EFL teachers' expectation of their students.

Therefore, if the outcome of writing in XWEC or SWECCL 1.0 is close to BAWE, it may mean that Chinese students' use of conjunctions are the same as British students'. However, if there is a significant difference between the two Chinese corpora and BAWE, it may mean that Chinese students use conjunctions differently in their writings. A recommendation was provided for teaching formal conjunctions at the Sino-British University and other Chinese universities. WordSmith Tools 5.0 (Scott, 2010) was used to analyse the three corpora. Frequency of the use of conjunctions in the three corpora was counted and compared with the concord program in WordSmith 5.0. Additionally, this study used Chi-Square in SPSS to test whether the differences in the corpora are statistically significant (i.e. $p < 0.05$). Research questions in this study were:

1. Did students at the Sino-British University improve their use of conjunctions after completing Year One of their English learning?
2. Are there any differences or similarities in the use of conjunctions between Chinese and British students based on the three corpora?

7.3   Results

7.3.1   Causal conjunctions

Causal conjunctions, such as 'therefore', 'thus', 'hence', 'so', 'accordingly', 'consequently', 'as a result', and so forth, are vital for linking results between sentences. Some of them may not be used frequently in formal written English – for example, 'so'. The table below illustrates the use of these conjunctions by students in the UK and China in the three corpora.

As can be seen in Table 7.2, the top three most used causal conjunctions in BAWE are 'therefore', 'thus', and 'hence'. This indicates that English native speakers or high-level academic writers at British universities often use these three words to lead to results. In the first XWEC-Y1 essay, it can be seen that 'so' is top, followed by 'therefore', and 'thus'. 'Hence' is bottom. The final Y1 report shows that 'therefore' and 'thus' are the top two. 'Hence' is in the top 'five', compared to being in the bottom position in Year One. This suggests that students make some progress by the end of their Year One study in the use of causal conjunctions – which is similar to the BAWE. In spite of this, the statistics description (Chi-Square) in Table 7.3 illustrates that there is still a strongly significant difference between BAWE and the XWEC-Y1 final reports (p = 0.000) in using 'therefore', 'thus', and 'hence', which are under-used by students at XJTLU. This means that Chinese students still need to use these conjunctions more regularly. Although 'so' is still in the top three, close to the top-four use of 'so' in BAWE, it is still used more frequently by students at XJTLU.

In SWECCL 1.0-Y1 and SWECCL 1.0-Y2, the findings show that using 'so' as the top conjunction is certainly not unique to Chinese students at the Sino-British University; it is frequently used by students in other Chinese universities, followed by 'therefore', 'as a result', or 'thus'. 'Hence' is not regularly used. However, in SWECCL 1.0-Y4, 'therefore' is used most and 'thus' is in second place. This shows that students in Y4 increase their use of 'therefore' and 'thus', which are the most used in BAWE, as in the XWEC-Y1 final report. Nevertheless, 'so' is still in the top two used by students in Y4, and 'hence' is less used.

The results above indicate that Chinese students very frequently use 'so', which is informal, in the first essay in XWEC-Y1 and first two years in SWECCL 1.0, compared with the other top three uses of conjunctions in BAWE. This is possibly because Chinese students use 'so', which was familiar to them when they were in high school. Students adapt their use of these conjunctions after one year of study in XWEC and four years in SWECCL 1.0. The reason could be that the Sino-British University adopts the same EAP teaching materials as British universities and aims to help students cope with their academic study in English-medium universities. Although Y4 students make some progress in SWECCL 1.0, many of them still like to use 'so' due to its familiarity and the influence of its oral use, as claimed by He and Xu (2003), Wen et al. (2003), and Zhao (2011).

Table 7.2 The use of causal conjunctions by the three student groups

BAWE	XWEC-Y1 1st	XWEC-Y1 final	SWECCL 1.0-Y1	SWECCL 1.0-Y2	SWECCL 1.0-Y4
therefore 0.116	so 0.194	therefore 0.091	so 0.290	so 0.245	therefore 0.097
thus 0.066	therefore 0.067	thus 0.040	therefore 0.027	therefore 0.048	so 0.041
hence 0.031	thus 0.031	so 0.034	as a result 0.025	thus 0.020	thus 0.018
so 0.019	as a result 0.016	as a result 0.024	thus 0.013	as a result 0.018	as a result 0.013
as a result 0.019	for this reason 0.007	hence 0.016	consequently 0.006	consequently 0.004	consequently 0.007
consequently 0.012	consequently 0.006	as a consequence 0.013	hence 0.003	hence 0.001	for this reason 0.003
accordingly 0.003	hence 0.004	consequently 0.010	as a consequence 0.001	in consequence 0.001	hence 0.001

Table 7.3 Chi-Square for causal conjunctions between BAWE and the XWEC-Y1 final reports

Word	Freq in BAWE	Freq in XWEC Y1 final report	Chi-Square	Significance (p)	Use more/ less regularly
therefore	7,807	396	20.465	0.000*	–
thus	4,472	175	41.590	0.000*	–
hence	2,098	71	28.837	0.000*	–
so	1,330	149	43.137	0.000*	+
as a result	1,276	105	6.168	0.013*	+
consequently	807	46	0.583	0.445	
accordingly	222	16	0.211	0.646	

Note: * indicates significant level; + and – indicate: used 'more regularly' and 'less regularly'.

Moreover, the Chi-Square result shows that there is a significant difference in the use of 'thus' (p = 0.007 < 0.05) and 'hence' (p = 0.001 < 0.05) between XWEC-Y1 and SWECCL 1.0-Y4. However, the statistical data also suggests that there is no difference for other causal conjunctions. This means that while students in XWEC-Y1 use 'thus' and 'hence', which are the second and third most used in BAWE, students in SWECCL 1.0-Y4 may not often use them. This finding supports the idea that students in XWEC use 'thus' and 'hence' significantly more frequently than students in SWECCL 1.0-Y4.

7.3.2 Additive conjunctions

In terms of additive conjunctions, the data in Table 7.3 reveal interesting findings. It can be seen that 'further', 'furthermore', and 'in addition' are the top three frequently used by students in BAWE. 'And', 'too', 'what's more', and 'what's worse' are not often used. In the first essay in XWEC, it can be seen that 'and', 'further', and 'in addition' are the top three used. In the final report in Y1 in XWEC, the top three most frequently used conjunctions are 'in addition', 'further', and 'furthermore' which are almost the same as in BAWE. Moreover, 'and' does not often appear in the sentence-initial position. This result indicates that students at XJTLU, after one year of study, use the three top conjunctions in a similar fashion to students in BAWE.

However, Table 7.4 also shows that the top three used conjunctions from Y1 to Y4 in SWECCL 1.0 are 'what's more', 'and' (sentence-initial), and 'too' (sentence-end), which are used far less in BAWE. 'Besides' is

Table 7.4 Additive conjunctions among the three corpora

BAWE	XWEC-Y1 1st	XWEC-Y1 final	SWECCL 1.0-Y1	SWECCL 1.0-Y2	SWECCL 1.0-Y4
further 0.054	and (initial) 0.132	in addition 0.095	what's more 0.724	what's more 0.749	what's more 0.888
furthermore 0.020	further 0.095	further 0.073	and (initial)	and (initial) 0.201	and (initial) 0.181
in addition 0.018	in addition 0.065	furthermore 0.057	too (end) 0.155	too (end) 0.111	too (end) 0.097
also (initial) 0.016	besides 0.041	moreover 0.044	besides 0.036	besides 0.030	besides 0.028
moreover 0.015	also (initial) 0.039	and (initial) 0.037	also (initial) 0.019	also (initial) 0.017	also (initial) 0.024
and (initial) 0.011	moreover 0.027	besides 0.026	moreover 0.014	further 0.016	moreover 0.024
additionally 0.005	furthermore 0.026	additionally 0.017	in addition 0.014	in addition 0.013	further 0.011
besides 0.004	too (end) 0.014	also (initial) 0.016	further 0.013	moreover 0.011	in addition 0.007
too (end) 0.002	additionally 0.001	too (end) 0.001	furthermore 0.006	furthermore 0.006	furthermore 0.003
what's more 0.000	what's more 0.000	what's more 0.000	what's worse 0.001	what's worse 0.002	what's worse 0.000
what's worse 0.000	what's worse 0.000	what's worse 0.000	additionally 0.000	additionally 0.002	additionally 0.000

also often used, but less frequently in BAWE and the Y1 final report in XWEC. 'Further', 'furthermore', and 'in addition', which are frequently used in BAWE and XWEC, are used very occasionally in SWECCL 1.0. This suggests that students in the nine universities of China are taught differently from students in British universities and the Sino-British University. It might also be because Chinese students are influenced by oral and informal English. Similar to SWECCL 1.0, 'and' (sentence-initial) is the most used in XWEC when students are writing their first essay because they are in the same English teaching context as when they were in high school. After one year, the use of 'and' at the beginning of the sentence declines because EAP teaching at XJTLU complies with the standard of British universities; the learning outcome is therefore similar to students in Britain.

Moreover, the results in Table 7.4 demonstrate that the frequency of the majority of additive conjunctions that students employ in the final report in Y1 in XWEC is more than that in BAWE. The Chi-Square result in Table 7.5 shows that there is a significant difference in the use of 'further', 'furthermore', 'in addition', 'moreover', 'and' (sentence-initial), 'additionally', and 'besides'. This indicates that students in XWEC over-use these additive conjunctions, compared to students in BAWE. There is no significant difference in the use of 'also', 'too' (sentence-end), 'what's more' and 'what's worse' between the two corpora. This indicates that the final report in XWEC used these conjunctions in the same manner as in BAWE writings.

Surprisingly, our results show that 'what's more' and 'what's worse' are not used by students in BAWE and XWEC, but the percentage use of 'what's more' increases from Y1 to Y4 in SWECCL 1.0. 'What's worse' is used in Y1 and Y2, but not used in Y4. This suggests different teaching standard requirements between British universities and Chinese universities in the use of 'what's more' and 'what's worse'. In the British academic mode, the two phrases are considered informal. Since the Sino-British University has to strictly adhere to the standards of British universities, there is no doubt that the written learning outcome is similar between the two teaching contexts. However, the two conjunctions are acknowledged as formal in the English teaching mode in China because they may be included in the English teaching syllabus at the nine universities. This teaching preference presents a potential challenge in English academic teaching in China.

The statistical data in Chi-Square show significant differences between XWEC-Y1 and SWECCL 1.0-Y4 in the use of 'furthermore' ($p = 0.00 < 0.05$), 'further' ($p = 0.00 < 0.05$), 'in addition' ($p = 0.00 < 0.05$), and

Table 7.5 Chi-Square for additive conjunctions between BAWE and the XWEC-Y1 final report

Word	Freq in BAWE	Freq in XWEC Y1 final report	Chi-Square	Significance (*p*)	Use more/less regularly
further	3,686	316	25.081	0.000*	+
furthermore	1,371	249	250.923	0.000*	+
in addition	1,223	411	1059.058	0.000*	+
also (initial)	1,104	70	0.005	0.940	
moreover	1,060	192	192.469	0.000*	+
and (initial)	753	163	224.914	0.000*	+
additionally	359	74	93.973	0.000*	+
besides	276	114	371.899	0.000*	+
too (end)	140	7	0.408	0.523	
what's more	0	0			
what's worse	0	0			

Note: * indicates significant level; + and – indicate: used 'more regularly' and 'less regularly'.

'moreover' (p = 0.02 < 0.05). These four conjunctions are the top four used by XWEC-Y1 students, which are also frequently used in BAWE, but not often used by SWECCL 1.0-Y4 students. On the other hand, there are also significant differences in the use of 'and' (sentence-initial) (p = 0.00 < 0.05), 'too' (sentence-end) (p = 0.00 < 0.05), and 'what's more' (p = 0.00 < 0.05). These findings support the results above – that while SWECCL 1.0-Y4 students use these informal additive conjunctions frequently, students in XWEC-Y1 do not adopt them in their writing. These results indicate that students in the Sino-British University use more formal additive conjunctions than students in the nine Chinese universities.

7.3.3   Contrastive and concession conjunctions

In contrastive and concession conjunctions, it can be seen in Table 7.6 that 'however', 'although', and 'though' are the top three used in BAWE. 'However', 'but' (sentence-initial), and 'though' are the top three used in the XWEC-Y1 first essay. After one year of study, 'however', 'although', and 'though' are the top three used by students. This means that students at the Sino-British University tend to use the same top three contrastive and concession conjunctions as students in British

Table 7.6 A comparison of the use of contrastive and concession conjunctions

BAWE	XWEC-Y1 1st	XWEC-Y1 final	SWECCL 1.0-Y1	SWECCL 1.0-Y2	SWECCL 1.0-Y4
however 0.181	however 0.105	however 0.164	but (initial) 0.326	but (initial) 0.275	but (initial) 0.150
although 0.068	but (initial) 0.094	although 0.044	however 0.115	however 0.124	however 0.131
though 0.030	though 0.026	though 0.036	though 0.062	though 0.051	although 0.024
despite 0.024	although 0.011	but (initial) 0.020	although 0.041	although 0.045	though 0.024
but (initial) 0.019	yet 0.009	whereas 0.011	even though 0.009	even though 0.009	whereas 0.005
whereas 0.016	nevertheless 0.006	even though 0.010	despite 0.009	despite 0.007	despite 0.003
even though 0.009	even though 0.006	despite 0.007	yet 0.004	in spite of 0.004	even though 0.003
yet 0.007	nonetheless 0.002	nevertheless 0.007	nevertheless 0.002	nevertheless 0.003	yet 0.003
nonetheless 0.003	in spite of 0.002	in spite of 0.003	in spite of 0.002	whereas 0.002	nevertheless 0.001
nevertheless 0.002	despite 0.001	nonetheless 0.000	whereas 0.001	yet 0.002	nonetheless 0.000
in spite of 0.002	whereas 0.000	yet 0.000	nonetheless 0.000	nonetheless 0.000	in spite of 0.000

universities. In particular, 'but' (sentence-initial) is frequently used, in the top two, in the first essay when they arrive at the university, with a similar result in SWECCL 1.0. Whereas the use of 'but' (sentence-initial) decreases in the final assignment in Y1 in XWEC.

It can be seen in SWECCL 1.0 that the top three contrastive and concession conjunctions across Y1–Y4 are almost the same. 'But' (sentence-initial) is used as the top one in all the years. The Chi-Square shows a significant difference between XWEC-Y1 final and SWECCL 1.0-Y4 in the use of 'but' (sentence-initial) (p = 0.00 < 0.05). This indicates that students in the nine Chinese universities use 'but' extensively at the beginning of the sentence, though it is used less by students in British universities and the Sino-British University. This might be due to the fact that Chinese students are more familiar with the use of 'but' at the beginning of sentences than any other contrastive conjunctions.

In SWECCL 1.0-Y4, 'however', 'although', and 'though' are also frequently used. This shows that students in the nine universities used the three conjunctions in the same manner as students in BAWE and XWEC. In terms of the use of 'whereas', which is frequently used in BAWE, the results show that after one year's study at XJTLU and four years' study at Chinese universities, it is also increasingly used.

However, the statistical descriptions of the BAWE and XWEC-Y1 final reports show differences in some contrastive and concession conjunctions. As can be seen in Table 7.7 below, Chi-Square displays significant differences between the two corpora in the use of 'although', 'despite', and 'nevertheless'. The data also show that students in XWEC underuse 'although' and 'despite', but over-use 'nevertheless', compared to BAWE. This suggests that students in XWEC can be encouraged to use 'although' and 'despite' more frequently and 'nevertheless' less frequently. Meanwhile, there are slight differences between the two corpora in the use of 'however', 'though', 'whereas', and 'yet' (sentence-initial). There is no difference in the use of 'but' (sentence-initial), 'even though' and 'nonetheless'. These results indicate similar usage of these conjunctions in the XWEC-Y1 final reports and by students in BAWE.

7.3.4 Temporal conjunctions

With respect to temporal conjunctions, the results in Table 7.8 demonstrate that the percentage of the use of temporal conjunctions in BAWE is very low, which indicates that students in British universities do not often use temporal conjunctions. In the Y1 first essay in XWEC, it can be seen that students use temporal conjunctions quite

Table 7.7 Chi-Square for contrastive and concession conjunctions between BAWE and the XWEC-Y1 final reports

Word	Freq. in BAWE	Freq. in XWEC-Y1 final report	Chi-Square	Significance (*p*)	Use more/less regularly
however	12,236	709	6.624	0.010*	–
although	4,579	191	34.121	0.000*	–
though	2,035	157	5.112	0.024*	+
despite	1,618	34	45.754	0.000*	–
but (initial)	1,313	90	0.398	0.528	+
whereas	1,081	51	4.561	0.033*	–
even though	628	47	1.074	0.300	
yet (initial)	80	0	5.119	0.024*	–
nonetheless	33	3	0.342	0.558	
nevertheless	22	28	221.009	0.000*	

Note: * indicates significant level; + and – indicate: used 'more regularly' and 'less regularly'.

often, particularly 'nowadays', 'now', and 'today'; exactly the same as students in Y1–Y4 in the nine Chinese universities (SWECCL 1.0). This suggests that Chinese students like to use these temporal conjunctions and might be heavily influenced by the traditional Chinese writing style in which the temporal conjunctions 'now', 'nowadays', and 'today' are used with high frequency. Since some Chinese students' essays are included in BAWE, the small percentage of the use of temporal conjunctions might be used by Chinese students due to the traditional style in Chinese writing, although their scores are more than 60, which is a high level in the British university system. Interestingly, the data in Table 7.8 shows a decline in the percentage of use of temporal conjunctions by students in the Y1 final report in XWEC, although 'nowadays' is still the most used. This implies that use of temporal conjunctions by students at XJTLU lessens because they have been taught in EAP lessons to reduce their usage of temporal conjunctions, although to some extent they might still be influenced by their Chinese writing style.

The Chi-Square also displays significant differences between XWEC-Y1 and SWECCL 1.0-Y4 in the use of 'now', 'nowadays', and 'today' (p = 0.00 < 0.05). This means that students in XWEC-Y1 use the three temporal conjunctions far less than students in SWECCL 1.0-Y4, and this difference is significant.

Table 7.8 A comparison of the use of temporal conjunctions

BAWE	XWEC-Y1 1st	XWEC-Y1 final	SWECCL 1.0-Y1	SWECCL 1.0-Y2	SWECCL 1.0-Y4
currently 0.009	nowadays 0.035	nowadays 0.005	nowadays 0.094	nowadays 0.091	now (initial) 0.050
now (initial) 0.005	now (initial) 0.028	at present 0.003	now (initial) 0.050	now (initial) 0.043	nowadays 0.037
at present 0.002	today (initial) 0.005	today (initial) 0.001	today (initial) 0.011	today (initial) 0.010	today (initial) 0.031
today (initial) 0.002	at present 0.002	currently 0.001	at present 0.005	at present 0.004	at present 0.000
nowadays 0.002	currently 0.002	now (initial) 0.001	currently 0.001	currently 0.000	currently 0.000

Table 7.9 Chi-Square for temporal conjunctions between BAWE and the XWEC-Y1 final report

Word	Freq in BAWE	Freq in XWEC Y1 final reports	Chi-Square	Significance (*p*)	Use more/less regularly
currently	638	5	31.197	0.000*	−
now (initial)	345	5	13.021	0.000*	−
at present	173	13	0.312	0.576*	+
today (initial)	157	6	1.570	0.210*	−
nowadays	142	23	18.333	0.000*	+

Note: *indicates significant level; + and − indicate: used 'more regularly' and 'less regularly'.

Simultaneously, in Table 7.9, Chi-Square shows that there are significant differences between BAWE and the XWEC-Y1 final reports in the use of 'currently', 'now' (sentence-initial), and 'nowadays'. The data also reveal that students in XWEC under-use 'currently' and 'now (sentence initial)', but over-use 'nowadays'. There is no difference in the use of 'at present' and 'today (initial)' between BAWE and the XWEC-Y1 final reports.

7.3.5 Preposition and phrasal conjunctions

Regarding prepositional and phrasal conjunctions used at the beginning of sentences such as 'about', 'in terms of', 'with respect to', 'in regard to', 'regarding', and 'concerning', the findings in Table 7.10 display some differences among the three types of corpora. In BAWE, the results show that students in Britain prefer to use 'in terms of', followed by 'with respect to', 'regarding', and 'concerning'. Students in their first essay in XWEC use 'concerning' most, followed by 'in terms of' and 'about' at the beginning of sentences. In their final assignment in XWEC, students prefer to use 'in terms of' most, the same as in BAWE. Y1 and Y2 SWECCL 1.0 students most often choose to use 'about' at the beginning of a sentence, and then use 'in terms of', which is similar to BAWE and XWEC, whereas students in Y4 in SWECCL 1.0 do not use these phrases at all. The data also shows that students in BAWE often use 'with respect to' and 'regarding', which are used minimally or not at all by Chinese students. This indicates that Chinese students are more familiar with 'about' than other phrases used by students in Britain at the beginning

Table 7.10 A comparison of the use of prepositional and phrasal conjunctions

BAWE	XWEC Y1 1st	XWEC-Y1 final	SWECCL 1.0-Y1	SWECCL 1.0-Y2	SWECCL 1.0-Y4
in terms of 0.025	concerning 0.073	in terms of 0.007	about 0.003	about 0.002	about 0.000
with respect to 0.004	in terms of 0.002	about 0.001	in terms of 0.000	in terms of 0.001	in terms of 0.000
regarding 0.001	about 0.002	concerning 0.000	in regard to 0.000	concerning 0.000	concerning 0.000
concerning 0.001	in regard to 0.000	regarding 0.000	concerning 0.000	in regard to 0.000	in regard to 0.000
about 0.001	regarding 0.000	in regard to 0.000	regarding 0.000	regarding 0.000	regarding 0.0000
in regard to 0.000	with respect to 0.000	with respect to 0.000	with respect to 0.000	with respect to 0.000	with respect to 0.000

Table 7.11 Chi-Square for prepositional and phrasal conjunctions between BAWE and the XWEC-Y1 final reports

Word	Freq in BAWE	Freq in XWEC Y1 final report	Chi-Square	Significance (*p*)	Use more/ less regularly
In terms of	1731	30	57.9069	0.000*	–
With respect to	320	0	20.4785	0.000*	–
Regarding	69	2	1.2842	0.257	–
Concerning	68	4	0.0268	0.870	–
About	65	5	0.1577	0.691	+
In regard to	48	1	1.3687	0.242	–

Note: * indicates significant level; + and – indicate: used 'more regularly' and 'less regularly'.

of sentences. This also points to a lack of variation in the use of prepositional and phrasal conjunctions by Chinese students. The statistics description (Chi-Square) illustrates a significant difference between XWEC-Y1 and SWECCL 1.0-Y4 in the use of 'in terms of' (p = 0.008 < 0.05). This indicates that whereas students in XWEC use 'in terms of', students in SWECCL 1.0-Y4 do not tend to use it.

Chi-Square in Table 7.11 shows that there are significant differences between BAWE and the XWEC-Y1 final reports in the use of 'in terms of' and 'with respect to', and students in XWEC under-used the two conjunctions. This indicates that students in XWEC should use 'in terms of' and 'with respect to' more regularly. However, there is no difference in the use of 'regarding', 'concerning', 'about' (sentence-initial), and 'in regard to'. This indicates that students in XWEC and BAWE use these conjunctions with a similar frequency.

7.3.6 Conjunctions of summary

Concerning conjunctions of summary, the results in Table 7.12 reveal similarity amongst the three groups of students. As with the students in Britain, students at the Sino-British University and other Chinese universities in China often use 'in all', 'in conclusion', 'in short', and 'to sum up'. The statistics description (Chi-Square) does not illustrate any significant difference in using these conjunctions between students in the two Chinese contexts. This result demonstrates that students in the three groups use these conjunctions of summary similarly.

Table 7.12 A comparison of the use of conjunctions of summary

BAWE	XWEC-Y1 1st	XWEC-Y1 final	SWECCL 1.0-Y1	SWECCL 1.0-Y2	SWECCL 1.0-Y4
in all 0.010	in conclusion 0.066	in all 0.006	in all 0.010	in all 0.017	in all 0.007
in conclusion 0.006	to sum up 0.016	to sum up 0.003	to sum up 0.003	all in all 0.009	in conclusion 0.007
in short 0.001	in all 0.013	in short 0.003	in conclusion 0.002	to sum up 0.009	in short 0.007
to sum up 0.000	all in all 0.005	in conclusion 0.003	in short 0.001	in conclusion 0.005	to sum up 0.007
in summary 0.000	in summary 0.004	in summary 0.002	all in all 0.001	in short 0.003	all in all 0.000
to summarize 0.000	in short 0.003	to summarize 0.000	in summary 0.000	to summarize 0.000	in summary 0.000
all in all 0.000	to summarize 0.002	all in all 0.000	to summarize 0.000	in summary 0.000	to summarize 0.000

Table 7.13 Chi-Square for conjunctions of summary between BAWE and the XWEC-Y1 final report

Word	Freq. in BAWE	Freq. in XWEC-Y1 final reports	Chi-Square	Significance (p)	Use more/less regularly
in all	671	29	4.3379	0.037*	–
in conclusion	427	14	6.2919	0.012*	–
in short	109	16	10.1823	0.001*	+
to sum up	63	16	28.3351	0.000*	+
in summary	63	9	5.3578	0.021*	+
to summarize	58	4	0.0210	0.885	+
all in all	30	0	1.9198	0.166	–

Note: * indicates significant level; + and – indicate: used 'more regularly' and 'less regularly'.

At the same time, Chi-Square in Table 7.13 demonstrates that there is no difference in the use of 'to summarize' and 'all in all' between BAWE and the XWEC-Y1 final reports. However, there are significant differences between BAWE and the XWEC-Y1 final reports in the use of 'to sum up', and students in XWEC over-used it. There are slight differences in the use of 'in all' (under-use), 'in conclusion' (under-use), 'in short' (over-use), and 'in summary' (over-use).

7.4 Discussions and conclusion

As discussed above, the students from the Sino-British University use conjunctions in their academic writing after one year of English learning in a similar way, to some extent, to BAWE students. In terms of causal conjunctions, students at the Sino-British University use 'therefore' and 'thus' more than 'so' after their first year of English study. Also, 'hence' is used more than before. Students in other Chinese universities tend to use 'so' quite often, though it is used less than 'therefore', 'thus', and 'hence' by students in Britain. Y4 students use 'therefore' most, but 'so' is still in the top two. This means that 'so' is used by many Chinese students, a written usage which might be influenced by their oral English. Therefore, Chinese students could be advised not to use 'so' frequently, since it might be informal; whereas students could be encouraged to use 'therefore', 'thus', and 'hence' regularly.

In terms of additive conjunctions, the results show that students at the Sino-British University also make considerable progress. After one year of English learning, they use 'further', 'furthermore', and 'in addition' frequently: the top three used by students in Britain. However, students in other Chinese universities use 'what's more' 'and' and 'too', which are seldom used by students in Britain, as their top three. This suggests that students in other Chinese universities could be encouraged to consider using 'further', 'furthermore', and 'in addition' more often.

With respect to contrastive and concession conjunctions, the results indicate that students at the Sino-British University use them in the same fashion as BAWE students. In particular, 'but' is not in the top three used at the beginning of sentences in the final reports. However, 'but' is preferred by many Chinese students from Y1 to Y4 in the nine universities. Thus, it is suggested that use of 'but' could be reduced at the beginning of sentences. Despite this, there are similarities in the use of 'however', 'though', and although' amongst the three groups of students.

Regarding temporal conjunctions, the results suggest that the percentage of use by students in Britain is low, but is very high among Chinese students. Chinese students seem to prefer to use 'now', 'nowadays', and 'today'. This indicates that Chinese students should be discouraged from using temporal conjunctions. If Chinese students want to use them, 'currently' – the one most often used in BAWE – could be taken into consideration.

Concerning prepositional and phrasal conjunctions, the findings reveal that students in BAWE employ them in various ways. However, Chinese students use 'about' frequently at the beginning of sentences. It is suggested that Chinese students should use a variety of prepositional and phrasal conjunctions in order to enrich sentence structures. In regard to conjunctions of summary, the results show that Chinese students use them just as students in Britain do.

In conclusion, the students in the Sino-British University use more formal conjunctions frequently than the nine universities in China due to the fact that the English course in the Sino-British University adheres to the criteria of British universities. Nevertheless, there is still poor usage of some conjunctions. Students from other Chinese universities have also adopted some similar conjunctions to BAWE students. Despite this, as a result of the strong impacts of spoken English, Chinese culture, and EFL teaching methods in China, students in the nine universities seem to use more informal conjunctions than students in the UK and the Sino-British University. This is possibly because many Chinese students may be unaware of the distinction between informal and formal conjunctions in an academic context, as with other EFL learners (e.g. Altenberg & Tapper, 1998). In the meantime, some informal conjunctions are used more frequently, since many Chinese students may be highly familiar with them. It is suggested that some amendments could be taken into account in academic teaching by teachers in China. It would be valuable for students to adjust unsuitable under- or over-use of conjunctions in their assignments. It is anticipated that the results in this research could help EFL teachers in China to re-evaluate teaching of conjunctions. Positive results in students' learning outcomes in the use of conjunctions can be maintained, but incorrect usage of conjunctions should be adjusted and modified in EAP contexts. Moreover, it is hoped that this study can help EFL learners utilize conjunctions appropriately in their academic English writing.

Nevertheless, there are some limitations in this study. Compared with the other two corpora, the corpus of XWEC at the Sino-British University covered only limited students and examples, which may affect the results and analysis. Secondly, using BAWE as a standard mode might be restricted and biased. Comparing 'native speaker' and 'learner' corpora may not be significantly meaningful as they may have different genres for academic writing, though it would be an ideal achievement if ESL/EFL learners could perform similar levels of the use of academic vocabulary. Next, only certain conjunctions are compared in this study; some other conjunctions are not. Therefore, more examples in XWEC should be collated for future research in order to achieve a balance with the other two corpora. More conjunctions could be compared among the three corpora. More standard modes of academic corpus – for example, the Michigan Corpus of Written Academic English (MICAWE) – could be added and compared in order to achieve convincing results in future research.

Note

The data in the British Academic Written English (BAWE) corpus used in this study was developed at the Universities of Warwick, Reading, and Oxford Brookes under the directorship of Hilary Nesi and Sheena Gardner (formerly of the Centre for Applied Linguistics [previously CELTE], Warwick), Paul Thompson (Department of Applied Linguistics, Reading) and Paul Wickens (Westminster Institute of Education, Oxford Brookes), with funding from the ESRC (RES-000-23-0800).

References

Alsop, S. & Nesi, H (2009). Issues in the development of the British Academic Written English (BAWE) corpus. *Corpora*. 4 (1): 71–83.

Altenberg, B. & Tapper, M. (1998) The use of adverbial connectors in advanced Swedish learners' written English. In S. Granger (ed.). *Learner English on Computer* (pp. 80–93). Abingdon, UK: Routledge.

Celce-Murcia, M. & Larsen-Freeman, D. (1999). *The Grammar Book: An ESL/EFL Teacher's Course* (2nd ed.). Boston: Heinle & Heinle Publishers.

Furuta, Y. (2012). A Corpus-Driven Approach to English Expressions Based on Comparison: Not so Much A as B and Not so Much A but B. *International Journal of Computer-Assisted Language Learning and Teaching*, 2 (1): 24–34.

Granger, S. (1994). The Learner Corpus: a revolution in applied linguistics. *English Today*, 10 (3): 25–33.

Granger, S. & Tyson, S. (1996) Connector Usage in the English Essay Writing of Native and non-Native EFL Speakers of English. *World Englishes*, 15 (1): 17–27.

Granger, S., Kraif, O., Ponton, C., Antoniadis, G. and Zampa, V. (2007) Integrating learner corpora and natural language process: A crucial step towards reconciling technological sophistication and pedagogical effectiveness. *ReCALL*, 19 (3): 252–268.

Greaves, C. & Warren, M. (2007) Concgramming: A computer driven approach to learning the phraseology of English. *ReCALL*, 19 (3): 287–306.

Halliday, M. A. K. & Hasan, R. (1976) *Cohesion in English [M]*. London: Longman.

He, A. P. (2004) *Corpus Linguistics and English Teaching*. Beijing: Foreign Language Teaching and Research Press.

He, A. P. & Xu, M. F. (2003) A study of oral English small words by Chinese College students. *Foreign Language Teaching and Research*, 6: 446–452, 481.

Huang, L. (2010) The potential influence of L1 (Chinese) on L2 (English) communication. *ELT Journal*, 64/2: 155–164.

Muo, J. H. (2005) A corpus-based study of Chinese College students' use of conjunctions in argument essays. *Foreign Language Teaching*, 5: 45–50.

Narita, M., Sato, C., & Sugiura, M. (2004) Connector usage in the English essay writing of Japanese EFL Learners. *The Proceedings of the Fourth International Conference on Language Resources and Evaluation* (pp. 1171–1174).

Nesi, H., Heuboeck, A. & Holmes, J. (2007) The British Academic Written Corpus Manual (BAWE) the University of Reading, UK. http://www.reading.ac.uk/AcaDepts/ll/app_ling/internal/bawe/BAWE.documentation.pdf.

Nesi, H. (2011) BAWE: an introduction to a new resource. In: Frankenberg-Garcia, A., Flowerdew, L. & Aston, G. (eds) *New Trends in Corpora and Language Learning* (pp. 213-228). London: Continuum.

Quirk, R., Greenbaum, S., Leech, G., & Svartvik, J. (1985). *A comprehensive grammar of the English language*. London: Longman.

Scott, M. (2010) *WordSmith Tools*, Version 5.0. Oxford: OUP.

Wen, Q. F., Ding, Y. R., Wang, W. Y. (2003) Oral English trend in Chinese College students' written English. *Foreign Language Teaching and Research*, 4: 268–274.

Wen, Q. F., Wang, L. F. & Liang, M.C. (2009) *Spoken and Written English Corpus of Chinese Learners (SWECCL)*. Beijing: Foreign Language Teaching and Research Press.

Zhao, X. (2011) The use of casual connectives in non-English majors' writings: A study based on picture compositions and the SWECCL corpus. *Foreign Language Education in China*, 4(2): 12–20.

8
Application of Corpus Analysis Methods to the Teaching of Advanced English Reading and Students' Textual Analysis Skills

Haiping Wang, Yuanyuan Zheng, and Yiyan Cai

8.1 Introduction

Quite a number of studies have addressed deficiencies in traditional methods of teaching reading in English as they relate to improving students' textual analysis skills and hence reading competence. As Huang (2011: 5) points out, the teaching of reading in English has been going on a long time, but has 'regrettably fallen short of people's expectations', and reading comprehension remains a problem for most students today.

English majors are no exception. According to the survey of needs analysis prior to this study, students involved in the survey admitted that they lacked a vocabulary large enough for advanced reading. During the process of reading, students encounter problems such as inadequate mastery of the text theme, lack of skills to locate topic sentences and key words, and inability to do textual analysis; therefore they might gradually lose their interest in reading. Meanwhile, teachers providing advanced reading instruction may have difficulties searching for examples to explain the use of specific words, may lack the background knowledge to assist textual analysis, and may inadequately emphasize the structure of a text and overemphasize explanation of individual words or sentences instead of piecing them together in the context.

Recognizing the critical role of reading and difficulties in teaching and learning reading skills, this study investigated the effects of employing a new teaching method of advanced reading. That is to say, students are involved in the construction of a textbook-related reading corpus and asked to select and tag texts through close reading and finally present their analysis of the tagged texts, with the teaching purpose of improving their textual analysis skills and reading comprehension ability.

8.2 Corpus-based discourse analysis and the teaching of English reading

Two recent studies on corpus-based discourse analysis utilize very different approaches. The first, a quantitative approach, centres upon the distribution of certain linguistic forms and features. For example, corpus linguistics can help the study of language use in a particular text genre, in a particular kind of discourse, or in a particular social or communicative context (Barlow, 2011). Alternately, a qualitative approach focuses on organization and structure of texts, mainly on the discourse level beyond words and sentences restricted to a few texts from a single genre (Upton, 2009: 586). The difference between the two is that a researcher conducting a corpus-supported analysis usually resorts to a theoretical framework, whereas a researcher conducting a corpus-driven analysis approaches the data with very few preconceptions (Lee, 2008). Then, how to integrate corpus analysis methods and discourse analysis that focuses on the structural organization of texts poses one of the challenges to corpus linguists. Therefore, Biber et al. (2007: 10) have attempted to seek the interface of these two perspectives by proposing an applicable structured, seven-step, corpus-based approach to discourse analysis, starting from the development of an analytical framework to understand the function of texts in the corpus and leading to a closer examination and description of concrete linguistic characteristics and features reflected by the corpus. Biber et al. (2007) refer to this as a 'top-down approach' to the analysis of discourse structure, which is different from a 'bottom-up' approach that starts with lexical and linguistic form-focused corpus analysis.

To facilitate the top-down approach of corpus-based discourse analysis, developing a feasible analytical framework and tagging system is the key. Recently, quite a few corpus studies that rely on tagging for the identification of move structure patterning have been carried out for ESP genre analysis (Upton & Connor, 2001; Connor et al., 2002; Flowerdew & Dudley-Evans, 2002). The tagging of larger stretches of text, such as move structures, for rhetorical features makes it possible to do corpus-based discourse analysis beyond the sentence level, which succeeds in complementing the 'bottom-up' approach (Flowerdew, 2005: 326–327). It is evident that corpus-based discourse analysis is different from the traditional paragraph-based approach, and the corpus-based approach helps quantify and describe discourse features reflecting certain organizational patterns of texts that serve the function of conveying the author's purpose of writing.

Previous studies have shown that reading is a complicated process including top-down processing and bottom-up processing. Bottom-up processing is a serial model where readers begin with printed words, recognize graphic stimuli, decode them to sound, recognize words and decode meanings (Alderson, 2000: 16). On the other hand, other studies have emphasized the importance of the reader's background knowledge in the reading process and models of reading stressing this type of knowledge are termed schema models; in other words, the reader's relevant schemata might be activated when s/he comes to a text. The more relevant the schemata turn out to be, the more successful the reading is. Top-down reading processing emphasizes the importance of these schemata and the reader's contribution. According to Carrell (1983), readers' comprehension is dependent upon linguistic schemata, rhetoric schemata and content schemata. Linguistic schemata and rhetoric schemata belong to schemata of different formality levels that refer to readers' linguistic knowledge of vocabulary, idioms, grammar, and knowledge of text types, discourse structure, and text organization respectively. As a counterpart to formal schemata, content schemata refer to readers' knowledge of the subject matter and content of a text. Traditional views on reading follow the serial model of bottom-up processing, from words and phrases to sentences and passages. This view of reading has laid a solid foundation for the traditional way of teaching reading, which successfully draws students' attention to memorization of new vocabulary and analysis of single sentences instead of mastering the macro-structure and coherent organization of the whole text. Therefore, the teaching of reading is replaced by explanation of separate grammar points and students act as passive receivers, mechanically copying down teachers' talk. As a result, the students' reading competence does not demonstrate a leap forward.

The reason behind the aforementioned students' reading difficulties might lie in Carrell's statement that 'some students' apparent reading problems may be problems of insufficient background knowledge' (Carrell, 1988: 245). The same conclusion is also drawn by Chinese scholars. The reading process is often considered an interactive model where bottom-up processing and top-down processing interact with each other. Students' lack of content schemata will influence their top-down reading processing and lead to a halt of the interactive model; thereafter, students have to rely wholly upon bottom-up reading processing, leading to difficulty in mastering the holistic content and macro structure of the text. Therefore their reading speed and accurate textual comprehension will be decreased (Duan, 2010: 128). Furthermore, in real teaching situations, the fact is revealed that English majors have insufficient background knowledge, in spite of their rich linguistic knowledge. In terms of top-down reading processing, the deficiency in content schema, namely lack of background knowledge, could lead to reading comprehension failure. Top-down processing allows readers to develop 'expectations' about text structures and meanings by using prior knowledge, and the 'expectation' plays an important role in the reading process (Gui, 2000: 112). Through top-down processing, readers actively employ their world knowledge in the form of various kinds of schemata that can help them predict what might happen in the following discourse and hence their brain function will shift from receiving information passively to processing information actively.

Meanwhile, discourse analysis has already found its way into pedagogical settings, especially in the classroom teaching of reading. McCarthy and Carter (1994: 172) believe language must be described from the perspective of discourse, and they emphasize discourse competence as a reading skill. But how to effectively employ corpus-based discourse analysis in the teaching of reading remains a challenge. Relevant studies show that corpus-based discourse analysis can foster the process of schema acquisition, which is in fact the process of composition and decomposition of pre-existing schemata (Aston, 1995: 262). Aston believes that corpora provide us with 'context-specific' word use and concrete 'contextual repetitions' which are considered essential to enhancement of students' weak cognitive schemata and eventually turning them into part of their permanent memory (Aston, 1997: 56). Therefore, corpora and corpus tools can help students with their schemata construction and reconstruction in the process of English reading. For example, Aston (1997: 56–64) constructed a reading corpus composed of a wide selection of newspaper and magazine articles, providing a large amount of informative and current natural language that enriched students' cognitive schemata and also managed to improve their interest in reading and the corresponding autonomous learning ability. In fact, schema construction calls for a reasonably-designed syllabus, appropriately-selected teaching materials, and cross-disciplinary cooperation between language teachers and corpus linguists, which will help students cultivate their interest in reading, enrich their content schemata and then improve their reading competence.

Until recently, top-down approaches (including move analysis) of corpus-based discourse analysis have not been popular with language teachers because it is highly labour-intensive to apply a top-down analytical framework to a large corpus. However, if the corpus is maintained at a reasonable size, 'this investment of labor pays off by enabling more detailed but generalizable analysis of discourse structure across a representative sample of texts from a genre' (Upton, 2009: 588).

The present study calls for attention to students' active participation in corpus construction and their contribution to the tagging of texts, which are oriented toward improvement of their textual analysis skills. Actually, quite a few pioneers who have endeavoured to narrow the gap between corpus-based discourse analysis and language teaching have attempted to apply students' self-compiled corpora to teaching. For example, Noguchi (2004) required his students majoring in science and technology to construct an EAP (English for Academic Purposes) corpus, which is composed of academic reports and theses, and then instructed them to conduct their own research upon concrete genre features and typical collocations and concordances. Lee and Swales (2006) entitled their EAP course 'Exploring your own discourse world', requiring students to edit their own specialized corpora after familiarizing themselves with the corpora and to explore the register characteristics through corpus tools. Since students' contribution to corpus construction for pedagogical uses has already been applied in the field of teaching ESP (English for Specific Purposes) and EAP, we may also borrow this new teaching concept and apply it to the teaching of advanced English reading, which might in turn enhance students' close reading ability and cultivate their data-driven autonomous learning habits.

8.3   Motivation for this study

Plenty of studies (e.g., Conrad, 2004) have pointed out that corpus linguistics will revolutionize language teaching, by fundamentally changing the ways of teaching materials development, curriculum design, teaching methodology and teacher training. But the connection of corpus linguistics with language teaching is still a comparatively new thing. The purpose of this study is to see whether the integration of corpus construction and corpus analysis methods with practical teaching is applicable.

Previous studies have suggested that applications of corpora in L2 teaching include both the use of corpus tools, including text collections and software packages for corpus access, and corpus methods, namely, the analytic techniques that are used while working with corpus data (Römer, 2011: 214). Therefore, corpus applications can be classified as direct applications, where students and teachers have direct access to corpora in the L2 classroom teaching, and indirect applications, that has an effect on teaching syllabus design and material development.

The project involves both direct and indirect application of corpora in the following ways: teachers design the teaching syllabus and materials based on corpora, which include corpus-driven teaching plans and processing of teaching materials, i.e. the examples chosen from corpora to explain the use of new words and analysis of texts must be processed first in order to aid students' comprehension. Teachers give demonstrations of textual analysis assisted by corpus tools, such as AntConc 3.2, and corpus analysis methods, such as selection and tagging of texts and presenting concrete linguistic features such as collocations, concordance lines, keyword lists, and tagged textual features with corpus tools, etc. Students need to refer to corpora (such as COCA – Corpus of Contemporary American English) whenever they meet any difficulty in understanding a word or phrase during the reading process. Students are also required to select and tag texts through autonomous reading which must match certain criteria teachers employ to construct the textbook-related corpus, and they are also required to make presentations based on the tagged texts to demonstrate their analytical reading abilities. Teachers guide students and give prompt and effective feedback during the whole process.

8.4   Method

8.4.1   Research Questions and Hypotheses

Research Question 1: What is the effect of students' contribution to reading corpus construction and tagging of corpus texts on their textual analysis skills?

Hypothesis 1: Students' active participation in corpus construction and text tagging, their access to corpora and corpus tools in the process of autonomous reading are central to the improvement of their textual analysis skills and hence their reading comprehension ability.

Research Question 2: To what degree are students motivated during the process of doing textual analysis based on corpus analysis methods and corpus tools?

Hypothesis 2: Students' active participation in construction of the textbook-related corpus and text tagging can improve their motivation in textual analysis and close reading in a formative process, because doing corpus-based textual analysis can motivate students to not only skim and scan reading materials but also closely read and analyse them.

8.4.2   Participants

The study involved two classes, altogether 72 Chinese EFL students (58 females and 14 males, 37 in the experimental class and 35 in the control class) enrolled in an Advanced English Reading course that lasted a whole semester at a major university in Shanghai, China. The main objective of the course was to develop students' English reading skills. The learners were between 19 and 22 years old. All of them were English majors and most of them had studied English in China for 8 to 11 years. The experimental class was randomly chosen; their average score in the final examination of the previous semester (75.6 on percentile grading) was below the average level of the whole grade of English majors (75.7). The average score in the control class was above the average level of the grade (76.3). The teacher who taught the experimental class was a teacher with seven years of experience in teaching Advanced English and she also had practical knowledge concerning the application of corpus in pedagogical settings, while the teacher who taught the control class had approximately the same amount of teaching experience but no knowledge about corpora. Throughout the whole semester, the experimental class teacher used a new teaching method, sparing no effort to link corpora and the classroom teaching of reading, while the control class teacher just followed the traditional way of teaching.

8.4.3   Syllabus design for the experimental class

Inadequacy of the background knowledge and textual analysis skills hamper English majors' reading comprehension; therefore, this study has emphasized the scientific design of a corpus-assisted teaching syllabus which could facilitate the construction of students' content schemata and meanwhile give them an opportunity to practise their textual analysis skills.

Therefore, first, the teaching sequence was changed. The original teaching sequence starting from the first unit to the last unit of the textbook (*An Integrative English Course for English Majors*, Book 6) was replaced by a new teaching sequence that followed theme-based modules. After classifying themes covered in the textbook, we designed four theme-based modules, i.e. modules on technology, education, American values and life philosophy respectively. Through this teaching sequence, all the texts chosen for classroom teaching, including texts taken from the textbook and materials taken from the textbook-related reading corpus constructed by the students, had to be relevant to the theme of those modules, and in this way, the students' content schema for each theme was enhanced step by step.

Second, students in the experimental class were required to compile an open-ended textbook-related reading corpus. During the corpus-construction process, they collected and tagged texts which had to match certain criteria the teacher had defined:

Criterion I. The word limit of each corpus text is 800–1,000 words;
Criterion II. There must be high correlation between the chosen texts and the corresponding module themes;
Criterion III. The chosen texts should fall in the same genre as that of the corresponding units in the textbook.

Students first logged on to the COCA corpus website, searched for concordance lines with the key theme words, traced back to the source stretches of texts containing those concordance lines and finally tried to locate the full source texts online. Eventually, we found that the source texts were mainly online newspaper and magazine articles taken from *Time, Newsweek* or the *New York Times*. All the source files were then converted to text format. Students in the experimental class were divided into six groups to handle these tasks, such as finding altogether 30 passages corresponding to each module of the textbook. This means that, for each module, each student in the experimental class was required to find just one to two related passages, which later proved to be a suitable work load. The initial size of the reading corpus contained around 120,000 words of 120-odd texts. Since the corpus was open-ended, more materials would be selected and added to the corpus in the following days. The topics of the corpus covered themes related to the original four teaching modules. Inevitably, students practiced their skimming and scanning reading skills in the process of locating 'proper' texts for compiling the relevant reading corpus.

Third, the teacher gave demonstrations of textual analysis assisted by corpus tools and corpus analysis methods and students followed teachers by doing text tagging and making presentations to demonstrate their textual analysis. In terms of tagging, after students located a suitable text for analysis, they had to insert embedded tags to indicate the genre, topic sentences, organizational patterns, cohesive devices, etc. For example, the embedded tag [psg_exp_time] means the text falls into the genre of exposition and the organizational pattern follows time order; [prg_tpc_1] signals the position of the topic sentence – the first sentence of the paragraph; [prg_lnk_comp] indicates the cohesive device used in the paragraph is comparison and contrast. Thereafter, all the tagged texts were processed by AntConc 3.2 with the aim of retrieving concordance lines containing embedded tags. For example, tags of topic sentences within one text could be retrieved to assist students' understanding of how topic sentences support the theme of the text; tags of linking devices across a series of texts within one genre could be retrieved to help students notice the main organizational patterns of a particular genre. To conclude each module, every group in the experimental class would give a presentation of their textual analysis based on the tagged texts and corpus tools, reporting the main idea of the text, analysing the line of thought, giving the genre and organizational pattern of the text, identifying the logical relationship between topic sentences and supporting details and demonstrating how effectively the detailed evidence supports the topic sentence.

By contrast, the teaching method employed in the control class remained traditional. That is to say, the teacher focused only on detailed explanation of new words, analysis of grammar, and paraphrase of complicated sentences. Therefore, the final differences that lie between the two classes' academic performances can mainly be attributed to the new teaching method.

8.4.4 Data collection procedure

For the experimental class, the students had to fulfil the checklist of reading tasks which included: (A) the teamwork of each group for text selection, tagging and presentation; (B) the delivery of a presentation based on tagged texts and corpus tools within each module; (C) a quiz after each module. In order to verify the aforementioned two research hypotheses, two types of data were collected: the pre-test and post-test quantitative data for the experimental class and control class, and the qualitative data from the learning feedback, questionnaires, and focus group interview of the experimental class.

In order to validate the effectiveness of the new teaching method, the analytical reading skills strengthened through doing the key corpus-based tasks needed to comply with the reading ability construct covered by both pre-test and post-test. Here, the tagging scheme, presentation criteria, and analytical reading skill index are presented as follows:

(A)   Tagging scheme
      The purpose of tagging is to help students build up a schema that helps them read the text closely and comprehend and analyse the text more effectively. The tagging scheme dimensions cover levels of passage, paragraph, and sentence:

      (a)   The first dimension – genre, theme, macrostructure, rhetorical devices, author attitude, and tone (at the passage level).

(b) The second dimension – cohesion and coherence, including tagging topic sentences, location of developmental paragraphs, linking devices (at the paragraph level).

(c) The third dimension – complex and compound sentence types (at the sentence level).

(B) Presentation criteria

(a) Summarize the main idea of the text and analyse macro-structure, genre, author's attitude, and the effectiveness of thesis statement (at the passage level).

(b) Analyse the line of thought, identify logical relationships between topic sentences and supporting details, and analyse how effectively the detailed evidence supports the topic sentence (at the paragraph level).

(c) Analyse impressive sentences and idiomatic use of lexical items (at the sentence level).

(C) A checklist of analytical reading abilities in the assessment

(a) The ability to summarize the thesis statement, identify the genre and macrostructure of the passage, and identify or infer the author's purpose of writing, attitude, tone, etc. (at the passage level).

(b) The ability to identify topic sentences, distinguish arguments from facts, analyse paragraph structure and writing order, and explore logical relationships between sentences (at the paragraph level).

(c) The ability to infer profound meaning of complicated sentences (at the sentence level).

Here, students' doing textual tagging and the follow-up presentation serves as an analytical process where their analytical skills and reading abilities are strengthened and the reading assessment functions as a tool to measure the effectiveness of the students' efforts involved in the process. Therefore, the tagging scheme and presentation criteria follow almost the same pattern as reflected by the construct of the reading assessment.

8.4.5 Data analysis procedure

The self-reported data contain students' regular feedback, the structured open-ended questionnaire and the focus group interview. During the whole semester, students were required to give their learning feedback at least once a month. But there was no rigid format for the learning feed-back. Students were encouraged to give the feedback freely concerning the new teaching method, the effect of teaching reform and their own experience with corpora. At the end of the semester, all of the students in the experimental class were required to fill in a questionnaire with 10 short-answer questions which matched the two above-mentioned research questions. Finally, a focus group interview was organized to probe into students' real reflections on the teaching reform. Altogether 12 students who presented representative responses in the previous questionnaire survey were chosen to participate in the focus group interview. The focus group interview also pertained to the framework covering students' reflections on any development in their reading motivation and the effect of the corpus treatment on their reading skills, as well as their personal evaluation of the teaching reform.

To address the first research question, the same construct of analytical reading abilities and the same scoring system were adopted in the assessment of students' reading competence before and after the corpus treatment. The reading materials used in both the pre-test and post-test were taken from the reading section of TEM 8 (Test for English Majors, Band 8). The reading section of TEM 8 is regarded as the most represent-ative for assessing EFL learners' analytical reading abilities and the test has already been generally acknowledged as a valid and reliable national test which presents a consistent difficulty level. In this study, both the pre-test and the post-test tested students' analytical reading ability and both of them shared the same test format, containing four passages with five multiple choice questions for each passage. Altogether, both the pre-test and the post-test contained 20 questions, which equalled 20 points, one point for each question. The time limit for both tests was 40 minutes. In selection of test materials, passage size, passage genre, and subject matter were all considered so that the pre-test and post-test shared approximately the same test construct. In addition, there were three types of questions used in both the pre-test and the post-test: (1) general questions that tested students' identification of thesis state-ments, summary of texts, analysis of the author's purpose of writing and attitude, identification of the genre, and macrostructure of the passage; (2) detailed questions that tested students' ability to identify topic sentences and explore logical relationships between sentences and paragraphs; (3) inference questions that tested students' ability to infer profound meaning of complicated sentences. In order to avoid subjec-tive bias in scoring the test papers, we only used the multiple-choice question type in both reading tests.

The study required two separate mean comparison tests, namely, the Independent Samples T Test and Paired Samples T Test from the Statistical Package for Social Sciences (SPSS 13.0). Mean comparison tests were an appropriate statistical test for the study because: (a) they allowed testing for mean difference between two independent groups, i.e. between the experimental group and the control group and (b) they allowed testing for mean difference within the same group across a longitudinal time period, i.e. within the experimental group and the control group respectively.

8.5 Results

In this section of our chapter, the collected data pertaining to the above-listed research questions will be presented. Qualitative data and inferential statistics for the corresponding hypotheses are given below.

Hypothesis 1: Students' active participation in corpus construction and text tagging and their access to corpora and corpus tools in the process of autonomous reading are central to the improvement of their textual analysis skills and hence their reading comprehension ability.

The descriptive statistics for the pre-test and post-test appear in Table 8.1, the Independent Samples T Test results for the pre-test and post-test appear in Table 8.2, the results of Paired Samples Correlations for

Table 8.1 Descriptive statistics for pre-test and post-test

	Experimental Group (N = 37)		Control Group (N = 35)	
	Mean	Standard Deviation (SD)	Mean	SD
Pre-test	9.68	2.517	10.03	2.673
Post-test	11.38	2.639	10.06	2.086

Table 8.2 Independent Samples T Test for pre-test and post-test

	Levene's Test for Equality of Variances		T-test for Equality of Means				
	F	Sig.	t	df	Sig. (2-tailed)	Mean Std Error	Difference Difference
Pre-test	.001	.973	−.577	70	.566	−.353	.612
Post-test	.721	.399	2.348	70	.022	1.321	.550

Table 8.3   Paired samples correlations for experimental group and control group

	Number	Correlation	Sig.
Experimental Group	37	.345	.036
Control Group	35	.506	.002

Table 8.4   Paired samples T Test for experimental group and control group

	Paired Differences			t	df	Sig. (2-tailed)
	Mean	Std. Deviation	Std. Error Mean			
Experimental Group (N=37)	−1.703	2.817	.463	−3.676	36	.001
Control Group (N=35)	−.029	2.419	.409	−.070	34	.945

both the experimental group and the control group appear in Table 8.3 and the results of Paired Samples T Test for the experimental group and the control group appear in Table 8.4.

First, we see the descriptive statistics for the two groups of both tests. Judging from the mean scores, it is easy to find that the mean difference for the experimental group is higher than that of the control group (1.7 vs. 0.03). This means that the students in the experimental group have, on average, a higher reading score than those of the control group.

In terms of Independent Samples T Test of the pre-test outcome, we shall look at Levene's Test for Equality of Variances first. Table 8.2 shows that Levene's Test is not significant because the p-value is much greater than .05 (p = .973) for the pre-test and this tells us we have met our second assumption: the variances of the two groups are approximately equal. In other words, the two groups have approximately equal variance on the dependent variable. So the top line of t value was put into the table. The t-value of the pre-test is −.577 with the significance level more than .05 (p = .566), which means there is no significant difference between the reading scores of the experimental group and the control group. In contrast, when we follow the same steps to analyse the statistics of the post-test outcome, we find that the t-value of the post-test is 2.348 with the significance level less than .05 (p = .022), which means there is a significant difference between the reading scores of the experimental group and the control group in their post-test. Therefore, we can conclude that the students in the experimental group have performed significantly better in the post-test than those in the control group who have done the same test.

Table 8.3 shows the correlation between the pre-test and post-test for the experimental group and the control group. Because this is a repeated measure analysis, the same participants of each group are measured twice. Theoretically, a high degree of correlation between the pre-test and post-test scores is expected, even if everyone improves by a different amount. Here the correlations between the two sets of scores for both the experimental group and the control group are around the midlevel at the significance level below 0.05. Though the correlation coefficient is not that high, at least the two sets of scores are related and the following Paired Samples T Test is appropriately chosen. The reason for the fact that the correlation between the pre-test and post-test for the experimental group is lower than that of the control group might be that the experimental group experienced a new kind of teaching method for a whole semester. This could result in the instability of some individuals' performance while the control group students present a more stable performance since there was no change in the teaching methods in their classroom.

Table 8.4 shows the statistics of the Paired Samples T Test for the experimental group and the control group. The mean difference between the pre-test and post-test of the experimental group is 1.7 and $|t|$ in the Paired Samples T Test equals 3.676 at the significance level 0.01 ($p < 0.05$), which means the mean difference between the pre-test and post-test of the experimental group is statistically significant. On the other hand, the mean difference between the pre-test and post-test of the control group is 0.03 and $|t|$ in the Paired T Test equals 0.07 at the significance level 0.945 ($p > 0.05$), which means the mean difference between the pre-test and post-test of the control group is not statistically significant. Therefore, we can draw the conclusion that there is strong evidence showing that the new corpus treatment enhances the analytical reading ability of the students in the experimental group and hence their performance in the post-test is significantly better than that of the control group.

Meanwhile, the questionnaire data showed that 85% of the students in the experimental class thought their skimming and scanning skills had improved; 62% felt they had speeded up their reading and could make sense of the main idea more quickly; 85% believed they had strengthened their skill in identifying topic sentences and 65% believed they had improved their ability to identify key words and sentences; 47% reported they had learned to identify the author's purpose of writing, attitude, tone, etc.; 59% thought they had improved their skill in exploring logical relationships between sentences and paragraphs; 50% reported they could identify the genre of the text and 29% believed that corpus helped them master the macro-structure of the passage.

The key words and key content of the qualitative data from the students' feedback and focus group interview are listed in Table 8.5.

Hypothesis 2: Students' active participation in the construction of the textbook-related corpus and text tagging can improve their motivation in textual analysis and close reading in a formative process, because doing corpus-based textual analysis can motivate students to not only skim and scan reading materials but also closely read and analyse them.

Data from the questionnaires showed that 27 students (74%) believed that corpora could improve their autonomous reading ability and they felt gradually motivated to do text tagging and textual analysis presentations based on corpus analysis methods and corpus tools, because 88% of them felt that 'corpus strengthened understanding of word use in the context' and 94% were sure that a 'keywords list enhanced their impression of a passage'. Meanwhile, according to their report, the

Table 8.5 Students' feedback related to Hypothesis 1

Key words	Feedback
Line of thought	*Through tagging every passage, I got a clearer outlook of it and it helped me analyse the author's line of thought. Before, we were told that the text was well written, but now, we came to know why it was well written and how and what we could learn from the organizational pattern …*
Identify topic sentences	*While tagging an article, we should understand the main idea first and must find out the topic sentence that gives the main idea …*
Identify key words and sentences	*To identify key words and sentences is equal to do intensive reading. I must remind myself of rationalizing my analysis of the text with substantial evidence …*
Explore logical relationships	*It helps me improve close reading, which means I must read carefully to understand each paragraph and analyse sentences so that I can get the main idea and coherence of the passage. Through tagging and doing presentation, my analytical skills are improved and I am aware of using evidence to support my idea and get to know the persuasiveness of an argumentation and learn from good articles …*

Table 8.6 Students' feedback related to Hypothesis 2

Key words	Feedback
Word use in the context	*Corpus helps me identify synonyms. For example, with COCA, I can easily identify the connotation of a word and its frequent collocation … it facilitates my autonomous reading …*
Keyword list	*Key words and text structure offer the line of thought of a text. While reading a passage myself, keyword list display can help me get the main idea faster, and help me understand the structure of the text, the author's attitude, primary purpose better …*
Motivation for autonomous reading	*At least doing the reading tasks helps me improve my awareness of autonomous extracurricular reading… the tasks of tagging and doing presentation improved my autonomous reading. I was pretty much at a loss when first required to analyse a text, but after repetitive practice, I came to realize some rules on how to identify topic sentences and logical relationships, so reading efficiency was also improved step by step …*
Presentation	*We are motivated to do presentation every time. Group members were assigned clear tasks: who selected materials, who did the text tagging and who made the PPT. We shifted our tasks every time to ensure everybody's participation. Doing presentation strengthened our analytical skills and we also practiced our skills of using corpus tools, such as COCA corpus, WORDNET, AntConc, etc.*

students in the experimental class spent 4.25 hours per week on corpus-related reading tasks on average.

The qualitative data from the students' feedback and the focus group interview are listed in Table 8.6.

8.6 Discussion

Up to now, three principal domains for the application of corpus linguistics to language teaching research have emerged: (1) Language description, (2) Language analysis in the classroom and (3) Learner corpora (Keck, 2004: 84). This research attempts to integrate corpus linguistics and teaching material development and also applies the newly designed corpus-based teaching materials to classroom teaching, that is to say, it touches upon the first two major domains. The results of this study indicate that students' contribution to the construction of a textbook-related corpus and the application of corpus analysis methods to the teaching of advanced English reading can improve students' textual analysis skills and reading comprehension ability.

First, the investigations of language use and construction of a textbook-related reading corpus served as an extension of language teaching textbooks. In terms of application of corpus linguistics to the classroom setting, not only was the teacher required to fully employ corpus tools and have insight into corpus-based language analysis, but also the learners were encouraged to take charge of their own learning, and thus 'motivation was increased' (Aston, 2001).

Second, this study went beyond the traditional DDL (data-driven learning) introduced by Tim Johns (1991). Traditional DDL enjoined teachers to select and edit concordance lines for students who were engaged in the concordance line analysis and thus would pay due attention to natural patterns of language use. The study encouraged students to explore ways in which they might select and tag materials to construct the textbook-related reading corpus and generate their own concordance data in their presentation on the tagged texts. Therefore, learners were engaged in autonomous discovery learning. Seidlhofer (2000: 207) also discussed 'using learner corpora for learning', and the finding was that the 'localized' corpora could motivate the students in the learning process. In this study, according to the learners' self-reported data, the majority of them believed they gradually formed an effective discovery learning habit and also witnessed a development in their autonomous learning. The focus group interview data further validated this by providing reasons. First, during the process of corpus construction and analysis, students cultivated the habit of reflecting upon the new learning style, and they started to compare the traditional way of learning and the new corpus-assisted way of learning. Though many of them first reported an awkward experience with corpora, ultimately, they still held firm beliefs that this data-driven learning style would benefit their language learning in the long run. Second, the students gradually identified with the education reform. Motivated by the awareness of the importance of improving their reading skills required by TEM 8, the students played an active part in the corpus construction and analysis.

Third, quantitative results proved that the students' analytical reading ability was significantly improved, because the checklist of reading abilities exactly echoed the pre-designed reading skills which should be strengthened in the process of students' participation in corpus construction and analysis. It is also worth noticing that many students reported that in traditional ways of teaching, they only received information passively and had a vague idea of a passage, while having experienced the new teaching method, they automatically tried to probe into the structure of the passage and the hidden ideas. In the process of selecting and tagging materials, they read the text thoroughly, explored the thesis statement and analysed the text by reading between the lines. Some students also reported that they were more aware of the genre or register-specific features of passages and they believed the new method helped them to think in English.

Finally, the teacher in the experimental class made great efforts to maintain and improve students' motivation in the project. Students with higher autonomous reading ability were given the opportunity to go further while quite a few students mentioned their reluctance to change the original passive learning habit. Though the inactive students' motivation was maintained by the teacher's implementing formative evaluation systems, such as quizzes, those students failed to witness improvement in the post-test. It is worth mentioning that students' low motivation is often associated with words like 'corpus' or 'technology' in their feedback. Unfamiliarity with corpus tools might help explain their low motivation in doing corpus-mediated reading, yet we cannot assume they are not motivated to do paper-mediated reading. Corpus-mediated reading might help improve students' motivation in reading paper-mediated materials after their content schemata are enriched. In this regard, further empirical studies are needed to address the issue.

8.7 Limitation of the Study

The present study is a case study and the number of participants is rather limited. Therefore, care must be taken in generalizing these findings to a larger or different population. Both the sample size and the context of the study may limit the generalizability of the findings. To the extent that a limited number of participants were employed in this study and factors influencing language learning were hard to control, the findings here are necessarily limited in generalizability.

8.8 Conclusion

In conclusion, this study has demonstrated that students' active participation in the construction and analysis of the textbook-related corpus and their contribution to the teaching of reading are central to the improvement of their textual analysis skills and reading competence.

On the one hand, there exists great potential for the application of corpus linguistics in the area of language teaching and, on the other hand, the teaching of English reading is still in need of further reform and development. Therefore, teachers teaching reading are anxious to know how to effectively apply corpus tools and corpus analysis methods to their daily teaching practice, and its possible effect on learners' performance. Teachers' urgent needs call for more empirical studies to address this issue. It is hoped that insights from this study will pave the way for more future studies that can promote the campaign to narrow the gap between corpus linguistics and the teaching of reading.

References

Alderson, J. C. (2000). *Reading assessment.* New York: Cambridge University Press.

Aston, G. (1995). Corpora in language pedagogy: Matching theory and practice. In G. Cook & B. Seidlhofer (eds), *Principles and practice in applied linguistics* (pp. 257–270). Oxford: Oxford University Press.

Aston, G. (1997). Enriching the learning environment: Corpora in EFL. In A. Wichmann, S. Fligelstone, T. McEnery, & G. Knowles (eds), *Teaching and language corpora* (pp. 51–64). London, UK: Longman.

Aston, G. (2000). Corpora and language teaching. In L. Burnard & T. McEnery (eds), *Rethinking language pedagogy from a corpus perspective* (pp. 7–18). New York: Peter Lang.

Aston, G. (2001). Learning with corpora: an overview. In G. Aston (ed.), *Learning with corpora* (pp. 7–45). Houston, TX: Athelstan.

Aston, G. (2002). The learner as corpus designer. In B. Kettemann & G. Marko (eds), *Language and computers: Studies in practical linguistics* (pp. 9–25). Amsterdam: Rodopi.

Barlow, M. (2011). Corpus linguistics and theoretical linguistics. *International Journal of Corpus Linguistics, 16*(1), 3–44.

Bernardini, S. (2000). Exploring new directions for discovery learning. In B. Kettemann & G. Marko (eds), *Teaching and learning by doing corpus analysis: Proceedings of the Fourth International Conference on Teaching and Language Corpora* (pp. 165–182). New York: Rodopi.

Biber, D., Connor, U. & Upton, T. (2007). *Discourse on the move: Using corpus analysis to describe discourse structure.* Amsterdam: John Benjamins.

Carrell, P. L. & Eisterhold, J. C. (1983). Schema theory and ESL reading pedagogy. *TESOL Quarterly, 4,* 553–569.

Carrell, P. L. (1988). Interactive text processing: Implications for ESL/second language reading classrooms. In P. L. Carrell, J. Devine & D. E. Eskey (eds), *Interactive approaches to second language reading* (pp. 239–259). Cambridge: CUP.

Connor, U., Precht, K., & Upton, T. (2002). In S. Granger, J. Hung, & S. Petch-Tyson (eds), *Computer learner corpora, second language acquisition and foreign language teaching* (pp. 175–194). Amsterdam: John Benjamins.

Conrad, S. (2004). Corpus linguistics, language variation, and language teaching. In J. M. Sinclair (ed.), *How to use corpora in language teaching* (pp. 67–85). Amsterdam: John Benjamins.

Duan, Z. C. (2010). On the relation between content schema and the cognitive strategies in advanced reading. *Foreign Language and Literature, 26*(5), 126–129.

Flowerdew, L. (1998). Corpus linguistic techniques applied to textlinguistics. *System, 26*(4), 541–552.

Flowerdew, J., & Dudley-Evans, T. (2002). Genre analysis of editorial letters to international journal contributors. *Applied Linguistics, 23*(4), 463–489.

Flowerdew, L. (2005). An integration of corpus-based and genre-based approaches to text analysis in EAP/ESP: countering criticisms against corpus-based methodology. *English for Specific Purposes, 24*, 321–332.

Gui, S. C. (2000). *A new psycholinguistics course.* Shanghai: Shanghai Foreign Languages Education Press.

Huang, Y. S. (2011). The role of college English reading. *Foreign Language World, 143*(2), 5–10.

Hunston, S. (2002). *Corpora in applied linguistics.* Cambridge: Cambridge University Press.

Johns, T. (1991). Should you be persuaded: two examples of data-driven learning. In T. Johns & P. King (eds), *Classroom concordancing. E L R Journal Vol. 4* (pp. 1–16). Birmingham: Birmingham University Press.

Keck, C. M. (2004). Book review: Corpus linguistics and language teaching research: bridging the gap. *Language Teaching Research, 8*(1), 83–109.

Kirk, J. (2000). Teaching critical skills in corpus linguistics using the BNC. In B. Kettemann & G. Marko (eds), *Teaching and learning by doing corpus analysis: Proceedings of the Fourth International Conference on Teaching and Language Corpora* (pp. 155–164.). New York: Rodopi.

Lee, D. &. Swales, J. M. (2006). A corpus-based EAP course for NNS doctoral students: Moving from available specialized corpora to self compiled corpora. *English for Specific Purposes, 25*(1), 56–75.

Lee, D. (2008). Corpora and discourse analysis: New ways of doing old things. In V. K. Bhatia, L. Flowerdew, & R. H. Jones (eds), *Advances in discourse studies* (pp. 86–99). London: Routledge.

McCarthy, M. & Carter, R. (1994). *Language as discourse: Perspectives for language teaching.* Harlow: Longman.

Noguchi, J. (2004). A genre analysis and mini-corpora approach to support professional writing by non-native speakers. *English Corpus Studies, 11*, 101–110.

Römer, U. (2011). Corpus research application in second language teaching. *Annual Review of Applied Linguistics, 31*, 205–225.

Seidlhofer, B. (2000). Operationalising intertextuality: using learner corpora for learning. In L. Burnard & T. McEnery (eds), *Rethinking language pedagogy from a corpus perspective* (pp. 207–224). Frankfurt am Main: Peter Lang.

Sinclair, J. (2004). *Trust the Text: language, corpus and discourse.* London: Routledge.

Upton, T. & Connor, U. (2001). Using computerised corpus analysis to investigate the textlinguistic discourse moves of a genre. *English for Specific Purposes, 20*(4), 313–329.

Upton, T. & Cohen, M. (2009). An approach to corpus-based discourse analysis: The move analysis as example. *Discourse Studies, 11*(5), 585–605.

van Dijk, T. (2008). *Discourse and context: A socio-cognitive approach.* Cambridge: Cambridge University Press.

9

An Appraisal Analysis of Reports about Chinese Military Affairs in the *New York Times*

Zhaoyang Mei, Ren Zhang, and Baixiang Yu

9.1 Introduction

News journalism ranges across the greatest diversity of discourses, including not only those of politics, the law, and the emergency services, but those of economics, bureaucracy, medicine, religion, the social and physical sciences, the humanities, and education (White, 1998: 266). News reporting is seen by some as a vital mechanism for the dissemination of information by which an informed and meaningful public discourse may be established and maintained.

Husson and Robert, commenting favourably on the manner of English language news reporting, asserts that the professional news reporter is 'precise and neutral', eliminates all subjectivity and constructs texts where 'the only things on show are the raw facts' (Husson & Robert, 1991: 63). The notion that the news item should be 'neutral' and 'factual', at least in principle, is sometimes encountered even in the media studies literature. However, in contrast to the view that news should be 'neutral', some media theorists regard the news as a mechanism of social control – a discourse which naturalizes the regimes of 'common sense' which sustain social inequalities and supports the interests of various economic and political elites. Some early influential analyses coming from the Chicago School of urban sociologists, especially the work of Hughes (1940, 1942), consider that 'news is seen as exemplifying and animating social and ideological values'.

Evaluation has attracted considerable attention from linguists in recent years. One reason for this is that evaluation is an important aspect and function of human language. Due to various factors, such as the environment, interpersonal relationships, and politics, our interpretation of the world cannot be completely objective. Our subjectivity will be more or less revealed by the language we use. According to Thompson and Hunston (2000: 25):

> evaluation is the broad cover term for the expression of the speaker or writer's attitude or stance towards, viewpoint on, or feelings about the entities or propositions that he or she is talking about. That attitude may relate to certainty or obligation or desirability or any of a number of other sets of values.

The reason for this is that evaluation can simultaneously be used to express the writer's opinion and in doing so to reflect the value system of that person and his/her community, to construct and maintain relations between the speaker/writer and hearer/reader, and to organize the discourse.

The main objective of our study is to analyse how the reports about Chinese military affairs express their stance and attitude towards Chinese military affairs and influence the image of Chinese military forces in US hearts. And we will focus on interpreting how the evaluative resources in the reports interact with each other to realize the textual communicative goals. The purpose is to understand how the various categories of evaluative meanings are proportioned and organized to achieve the communicative goals of this specific genre.

9.2 Theoretical backgrounds

In this section, linguistic studies of news media language will be briefly introduced.

9.2.1 Linguistic studies of journalistic discourse

9.2.1.1 *Journalistic discourse and stylistics*

Crystal and Davy (1969) set out to determine whether there is any linguistic basis to the folk belief in 'journalese' as a distinct style of English. Confining themselves to the language of news reporting (as opposed to features, editorials, reviews, etc.), they conclude that 'the concept of the "language of newspaper reporting" is not as meaningful as is generally assumed' and that '[t]here is not one, but a number of "journaleses"' (Crystal & Davy, 1969: 172). They note various common lexico-grammatical features:

- The texts make less frequent use of commas than would 'normally be expected' (1969: 172). (The authors don't specify the nature of this 'norm'.) This, Crystal and Davy suggest, is meant to avoid disturbing the tempo of reading more than is necessary.

- Frequent use is made of quotation marks, both to indicate attributed material and also to draw attention to individual items. The authors suggest this supplies the articles with verisimilitude and immediacy.
- The authors note a certain preference for alliteration (*depressing downpour, humble human*), which they suggest gives a sense of spoken language.
- Normal subject position may be reversed in the context of quotations (*..., said Dr Mason*).
- Adverbs are frequently located in a marked position at the front of the sentence. The authors suggest that this is motivated by a concern with varying emphasis within a given sentence. They contend this enables the interest and impetus of the text to be maintained.
- The texts feature much more complex pre- and post-modification in the nominal group than 'we normally hear or write' (Crystal and Davy, 1969: 186). The authors suggest this is done to add detail and colour.

9.2.1.2 *Journalistic discourse and Critical Discourse Analysis*

Critical Discourse Analysis (henceforth, CDA) is analysis of the dialectical relationships between discourse (including language, but also other forms of semiosis, e.g. body language or visual images) and other elements of social practices. Its particular concern is with the radical changes that are taking place in contemporary social life, with how discourse figures within processes of change, and with shifts in the relationship between semiosis and other social elements within networks of practice. Ideology is viewed critically in CDA. Ideological representations in texts must be studied in relation to social power.

Fairclough's (CDA) approach assumes that there is a dialectical relationship between language and other elements of social life. Although this approach draws on several older approaches, the new point is that it is based on various new theories about society and the relation between language, discourse, and society.

Recent work in CDA has focused upon the theoretical and methodological enhancement of the analysis of discourse within transdisciplinary research on social transformations variously referred to as 'globalization', 'new capitalism', 'knowledge-based economy and learning society', among others (Fairclough, 1999). The objective of recent CDA is mainly discourses of mass communication, such as discourses in television, advertisements, newspapers, official documents, and some other media, because CDA believes that language is a social reality and an eternal interposition of the order in society, which reflects the reality of various perspectives, and influences the social process through ideology – not a transparent or objective neutral transmission media, as researchers thought before. Outside China, the research on CDA has been developing rapidly, in both theory and application. Most studies in China have been carried out by Xin Bin (2004), Wang Yang (2003), and Ku Mei (2004); Wang Yang (2003) probes the transitivity means in Systemic Functional Grammar in critical discourse analysis and has demonstrated that the quantitative study of transitivity can be applied to selected news samples to supplement CDA, exposing ideology behind the news. Ku Mei (2004) employs Fairclough's theoretical framework to analyse political news and demonstrates that language and ideology are in a dialectical relationship.

9.2.2 Appraisal Theory

Appraisal Theory has been chosen here as the appropriate theoretical framework for the study of the evaluative features of news reports. It has been employed to analyse many spoken and written genres and has proved to be quite effective in identifying the evaluative features of texts. Most importantly, Appraisal Theory has a profound theoretical background since it is developed under the framework of Systemic Functional Linguistics.

According to Martin and Rose (2003: 22), 'appraisal is concerned with evaluation: the kinds of attitudes that are negotiated in a text, the strength of the feelings involved and the ways in which values are sourced and readers aligned'. In terms of meaning, Appraisal Theory divides the evaluative resources in the text into three systems: attitude, engagement, and graduation. They are respectively concerned with what have traditionally been dealt with under the headings of affect; epistemic modality and evidentiality; intensification and vague language (Martin & White, 2005: 2). It can be seen from Figure 9.1 that Appraisal Theory aims to group all aspects of evaluation under a unified framework and offer a new perspective on these phenomena.

Though Martin's Appraisal Theory provides an effective framework to analyse the evaluative features of various genres, it is far from perfect. First of all, language is the evaluative resource, and the manifestation of language is various. Studies on evaluative resources in the texts are confined to intra-text appraisal, which is the main method for the

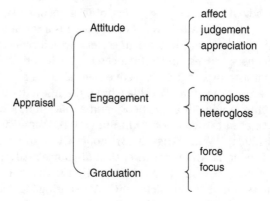

Figure 9.1   Basic framework of Appraisal Theory
Source: Adapted from Martin and White (2005).

writer/speaker to convey his/her attitudes, stances, and points of view. However, from the readers' perspectives, they are usually evaluating the text with the help of intra-text appraisal resources, which we term extra-text appraisal. Martin's Appraisal Theory is intra-text appraisal and does not give much attention to the social context. Secondly, evaluation without standards does not exist. The evaluative criterion is objective, containing parameters of historical and cultural orientation, personal experiences, and communicative aims, etc. The parameter system of evaluative criterion is infinite. Even if it is the same evaluative participant, they can frequently change their evaluative angles towards the same evaluative objective and therefore get different evaluative results. As the carrier of culture, language not only reveals the content of culture, but also influences the evaluative process. Finally, appraisal and discourse, evaluative participants' points of view, ideologies, and values are closely tied. Therefore appraisal cannot always be objective. The confirmation of evaluative criteria is also always influenced by discourse, points of view, ideologies, and values.

9.3   Methodology and data

Empirical investigations of general patterns in corpus are employed in the study. In addition to a close examination of appraisal resources in the texts of news reports, statistics related to the patterning of appraisal resources were calculated. The procedure is as follows: firstly, a certain number of news reports concerning Chinese military affairs were downloaded from the website of the *New York Times*; secondly, appraisal resources in the news were annotated, and a small-scale corpus was established; thirdly, a set of data concerning the patterning of appraisal resources was obtained and interpreted; finally, various types of appraisal resources were probed in context and their respective characteristics were identified. We will explain these steps in detail in the following sections.

9.3.1 The corpus

Since the *New York Times* is one of the most influential broadsheets in the US, its points of view and stances towards Chinese military forces will arouse much interest among scholars. Thus, we choose the *New York Times* as the target of our research. In this study, 20 news reports (11,068 words) were randomly selected from issues of the *New York Times* which were published between the years 2008 and 2010. In terms of theme, the news reports can be divided into three categories – Naval Missions in the Gulf of Aden (2,010 words), the US-China Military Relationship (4,541 words), and China's Military Development (4,517 words). Resources of appraisal in them are annotated according to the subtypes of appraisal resources they belong to. The corpus is employed to study the frequencies and proportions of various subtypes of appraisal.

9.3.2 Methods of annotation

The work of annotation is carried out by using the labels given in Table 9.1 ('+' and '–' represent respectively the positive and negative attitudinal resources).

In order to make readers get a clearer view of this annotation, instances are shown as follows:

1. ... he hoped [att:aff:+des] a visit to the region by Secretary of State Hillary Rodham Clinton would lead to a resumption of high-level [att:app:+val] military exchanges with China.
2. In October, the Pentagon announced the sale of $6 billion of advanced [att:app:+val] weapons to Taiwan, a move that prompted criticism [att:aff:–sat] from China.
3. But [eng:dis:coun] fighting submarines has been less of [gra:for:int] a military priority since then ...

Table 9.1   Labels used for annotation

Subsystem	Subcategory	Subtype
att:attitude	aff:affect	des:desire hap:happiness sec:security sat:satisfaction
	judg:judgement	norm:normality cap:capacity ten:tenacity ver:veracity prop:propriety
	app:appreaction	reac:reaction comp:composition val:valuation
eng:engagement	dis:disclaim	den:deny coun:counter
	pro:proclaim	con:concur pron:pronounce end:endorse
	ent:entertain	
	attr:attribute	ack:acknowledge dist:distance
gra:graduation	for:force	int:intensification qua:quantification
	foc:focus	sharp:sharpen soft:soften

Source: Zhang (2009: 13–14).

9.3.3   Methods of analysis

The quantitative analysis is mainly based on the data obtained by using the software WordSmith 4.0. By using the Concordancer (searching annotations) to list all occurrences of certain words or phrases, frequencies of certain types of appraisal resources can be obtained. Inscribed and evoked appraisal will also be analysed in the chapter.

It should be emphasized that our ultimate purpose is not to conduct a quantitative analysis of the data, but to account for the patterns found by means of a qualitative analysis. Statistics concerning the configuration of various appraisal subcategories have npnetheless been noted.

9.4 Analysis of appraisal resources in the reports

Up till now, various attempts have been made to study the evaluation of different genres. However, studies on news reports about Chinese military affairs are still at an early stage. Given the growing importance of the military relationship between China and the US, and the fact that the *New York Times* is one of the most influential newspapers in the US, its points of view and stances towards Chinese military affairs will arouse much interest among scholars. In this section, Appraisal Theory will be employed to analyse the reports specifically concerning China's military affairs in the *New York Times*, find out the characteristics of the appraisal resources, and then try to interpret how the Chinese military are presented in those news reports. Most importantly, the image of Chinese military is not depicted neutrally; we are supposed to build an objective image of the Chinese army in the media, as China is becoming increasingly influential in international affairs.

This part consists of three sections, which respectively characterize the three subcategories of appraisal (i.e. attitude, engagement, and graduation) in reports, by analysing 20 samples randomly selected from the *New York Times*. As noted above, the samples are divided into three categories – China's military development, the US-China military relationship, and the naval mission in the Gulf of Aden.

9.4.1 An introduction to the samples

All the samples are taken from the online version of the *New York Times*. Its reports cover many fields with a variety of content types. Thus, it has been named the 'Top Broadsheet in the United States' for its broad influence. Objectivity and fairness are the unchangeable pursuit of the *New York Times*. 'All the news that's fit to print' is the motto of the newspaper. However, as an institution, its personnel has a generally good relationship with the long-term members of the US government and also with the changing administrations. Often it is the place of choice for an administration to 'leak' ideas of possible future actions. Thus, the *New York Times* may basically reflect the government's foreign policies and its trends. The detailed information about the selected samples is shown in Table 9.2.

9.4.2 Characterization of attitude system

As has already been mentioned in the last section, the attitude system involves three semantic subcategories, that is, affect, judgement, and appreciation. Affect is concerned with reflecting positive and negative

186

Table 9.2 Information on the selected samples

Theme	Title	Author	Length	Published Dates
China's Military Development	China Signals More Interest in Building Aircraft Carrier	EDWARD WONG	405	December 23, 2008
	China's Secretive Military Opens Up in Cyberspace	MICHAEL WINES	357	August 21, 2009
	Chinese Submarine Fleet Is Growing, Analysts Say	DAVID LAGUE	619	February 25, 2008
	General Hints China's Navy Wants to Add Carrier	ANDREW JACOBS	333	November 17, 2008
	Naval Show to Feature Submarines From China	EDWARD WONG	600	April 21, 2009
	Chinese Military Seeks to Extend Its Naval Power	EDWARD WONG	795	April 23, 2010
	Watching Beijing's Air Power Grow	MICHAEL FORSYTHE	817	October 20, 2009
	China Says It Is Slowing Down Military Spending	MICHAEL WINES & JONATHAN ANSFIELD	591	March 4, 2010

(continued)

Table 9.2 Continued

Theme	Title	Author	Length	Published Dates
US-China Military Relationship	Arms Sales to Taiwan Will Proceed, US Says	EDWARD WONG	589	December 15, 2009
	China Warns U.S. Against Selling F-16s to Taiwan	ANDREW JACOBS	651	February 25, 2010
	Optimism Grows for US-China Military Talks	MARK McDONALD & KEITH BRADSHER	854	February 18, 2009
	China Allows US Port Call in Hong Kong	DAVID LAGUE	329	January 29, 2008
	U.S. and China Revive Military Talks	MICHAEL WINES	463	February 28, 2009
	U.S. Sees Chinese Military Rise, and a Need for More Contact	THOM SHANKER	535	March 25, 2009
	US-China Military Talks Resume	ANDREW JACOBS	536	June 24, 2009
	Chinese Military Impedes Ties to Pentagon, Gates Says	AUBREY BELFORD & THOM SHANKER	312	June 4, 2010
	Pentagon Says China's Boost to Space Plan Poses a Threat	THE ASSOCIATED PRESS	272	March 4, 2008
Naval Mission in Gulf of Aden	China Considers Naval Mission Against Pirates in Gulf of Aden	MARK McDONALD	762	December 17, 2008
	China's Navy to Join Pirate Patrols	MARK McDONALD	558	December 25, 2008
	China Confirms Its Navy Will Fight Somali Pirates	MARK McDONALD	690	December 18, 2008

emotions; judgement deals with attitudes towards human behaviour; and appreciation includes evaluations of text, process, or natural phenomena.

9.4.2.1   Configuration of affect, judgement and appreciation

News reporting employs attitudinal meaning as little as possible, for it is required to report current information in a fair, concise, and objective way. Reporters are usually restrained from showing too many personal opinions. That is why reporters tend to use as little attitude as possible.

The raw frequencies and respective proportions of the resources of affect, judgement, and appreciation in the samples are listed in Table 9.3.

In all the three subcategories of the reports, the proportions of judgement and appreciation are both considerably larger than that of affect. In other words, the news reporters prefer judgement and appreciation rather than affect to express attitude in most of the reports.

As affect is the most subjective among the three subcategories of attitude, while appreciation is the least, with judgement in between (X. Chen, 2007), the news reporters' preference is not random but purposeful. This can be explained by a comparison of the following examples:

A. When the helicopter fired around the Chinese boat, the pirates *pan-icked* and fled in a speedboat. Affect
B. ... Chinese naval ships off the coast of Somalia, where an increase in piracy has made the shipping lanes the most *dangerous* in the world. Appreciation
C. ...has Chinese and English versions, is another step by China's famously *secretive* armed forces to give outsiders a peek at their operations, or at .... Judgement

Table 9.3   Proportions of affect, judgement and appreciation

	Affect	Judgement	Appreciation	Attitude
China's Military Development	15(18.07%)	34(40.96%)	34(40.96%)	83(100%)
US-China Military Relationship	20(24.39%)	24(32.43%)	38(46.34%)	82(100%)
Naval Mission in Gulf of Aden	5(11.90%)	16(21.62%)	21(50.00%)	42(100%)
All the Reports	40(19.32%)	74(35.75%)	93(44.93%)	207(100%)

Appreciation is to interpret the valuation of things or affairs in the least subjective way. The news reporters can avoid expressing themselves and judging others' behaviour directly via appreciation. Therefore, appreciation can disguise personal opinions as much more objective facts (M. Chen, 2007). If the reporters adopt the first sentence in the above examples, it reveals the reporters' tendency to apply subjective attitudes, which is supposed to be avoided in news reporting, and it also makes the reader think the evaluation of the story is just a psychological reaction, not objective. The attitudinal expression in news reports adds somewhat interpersonal meanings. Nevertheless, news reporting does not need too much emotive expression and judgement of human behaviour. On the contrary, it should be the description of reality. Employing appreciation, reporters can express their own viewpoints more covertly, since reporters try to prove that their observation is capable of reflecting some social phenomena rather than their own opinions. Therefore it also convinces the readers that what they report is based on reality, not on their personal interpretations.

Newspapers express a certain emotive stance on events they are reporting in order to attract readers. However, affect expressing emotive stance directly is only used in a limited way. Since affect is too subjective and personal, it is not an effective device for persuading the reader into taking the same views towards the things evaluated as the reporters. Therefore, the proportion of affect is much lower than that of judgement and appreciation.

9.4.2.2 Characterization of affect, judgement, and appreciation

Table 9.4 reveals the raw frequencies of the four semantic subcategories of affect in the selected samples (the symbols '+' and '−' represent positive and negative values respectively).

Table 9.5 reveals the raw frequencies of the three semantic subcategories of appreciation in the selected samples.

It can be noted that the resources conveying negative meanings are more than those conveying positive meanings in the affect subcategories, and in appreciation, the valuation resource is much more than those of others. The samples were mostly published during the years 2008 to 2010, and during this period the trends of the foreign relationship between the US and China were influenced by Obama's meeting the Dalai Lama, US arms sales to Taiwan, and some commercial arguments. Thus, dissatisfaction with the China-US military relationship was at a high level. On the one hand, as China is developing rapidly and plays an increasingly important role in international affairs, China's

Table 9.4   Frequencies of the four subcategories of affect

	Desire		Security		Happiness		Satisfaction	
	+	–	+	–	+	–	+	–
China's Military Development	2	1	1	4	0	3	0	4
US-China Military Relationship	6	0	0	3	0	1	3	7
Naval Mission in Gulf of Aden	0	1	0	2	1	0	0	1
All Reports	8	2	1	9	1	4	3	12

Table 9.5   Frequencies of the three subcategories of appreciation

	Reaction		Composition		Valuation	
	+	–	+	–	+	–
China's Military Development	2	1	1	0	18	9
US-China Military Relationship	0	7	0	2	24	7
Naval Mission in Gulf of Aden	2	5	0	1	7	1
All Reports	4	13	1	3	49	17

military development and relationship with the US cannot be neglected any longer; on the other hand, exaggerating China's rapid military development will suggest to Americans that China is becoming a threat to their development. Perhaps these are the reasons why the frequency of the positive valuation category is relatively high.

4. China, **angered** [att:aff:–sat] over a major US arms deal with Taiwan, broke off senior-level military exchanges with Washington last October.
5. But [eng:dis:coun] he also expressed **frustration** [att:aff:–hap] over what the US military considers [eng:attr:ack] a continuing lack of transparency on the part of senior military officials in China.
6. Some [gra:for:qua] military analysts were **surprised** [att:aff:–sec] that China had built a second submarine of that class so soon after the first, in 2004.

7. China is continuing its rapid [gra:for:int] expansion of a submarine fleet that would [eng:ent] be particularly [eng:foc:shap] **useful** [att:app:+val] in a conflict with the United States over Taiwan, analysts and military officials said [eng:attr:ack].
8. ... a main goal of China's military buildup is to have **sufficient** [att:app:+comp] forces on hand in the event of war across the Taiwan Strait.
9. Stealthy submarines with torpedoes and antiship missiles would [eng:ent] pose a direct **threat** [att:app:–reac] to the deployment of American aircraft carrier battle groups, likely [eng:ent] the first line of response to a Taiwan crisis ...

In the examples selected from the samples, the reports position the reader attitudinally through *angered, frustration, surprised,* and through the negative associations of *threat, useful,* and *sufficient.* In *angered, frustration,* and *surprised,* we observe instances of attitudinal expressions. The reporters' subjective presence is made more salient as they intervene in the reports to assert these feelings. Although reporters refrain from overtly characterizing China's military development as a threat to American security, they indicate a positive disposition towards Taiwan and a negative view towards the transparency of the Chinese Defense Ministry. The words *useful* and *sufficient,* on the one hand, reveal a positive disposition towards China's military development; on the other hand, they invoke in the reader the sense that China is dedicated to developing military power rapidly to counterbalance that of America, and that the tension between China and the US is caused by China's military expansion. As a token, *China had built a second submarine of that class so soon after the first, in 2004* relies on socially and culturally conditioned connections and inferences on the part of reader – it takes only four years for China to build an advanced submarine. But the reporter still does not overtly condemn China as, for example, 'dangerous' or 'menacing'.

Judgement can be divided into social esteem and social sanction. Table 9.6 reveals the raw frequencies of the five semantic subcategories of judgement in the selected samples (the symbols '+' and '–' represent positive and negative values respectively).

The data presented in the above table show the following regularities: Values of social esteem (1+0+24+6+3+7=41) and values of social sanction (0+18+0+18=36) have adjacent proportions. Values of capacity (24+6=30) are the most frequently used among the five semantic subcategories of judgement. The distribution of negative and positive values is dramatically uneven in the subcategories of capacity (6 vs. 24), veracity

Table 9.6   Frequencies of the five subcategories of judgement

	Social esteem				Social sanction				
	Normality		Capacity		Tenacity		Veracity		Propriety	
	+	–	+	–	+	–	+	–	+	–
China's Military Development	1	0	8	2	1	3	0	9	0	7
US-China Military Relationship	0	0	5	0	1	4	0	7	0	9
Naval Mission in Gulf of Aden	0	0	11	4	1	0	0	2	0	2
All Reports	1	0	24	6	3	7	0	18	0	18

(18 vs. 0), and propriety (18 vs. 0). As capacity is about how capable someone is, the positive values in this subtype indicate that Chinese military forces are becoming increasingly capable of handling the relationship with the US, with their rapid military development. *Veracity* means how truthful someone is, while *propriety* means how ethical someone is. The negative values in these subtypes reveal that reporters try to convey the viewpoint that China's military development is a threat to the United States, or at least suspicious.

10. Some Taiwanese strongly [gra:for:int] advocate open independence, and **at times China has threatened the island with violence** [att:judg:–prop, Token] ...
11. The Pentagon released a study on March 25 that said [eng:attr:ack] that the Chinese government was seeking weapons and technology to disrupt [att:judg:–cap] the traditional advantages of the American military, and that **the veil of secrecy the Chinese government had thrown over its military could** [eng:ent] **lead to a miscalculation or conflict between the nations** [att:judg:–ver, Token].

Token is a term proposed by Martin and White (2005) to refer to indirect realizations which invoke attitude (that is, express attitude implicitly) in the context. Tokens, together with attributed judgement values, do not directly reflect journalists' attitude towards the evaluated person, but they can imply the reporters' attitude towards the evaluated person. The sentence prior to (10) in the original text shows the reporter's own negative view towards China's resolution of the Taiwanese issues. *China's main military concern, though, is Taiwan, the self-governing democratic island that China says must be reunited with the mainland and that the United States supports with arms sales.* Therefore, (10) can be interpreted as evidence of the reporter's own negative judgement of the Chinese military policies in the previous sentence. In example (11), the reporter quotes the Pentagon's study to reveal that what the Chinese government has done is against the principle of veracity, and harmful to the relationship with the US. With tokens and attributed attitudes, reporters can convey their attitudes towards Chinese military forces as covertly as possible, something which is also required in news report writing.

9.4.3   Characterization of engagement system

9.4.3.1 *Monoglossia*

Monoglossic statements in a narrative account of the content will close down the dialogic space between readers and reporters. As monoglossic statements are more likely to be challenged by readers with different views than heteroglossic ones, it is obvious that news reporters will try to use this kind of statement as little as possible in order to make their reports convincing and authoritative. Therefore, in this study, we will not discuss it specifically.

9.4.3.2 *Heteroglossia*

Frequencies of four subcategories of heteroglossia in samples are shown in Table 9.7, in which 'phw' represents 'per hundred words'. The words in the three groups total 4,517, 4,541, and 2,010.

The data presented in Table 9.7 show the following regularities: dialogistic contractive resources (111 disclaim + 5 proclaim = 116) are less frequently used than dialogistic expansive resources (112 + 299 = 411) in all three types.

One prominent feature is that the frequency of proclaim is drastically lower than the other three subcategories of heteroglossia. It seems that the news reporters do not think that utterance of proclaim is an effective device to convey their views, as utterances of proclaim limit the scope of alternative positions, and they are more likely to be challenged by readers with different points of view.

Another prominent feature is the higher frequency of attribute. It can be discerned in the reports that the frequency of attribute is more than two times that of entertain and disclaim, and nearly 50 times that of proclaim. The dramatically high frequency of attribute is due to the fact that the reporters want to be convincing and objective, so the proposition is disassociated from the authorial voice.

Table 9.7 Frequencies of the four subcategories of heteroglossia

	disclaim	proclaim	entertain	attribute
China's Military Development	49/1.08 phw	4/0.09 phw	49/1.08 phw	113/2.50 phw
US-China Military Relationship	54/1.19 phw	1/0.02 phw	43/0.95 phw	130/2.86 phw
Naval Mission in Gulf of Aden	8/0.40 phw	0/0 phw	20/1.00 phw	56/2.79 phw
All the Reports	111/1.00 phw	5/0.05 phw	112/1.01 phw	299/2.70 phw

Attribution is mostly accomplished through the grammar of directly and indirectly reported speech and thought. With attribution presenting some external voice, it is essential to find out whether or not it acts to disassociate the authorial voice from the current proposition. The reporters employ acknowledgements to present the authorial voice as engaging interactively with other voices, while distance acts to mark the internal authorial voice as explicitly separate from the cited, external voice (Martin & White, 2005: 113). They ground the viewpoint conveyed by the proposition in an explicit subjectivity, thereby signalling that it is individual and contingent, and therefore but one of a range of possible dialogic options (Martin & White, 2005: 113).

With attribution, it also presents a relatively impersonal and impartial façade to readers. Acknowledgements allow the reporters to remain aloof from any relationships of either alignment or disalignment. But in fact, the reason why reporters quote these citations is to imply that they either support or are opposed to the attributed value position. The following instances are extracted from the samples:

12. ... a **Defense Ministry spokesman** said [eng:attr:ack] Tuesday that the country was seriously considering 'relevant issues' [eng:attr:dist] in making its decision about whether to move ahead with the project, according to **Xinhua** [eng:attr:ack], the state news agency.

13. [eng:dis:coun] **the United States government** has said [eng:attr:ack] it may [eng:ent] come to Taiwan's defense in the event of hostilities with China.

14. **Experts** say [eng:attr:ack] the designs of the newest [gra:for:int] Chinese submarines show evidence of technical assistance from Russia.

15. It also showed [eng:attr:ack] that Chinese submarine technology had advanced [att:judg:+cap] more [gra:for:int] rapidly [att:app:+val] than some [gra:for:qua] experts had expected.

16. 'Piracy has become a serious [att:judg:–ver] threat [att:app:–reac] to shipping, trade and safety on the seas,' **Liu** said [eng:attr:ack] at a news briefing in Beijing. 'That's why we decided to send naval ships to crack down on piracy'.

From the above examples, the external sources of attribution in our reports samples can be divided into the following four groups: Chinese and foreign news agencies – as in the first sentence, the authorities concerned and individual representing it – as in (12) and (13), authoritative individuals – as in (14) and (16), and others – as in (15). High credibility can be achieved through the application of sources that have high status in the field, just like those in the above examples.

In reports concerning the US-China military relationship, a large number of quotations are specifically attributed to Chinese and American officers, as well as government officials, Chinese military, the Pentagon, and military analysts and experts and their studies or research reports (see the examples below). These sources can be regarded as having high status or authority, since the relationship between China and the US is very formal, and any mistake in reporting could raise tensions or disagreement between the two nations. However, reports about China's military development show that the external voices frequently appear as unknown, as for example in (15). It is also noteworthy that direct speech and indirect speech are frequently seen in news reports. That is, reporters typically bring in an external source to lend support to their arguments (Martin & White, 2005: 116).

9.4.4 Characterization of graduation system

From Table 9.8, we notice that resources of force are much more frequently used than those of focus. Among the resources of intensification in our samples, cases of upscaling are much more common than those of downscaling, perhaps because the reporters need to emphasize their viewpoints. Resources of quantification are more than any other subcategories. The reasons why reporters use a large number of vague words to define degree are to reduce the appearance of personal, arbitrary decisions and therefore to convince readers, especially their opponents, that what the reports describe is not a stage for expressing personal opinions but absolutely objective and fair; therefore reporters can succeed in covering any traces of personal viewpoints. The following instances demonstrate what we have discussed.

Table 9.8 Frequencies of subtypes within graduation system

	Force		Focus	
	intensification	quantification	sharpen	Soften
China's Military Development	37	64	8	1
US-China Military Relationship	28	39	5	0
Naval Mission in Gulf of Aden	12	15	1	0
All the Reports	77	118	14	1

21. The European Union recently began an anti-piracy operation in the gulf, and **several** [gra:for:qua] other nations have a naval presence there, including India, the United States and Russia.
22. China has more than [gra:for:qua] 30 advanced [att:app:+val] and increasingly [gra:foc:shap] stealthy [att:app:+val] submarines, and **dozens of** [gra:for:qua] older [att:app:–val], obsolete [att:app:–val] types.

As a subsystem of appraisal, graduation can modify all the evaluation resources through regulating force and focus. Upscaling of attitude frequently acts to construe the speaker/writer as maximally committed to the value position being advanced and hence strongly aligns the reader with that value position. Meanwhile, downscaling frequently has the opposite effect of construing the speaker/writer as having only a partial or an attenuated affiliation with the value position being referenced (Martin & White, 2005: 152–153). Therefore downscaling makes stances less aggressive and to some degree widens the space for negotiation. However, most instances of force in the reports collected in this study belong to upscaling rather than downscaling. For example,

23. Some analysts speculated, however, that China's **huge** [gra:for:qua] economic stimulus program and other efforts to address unemployment ...
24. In style and tone, the site is not **radically** [gra:for:int] different from some [gra:for:qua] Internet offerings by the Pentagon.
25. 'We **absolutely** [gra:for:int] welcome all nations, because as we've said all along, piracy is an international problem that requires an international solution,' ...

26. They may not seem out in front, but they work **extremely** [gra:for:int] hard in the back seat.
27. They are among **the most** [gra:for:int] powerful [att:app:+val] ships in the Chinese Navy.

The tendency to upscale reveals reporters' efforts to persuade readers in news reporting. However, observing the essence of upscaling, we discover that there exist some subtle varieties in upscaling devices, which show the application of different evaluative strategies. Firstly, upscaling can reveal appreciation of internal quality, which often appears in form of pre-modification, such as *a complex problem, an extremely boring process*. The high frequency of intensified appreciation values may have something to do with the fact that appreciation values are the most objective among the three subcategories of attitude. Therefore the application of intensification to appreciation values can stop the report from appearing too subjective. Secondly, comparative and superlative adjectives are much more frequent. This could provoke intense discussion in readers, which is also one of the ways in which the news media tries to be attractive.

9.5 Conclusions

We have discussed the evaluative features of the reports concerning Chinese military affairs, mainly including China's military development, the US-China military relationship, and the naval mission in Gulf of Aden – a specific operation indicating a great leap forward for the Chinese military.

9.5.1 Summary of major findings

Contrary to any claims to 'objectivity' on the part of the media industry, according to White, news reporting is a mode of rhetoric in the broadest sense of the word (2003: 1). News reports are a genre in which journalists try their best to avoid expressing their attitudes too directly, but news reports can also influence the media audience's assumptions and beliefs about the way the world is and the way it ought to be. Therefore, attitudinal resources appear infrequently, especially with affect – the least frequently used, and a strong preference across all the texts for attitudes is expressed as appreciation and judgement rather than affect. Reporters are supposed not to express their own opinions of the news event by talking about their own emotional reactions, because, to some degree, affect is too subjective to convince readers to believe what the reporters say. Thus evaluation of the affairs concerning Chinese military is mainly achieved by appreciation values and judgement aimed at Chinese military behaviours. Moreover, a large number of judgement values are realized by the evaluation of the participants through the subtypes of capacity and veracity. It is also worth noticing that the evaluation of the capability of the Chinese military is often positive, in that the Chinese military is recognized as an increasingly powerful armed force and is deliberately constructed as a huge threat to the US from the Americans' perspective. Social esteem tends to be explicit, while social sanction often tends to be implicit, or attributed, which demonstrates that social sanction in news reporting is confined. However, we should also note that news reports concerning Chinese military or government are not always real reflections of the events, and that reporters will be subconsciously influenced by the stance of the news agency.

In terms of engagement, monoglossic assertions are mingled with heteroglossic sentences. The reporters quote other authoritative words to support their standpoints and disassociate themselves from evaluative judgements, which creates readers' impressions of the merit of what the reporters depict. Therefore, the news reports can achieve the goal of neutrality and objectivity with partial impersonalization. Among the sentences framed as heteroglossia, dialogic expansions outnumber dialogic contractions. This kind of patterning indicates that reports are a highly objective genre, where the need to open up the dialogic space always outweighs the need to close it down. Another notable feature is that cases of proclaim are extremely rare in the reports. Perhaps proclaim statements are too absolute to convey viewpoints in reports.

Among the graduation resources in the reports about Chinese military affairs, those of force are much more frequently employed than those of focus. And most of the resources of force are used to achieve the effect of upscaling rather than downscaling.

9.5.2 Limitations of the present study

Evaluative analysis of the resources inevitably carries a certain degree of subjectivity. Appraisal is itself a very complicated linguistic phenomenon, so how the evaluative resources will be interpreted relates significantly to the readers. However, with the same theoretical foundation, researchers can agree to what subtype of appraisal has been realized in most cases. The news reports were annotated sentence by sentence, and then checked by three subject experts. Therefore, to some degree, the data concerning the proportions and frequencies of different evaluative resources are credible and reliable.

Secondly, annotation of the evaluative resources was done manually rather than automatically, so the annotated samples were confined to a narrow scope, and minor mistakes may still exist. As our interpretation is based on not only evaluative resources alone but also on the whole context, and the work of annotation is time-consuming and exhausting, we only selected 20 annotated samples.

Last but not least, the reports selected in this study are confined to those published by the *New York Times* and the themes of the selected news reports are also limited. Although the *New York Times* is one of the most influential newspapers in the US, it cannot represent all the other newspapers. The limited data inevitably results in the narrow scope of the research findings.

9.5.3 Suggestions for future research

To complement the current study, future studies could be carried out in the following areas:

On the one hand, more specific study of the evaluative resources concerning the subcategories of Appraisal Theory should be conducted. The quantitative analysis should focus on more detailed appraisal resources, and more linguistic approaches of journalistic discourse can also be applied to the evaluative research of language in the future.

On the other hand, the evaluative features of a wider range of news reports can be studies in the future. We could also investigate other newspapers or magazines such as the *Los Angeles Times, Washington Post, Christian Science Monitor*, etc., together with the *New York Times*, thus making the findings of the study more authoritative and convincing in describing how the Chinese military is seen through foreigners' eyes. Moreover, a study on a wide range of topics in news reports could present further understanding, and a comparative study of different entities from newspapers at home and abroad would also be worthwhile.

In a word, the analysis of appraisal resources in reports about Chinese military affairs in foreign news media is promising, and essential in the construction of 'displaying before the world the fine image of the People's Liberation Army as a mighty, civilized and peaceful force' (Hu, 2007). Language in news reports is not neutral but ideological. The options of words are controlled by power and ideology. Thus, when reviewing the information and stance in a news report, we should avoid taking a unilateral view, resist influences made by reporters or news agencies, and take an active position in the process of reading, through Appraisal Theory.

References

Chen, M. (2007) 'Appraisal Analysis of News Reports' Attitudinal Resources and its Translation'. *Shanghai Journal of Translators*, 1: 23–27.

Chen, X. (2007) 'A Contrastive Analysis of English and Chinese Editorial'. *Foreign Languages*, 3: 39–46.

Crystal, D. & Davy, D. (1969) *Investigating English Style*, London: Longman.

Fairclough, N. (1999) *Media Discourse*, London: Edward Arnold.

Hu, J.T. (2007) 'In celebration of the Chinese people's Liberation Army 80 anniversary'. *Qiushi*, 15: 3–7.

Husson, D. & Robert, O. (1991) *Profession Journaliste*, Paris: Eyrolles.

Hughes, H. M. (1940) *News and the Human Interest Story*, Chicago: University of Chicago Press.

Ku, M. (2004) *Language and Ideology – A Critical Study of Political News Discourse on Iraq War*. Thesis for Master's Degree, Shanxi University.

Martin, J. R. (2000) 'Beyond Exchange: Appraisal Systems in English'. In Hunston, S., & Thompson, G. (eds), *Evaluation In Text* (pp. 142–175). Oxford: OUP.

Martin, J. R. & Rose, D. (2003) *Working with Discourse*, London & New York: Continuum.

Thompson, G. & Hunston, S. (2000) *Evaluation in Text: Authorial Stance and the Construction of Discourse*, Oxford: Oxford University.

Wang, Y. (2003) *Transitivity and Critical Discourse Analysis of News Texts*. Thesis for Master's Degree, Shanxi Normal University.

White, P. R. R. (1998) *Telling Media Tales: The News Story as Rhetoric*, Sydney: Sydney University.

White, P. R. R. (2003) *Evaluative Semantics and Ideological Positioning in Journalistic Discourse – A New Framework for Analysis, Mediating Ideology in Text and Image: Ten Critical Studies*, Cambridge: Cambridge University Press.

Xin, B. (2004) 'Critical Discourse Analysis: Criticism and Discussion'. *Journal of Foreign Languages*, 5: 64–69.

Zhang, R. (2009) *An Appraisal Analysis of Book Reviews*, Henan: Henan Press.

Index

aboutness, 6, 86
abstracts, 78, 86, 87, 88
academic writing, 12, 78, 79, 87, 88,
    114, 116–18, 120, 122, 131, 134,
    136, 138, 153, 155
annotation, 4, 8, 98, 159, 183, 184, 199
    errors, 7
    by learners, 162, 163, 166, 167,
    172, 175
    POS, 5
appraisal theory, 12, 178, 181–2,
    185, 199
aspect, 35, 38, 44, 55
attribution, 194, 195
autonomous learning, 158, 161–3,
    169, 172–5

Baguwen, 77, 80
Beijing Language and Culture
    University, 4
Beijing Normal University, 4
Beijing University of Aeronautics &
    Astronautics, 3

Chinese characters, 4, 5, 22, 24, 32,
    41, 64, 66, 73, 76
chi-square test, 79–81, 139, 141, 143,
    146, 147, 149, 151, 153
classifiers, 5, 35, 37, 46–55, 67
coherence and cohesion, 167, 172
colligation, 5, 18, 19, 21, 29, 30, 102,
    105
collocation, 5, 7, 8, 10, 15, 17–19,
    21–8, 30, 57, 65, 67, 69, 70, 73–5,
    99, 100, 102, 105, 130, 158, 162,
    163, 173
conclusion sections, 59, 75, 82, 92–3,
    151, 175
concordances, 2, 10, 22, 24, 27–9, 43,
    63, 64, 66, 67, 69, 70, 75, 82, 98,
    100, 102, 105, 106, 108, 128–30,
    135, 162, 163, 165, 166, 174

conjunctions, 12, 134, 135–9,
    141, 143, 145, 147, 148, 151,
    153–5
contrastive analysis, 5, 35, 37, 54–9
control group, 169–71
corpora
    Academia Sinica Balanced Corpus, 5
    BAWE, 79, 114, 116–19, 121, 123,
    125, 128, 129, 134–9, 141, 143–5,
    146, 147, 149, 151, 154, 155
    British National Corpus (BNC), 27,
    36, 57, 79, 101, 102, 114, 116–19,
    121, 123, 125, 128–30
    Brown, 3
    CALLHOME, 5, 37
    Chinese, 2, 3, 5, 10, 22
    Chinese Learners English Corpus
    (CLEC), 7, 8
    COCA, 163, 165, 173
    College Learner English Spoken
    Corpus (COLSEC), 7, 8
    Freiburg-LOB corpus (FLOB), 5, 36,
    40, 51, 56
    Gigaword, 5, 63, 67
    JDEST, 6, 7
    Lancaster Corpus of Mandarin
    Chinese (LCMC), 5, 36, 40, 53, 56
    LOB, 3, 5, 36, 56, 74
    Modern Chinese Corpus, 3, 4
    SWECCL, 8, 134, 135, 137–9, 141,
    143, 146, 147, 149
    Written English Corpus of Chinese
    Learners (WECCL), 114, 116
    XJTLU Written English Corpus
    (XWEC), 114, 116, 135, 136
    zhTenTen, 22, 63
corpus analysis tools, 11, 74, 75, 80,
    85, 94, 158, 161–3, 165, 166, 169,
    172–6
    AntConc, 163, 165, 173
    ColloExplorer, 10
    ParaConc, 10

GPSR Compliance
The European Union's (EU) General Product Safety Regulation (GPSR) is a set
of rules that requires consumer products to be safe and our obligations to
ensure this.

If you have any concerns about our products, you can contact us on

ProductSafety@springernature.com

In case Publisher is established outside the EU, the EU authorized
representative is:

Springer Nature Customer Service Center GmbH
Europaplatz 3
69115 Heidelberg, Germany